EVIDENCE MATTERS

EVIDENCE MATTERS

Randomized Trials in Education Research

Frederick Mosteller
Robert Boruch
Editors

BROOKINGS INSTITUTION PRESS
Washington, D.C.

ABOUT BROOKINGS

The Brookings Institution is a private nonprofit organization devoted to research, education, and publication on important issues of domestic and foreign policy. Its principal purpose is to bring knowledge to bear on current and emerging policy problems. The Institution maintains a position of neutrality on issues of public policy. Interpretations or conclusions in Brookings publications should be understood to be solely those of the authors.

THE BROOKINGS INSTITUTION
1775 Massachusetts Avenue, N.W., Washington, D.C. 20036
www.brookings.edu

Library of Congress Cataloging-in-Publication data

Evidence matters : randomized trials in education research / Frederick Mosteller and Robert Boruch, editors.
p. cm.
Includes bibliographical references and index.
ISBN 0-8157-0204-3 (cloth : alk. paper) —
ISBN 0-8157-0205-1 (pbk. : alk. paper)
1. Education—Research. I. Mosteller, Frederick, 1916–
II. Boruch, Robert F.
LB1028 .E95 2002
370'.7'2—dc21 2001006573

9 8 7 6 5 4 3 2 1

The paper used in this publication meets minimum requirements of the American National Standard for Information Sciences—Permanence of Paper for Printed Library Materials: ANSI Z39.48-1992.

Typeset in Sabon

Composition by R. Lynn Rivenbark
Macon, Georgia

Printed by R. R. Donnelley and Sons
Harrisonburg, Virginia

Foreword

THE CENTER FOR EVALUATION at the Initiatives for Children program of the American Academy of Arts and Sciences is dedicated to the evaluation of social policies that relate to children. In the spring of 1998 Frederick Mosteller, director of the center and professor emeritus of mathematical statistics at Harvard University, and Howard Hiatt, director of the Initiatives for Children and professor of medicine at Harvard Medical School, began to talk about the evaluation of educational policies with Christopher Jencks, professor of public policy at the John F. Kennedy School of Government at Harvard. A leading topic of discussion was how to encourage more general evaluation of educational policies before they are widely implemented. When are randomized trials appropriate? What is the range of evaluation methodologies besides randomized trials? Aware of serious areas of disagreement on these and similar questions among groups concerned with education, they decided that a conference was needed to explore them. Participants should be invited whose views ranged—and diverged—as widely as possible. The Academy, they thought, would be an ideal convener of such a meeting. Institutionally neutral, it was not identified with any of the defended views, but rather with the spirit of open inquiry and exchange. We express appreciation to the American Academy of Arts and Sciences and its staff for their cooperation in hosting the conference.

At this point, the organizing committee joined forces with Paul Peterson, professor of government at Harvard, who was planning to hold a Harvard faculty seminar on the evaluation of social policies over the course of the coming academic year. The four agreed to convene the conference together. They would commission papers, inviting the authors to present draft versions at the seminar for comment and discussion, in order to polish the final products and focus the discussion for the conference. The provost of Harvard University, Harvey Fineberg, kindly made funds available from the Provost's Fund for Interfaculty Collaboration. The resulting seminar, entitled "University-Wide Research Seminar on Evaluation," was held at the Harvard Faculty Club under Paul Peterson's leadership in the 1998–99 academic year.

The conference took place at the American Academy in Cambridge, Massachusetts, in May 1999. It did, indeed, pull an unusually broad range of participants. One commented afterward that he had "never seen some of those people in the same room at the same time." Participants included academics, practitioners of different evaluation techniques, specialists in education, and representatives from government and foundations, which are the institutions that pay for the policies, programs, and projects and want to understand how to evaluate them effectively.

The conference was engaged and spirited, the discussion—for the most part—unusually candid. Many methodological issues were discussed, but one in particular became the focal point of the conference. Some participants expressed the concern that education research frequently did not employ randomized field trials in order to find out which education interventions were effective. When properly conducted, randomized field trials—often called the gold standard in research involving human subjects—allow for fairly precise estimates of programmatic effects. This approach, widespread in medical research, would seem equally applicable to the evaluation of education interventions. Others, however, wondered whether the use of randomized field trials in education research was viable, given the ethical, practical, and political issues that often arise. Out of these conversations emerged the essays in this volume.

For support of the conference, the conveners acknowledge with appreciation the Andrew W. Mellon Foundation, the Smith Richardson Foundation, the Spencer Foundation, the Planning and Evaluation Service of the U.S. Department of Education, and the W. T. Grant Foundation.

Howard H. Hiatt
Penny Janeway
Paul E. Peterson

January 2002

Contents

CHAPTER ONE

Overview and New Directions

ROBERT BORUCH
FREDERICK MOSTELLER

THIS BOOK PRESENTS some histories and current status of research on practices in education from several points of view. Our main goal is to help improve education in schools in the United States by encouraging the gathering of better evidence on the impact of educational practices.

That governments have become seriously interested in the quality of research in the education sector is plain. The U.S. Congress's Committee on Education and the Work Force, for example, has been concerned about the wide dissemination of flawed, untested educational initiatives that can be detrimental to children. In 2000 this concern led to the development of a bill designed to address problems in this arena: the Scientifically Based Education Research, Evaluation, and Statistics and Information Act of 2000. Among other things, the bill called for increased scientific rigor in education research and tried to specify what this meant. It called for controlled experiments and the use of properly constituted comparison groups in quantitative research and for scientifically based qualitative research standards.

That particular bill did not pass. But it is a clear signal of congressional interest. Partly as a consequence, the National Research Council has convened a committee titled Scientific Principles in Educational Research to help make explicit the standards of evidence that are appropriate. The National Academy of Education and the Social Science

Research Council have initiated a different related effort, focusing on the intellectual organization and state of educational research.

Examples from other countries are not difficult to identify. In the United Kingdom, for example, the Department for Education and Employment, in cooperation with the Economic and Social Research Council, has set up a new Centre for Evidence-Informed Policy and Practice at London's Institute of Education to improve the knowledge base. This move was driven partly by the country's concerns about ideology parading as intellectual inquiry and about the relevance and timeliness of research and the intelligibility of its results. The biennial Conferences on Evidence-Based Policy at Durham University (United Kingdom) anticipated much of this more recent governmental concern.

An appropriate approach to studying the value of an intervention depends on the question that is asked. This book focuses on evidence about what interventions work better. Some of the best evidence to address this question can be generated in randomized field trials (RFTs). By this, we mean situations in which individuals or entire organizations are randomly assigned to one of two or more interventions. The groups that are so constructed do not differ systematically. That is, there are no hidden factors that would lead the groups to differ in unknown ways. When the groups are statistically equivalent at the outset, we can then be assured that comparison of the relative effectiveness of the interventions will be fair. That is, the properly executed RFT will produce estimates of relative effects that are statistically unbiased. Furthermore, one can make legitimate statistical statements about one's confidence in the results.

This book also focuses on empirical studies of the relative effectiveness of programs in education. Other kinds of research are important in building up to controlled studies of program effectiveness, in augmenting such studies, and in adding to what we understand about education and its effects. These other kinds of research include sample surveys, designed to understand which children need assistance and to what extent. They include narrative studies of how children, their parents, their teachers, and policymakers make decisions about their needs. The other kinds of studies include exploratory research on new ideas about what might work. Even throat-clearing essays at times contribute to understanding.

Overview of the Chapters

Chapter 2, by Judith Gueron, discusses the difficulties in practice and their resolutions when randomization is used. The chapter includes counsel about carrying out randomized field trials, using the experiences of the Manpower Development Research Corporation as a guide. Judith Gueron's long and successful experience with such randomized trials brings reality to her advice about carrying out studies. Among the problems is the task of persuading the sponsors and participants of the value of this approach. Her organization has executed many such investigations by persuading sponsors that there is no easier way to get the answers to the right questions, by meeting legal and ethical standards, and by ensuring that each study is large enough in numbers and duration not to miss the effects being studied. Impacts often emerge over time. Gueron emphasizes the importance of giving people the services to which they are entitled, of addressing previously unanswered questions of sponsors and participants, and of having adequate procedures to assure participants of data confidentiality, and to ensure that the innovations offer more than the usual treatment. Although Gueron's advice is especially oriented toward RFTs, most of it has value for any investigator trying to study a sensitive social problem in the turmoil of the real world.

Chapter 3, by Robert Boruch, Dorothy de Moya, and Brooke Snyder, presents many examples of evaluation in education and elsewhere using RFTs. The authors emphasize the systematic study of field trials themselves in the world literature and offer a variety of viewpoints for considering these investigations. Internationally, the number of RFTs is increasing, presumably because the quality of evidence from these studies seems stronger than that from other kinds. Chapter 3 introduces several ways of considering the value of such trials: by looking at the severity of the problem, the realism of the investigation for policy guidance, and the ability to estimate costs and benefits. Attention is also given to the international Campbell Collaboration, which prepares systematic reviews of comparative studies in education, social science, criminal justice, and other areas. Cooperation between the older Cochrane Collaboration in health care and Campbell may be of help to both groups.

In chapter 4, David Cohen, Stephen Raudenbush, and Deborah Ball offer a historical view of progress in education since about 1960. For researchers in education, they argue, the question "Do resources matter?" is far less important than "What resources matter, how, and under what circumstances?" They push on to ask, "What instructional approaches, embedded in what instructional goals, suffice to ensure that students achieve the goals?" Adding resources to schools, they point out, does not automatically bring improved performance to the children. We need to attend to the environment that accompanies resources and to the interactions among such variables as money spent on instruction, years in school, depth of teachers' subject matter preparation, time on task, class size, and how instruction is actually carried out. The authors think that we need to move away from thinking about resources as money to considering environment, students, teachers, and their interactions. They want to see more research not on the components of instructional approaches, but on coherent instructional regimes. These regimes need to be compared for their effect on learning.

The remaining chapters turn to diverse topics, beginning with the pros and cons of using RFTs. The authors recognize the advantages of RFTs in relation to alternatives and ask why they are infrequently used in education. Thomas Cook and Monique Payne suggest that the rarity of RFTs is due to educational researchers' objections to randomized trials. They present arguments to refute these objections. Maris Vinovskis focuses on the institutional history of federally sponsored evaluations, arguing that the rarity of good studies is a function of weak political and administrative support for rigorous research. Gary Burtless focuses on chance, social convention, and major political impediments to randomized trials. And Carol Weiss discusses the practical difficulty of community-wide trials and identifies ways to study education in anticipation of RFTs or in parallel with them. A second topic of discussion is alternatives to experiments. Burtless and Cook and Payne cite evidence on defects in the design and results of nonrandomized trials, especially the difficulty of ensuring that estimates of relative effects are interpretable and statistically unbiased. All of the authors recognize that randomized trials are impossible at times, and they identify alternatives that may suffice, depending on the context of the evaluation. Weiss introduces some approaches that help to build understanding "before the randomizer arrives."

The essays also introduce refreshed ways of thinking about these topics and others. In chapter 5, Maris Vinovskis comments on the checkered history and role of the U.S. Department of Education (USDE) in rigorous evaluation of federal programs. He outlines major contributions such as the Coleman report and those of various political administrations, such as President Lyndon Johnson's enhanced investments in education. He also notes that other administrations, such as President Richard Nixon's, reduced investments in research. He describes how various institutional arrangements have emerged and then disappeared, institutions such as the National Institute of Education. To judge from Vinovskis's description, the National Center for Education Statistics has made substantial progress since the 1980s in the collection and dissemination of descriptive statistics, including student achievement data. According to Vinovskis, some senior executives at the U.S. Department of Education have supported rigorous evaluation, although the record in producing such evaluations has been spotty. The Even Start Family Program is used to illustrate a remarkable effort to sponsor and to execute a randomized field trial.

One reason for the scarcity of randomized trials, says Vinovskis, is that the USDE's Planning and Evaluation Service has focused on many short-term studies that assist the Department of Education. Hence the unit's resources are spread thinly. Similarly, he is concerned that regional laboratories and R&D centers spread their limited resources among many different small-scale projects rather then concentrating them on a few larger and longer-term initiatives. Vinovskis therefore urges policymakers to consider reconfiguration of the institutions responsible for program development and evaluations, beginning perhaps with a new National Center for Evaluation and Development in the USDE to handle large-scale evaluations and development projects. He would structure this new entity so as to reduce political influences on evaluations, for example, by providing for a six-year term of office for the center's commissioner. The proposed center would help consolidate evaluations across education programs and reduce what Vinovskis views as a fragmentation of federal monetary investments in evaluation and development.

In chapter 6, Thomas Cook and Monique Payne recognize that education research is strong in that it has produced high-quality description, survey methods and data, and achievement testing. They believe, however, that education research has been weak in establishing causal relationships. This weakness is based, they say, on some contemporary researchers' objections to using RFTs to understand such relationships. They present counterarguments and empirical evidence to meet these objections.

In response to criticism that RFTs stem from an oversimplified theory of causation, Cook and Payne point out that the purpose of such trials is "more narrow and practical—to identify whether one or more possible causal agents cause change in a given outcome." Opponents of RFTs, they add, have stressed qualitative methods that depend on different assumptions and involve a different objective: hypothesis generation rather than hypothesis testing. Cook and Payne also disagree that RFTs are inappropriate in the complex U.S. education system, noting that experiments can be designed and executed to take into account both the similarities among schools and their heterogeneity. Furthermore, they do not believe that randomized assignment is premature until a good program theory and mediational processes are developed, as some claim. They maintain that the value of randomized field trials depends not on having good program theory, but on making a fair comparison and protecting against statistical bias, regardless of the particular theory. Pointing to trials that have been mounted successfully, they disagree that randomization has been used and has failed. Such criticisms, they note, are often based on *non*randomized trials and on the imperfections of randomized trials in fields other than education.

Claims that RFTs involve trade-offs that are not worth making sometimes take the form of rejecting internal validity in favor of external validity. That is, the opponents of trials attach higher value to the generalizability of a study's results (external validity) and lower value to unbiased estimates of the relative effectiveness of programs (internal validity). Cook and Payne recognize that a given trial may or may not be designed to ensure that the results are generalizable from a particular sample to larger populations. They encourage the use of designs that "minimize the external validity loss."

In considering the complaint that RFTs are unethical, Cook and Payne recognize the legitimate tensions between a lottery and measures of merit as a device for allocating scarce resources. They maintain that randomization can be justified when we do not know which intervention is more effective, especially when resources for interventions are limited. They also examine the view that there are good alternatives to RFTs. They encourage the reader to recognize qualitative case studies as adjuncts to RFTs, rather than as substitutes for a randomized trial. They criticize another purported alternative, theory-based evaluation, which Weiss encourages, pointing out that theory-based approaches are rarely sufficiently explicit. Weiss offers some counterexamples. Furthermore, when there are multiple ways of making theory explicit, the theories are unspecific about timelines, reciprocal causal influences, and counterfactuals. Their concern about others' claims that quasi experiments are an alternative to randomized field trials lies in the fact that the phrase "quasi experiment" is often used promiscuously and that the quasi-experimental designs are often poorly conceived and executed.

In chapter 7, Gary Burtless notes that sizable RFTs have often been mounted to evaluate certain economic programs started on a pilot basis. Among the basic reasons for trials in these areas, he says, is that randomization ensures that we know the direction of causality and helps remove any systematic correlation between program status and unobserved characteristics of participants and nonparticipants. Burtless argues that RFTs can be designed to meet ethical standards while permitting policymakers to test new programs and new variations on old programs. In the area of welfare, says Burtless, some RFTs have been done where economists have found important defects in some of the statistical alternatives. These defects have led to wrong conclusions about the effects of programs.

Burtless also discusses political and professional influences on our willingness to do RFTs in the area of welfare and employment and training, as opposed to education programs. First, Butler notes that economists knowledgeable about RFTs have held important cabinet positions in the U.S. government in agencies such as the U.S. Department of Labor, but not in the U.S. Department of Education. Second, the influence depends on the extent of the federal role in financial, political, and regulatory environments. For instance, the federal government has a substantial role in drugs that are put on the commercial market partly because of regulations that require good evidence on the effects of new drugs. It does not have the same arrangement in place to determine whether education interventions are safe or effective. Burtless also recognizes that some target populations are politically weak, suggesting that their members then are not well positioned to oppose an RFT.

RFTs appear infrequently in education, Burtless suggests, partly because the federal financial share in education is small in relation to state and local investments. Consequently, the federal government has limited influence on mounting RFTs to test innovations in education. Another reason is that economists and other social scientists with a strong interest in rigorous evaluation have not held important positions in federal education departments or the legislative forums that shape policy on education programs. In addition, argues Burtless, teachers, parents, and others in the education community view RFTs as potentially denying benefits to children who need assistance. Furthermore, school administrators and teachers believe that they will lose control in some respects when a trial is undertaken. Finally, because the education community is politically influential, states Burtless, its members have the capacity to impede or stop a trial that they consider unethical or apt to reduce their authority.

In Carol Weiss's view, outlined in chapter 8, in some situations the sampling of individuals is not an appropriate basis for measuring program success. This would be the case in the study of community programs where the purpose is not to change the behavior of the individuals in the community but to change the community itself. One could sample communities, but this approach leads to large studies and the further difficulty that initial conditions in the chosen communities may differ substantially. Weiss offers a brief history of community studies in the United States. She also suggests a variety of alternatives to randomization, including the use of qualitative information to get at the rich structure of the activities and their outcomes.

Carol Weiss's main recommendations as alternatives to randomization are theory-based evaluation (TBE) and Ruling Out Alternative Explanations. By way of example, she describes a program expected to create jobs in a depressed community and a theory of change for an initiative to create a healthier atmosphere for adolescents (considering both positive and negative aspects). By spelling out the theories, Weiss argues, we are able to focus on events and consequences that demonstrate its weaknesses. We know what to pay attention to. We can gather data appropriate to the theory from the beginning and see if it is supported or whether some alternative theory is needed.

Weiss's second approach is to rule out alternative explanations, which she does by employing the usual requirements for indications of causality. For example, we may know the order in time that things should occur, and when they do not, we can eliminate an explanation. Or when it appears unlikely that a sequence of requirements can all be true, we can again eliminate an explanation.

New Directions

The central question addressed in this book is what areas of education might be suitable for mounting randomized trials or other studies of effectiveness? How do we go about selecting these areas? At least three kinds of answers are sensible. The first depends on the efforts of government and its advisers, including people who can put research into practice. The second depends on our own studies. The third kind of answer is a promissory note that international collaborative efforts such as the Campbell Collaboration can help in identifying research targets.

Government Efforts

The U.S. Department of Education's Strategic Plan for 2001–05 identifies three major goals that are pertinent here. It also identifies the specific objectives within each goal, and the programs that are being mounted to meet the objectives. More to the point, the strategic plan describes some of the evaluations that the department is planning or supporting, as described in a section of the plan called "Evaluation Highlights."

Goal 1 is to build a solid foundation of learning for all children. To this end, the department is supporting RFTs of the Even Start Family Program, for example. This program, intended to raise the literacy skills of families and young children, is being evaluated in twenty sites using RFTs. The department is also undertaking feasibility studies to determine whether RFTs of new programs can be mounted under the Reading Excellence Act. The department's trials on the Upward Bound Programs are well advanced. Some RFTs are being mounted in collaboration with the Department of Health and Human Services, notably on Head Start. Other programs targeted for evaluation under goal 1 pertain to Comprehensive School Reform, Talent Search, Career Academies, School to Work, and Title 1.

Goal 2 of the department's strategic plan is to reform the U.S. education system. A variety of evaluative activities are under way to assess whether objectives within this goal are being met. One program, the 21st Century Community Learning Centers, has been targeted for randomized trials supported by the department and at least one private foundation. This program funds after-school activity designed to raise academic achievement in schools in high-poverty areas. The department has also decided to study teacher development programs in mathematics and reading, teacher recruitment and retention programs, and programs that are sometimes controversial, such as charter schools and magnet schools.

Goal 3 of the Strategic Plan is to "ensure access for all to a high-quality post-secondary education and life-long learning." None of these evaluations involve a randomized trial. Instead, other kinds of studies are being deployed to generate evidence about the effectiveness of TRIO's Student Support Services for college students at risk, Vocational Rehabilitation Services, the Adult English as a Second Language Program, and the Adult Basic Education Program.

Evidence from Past Trials

Many topics in education merit study, in addition to the ones identified in the Strategic Plan. Some are already receiving attention. The effectiveness of summer school, for example, has been a subject of growing interest ever since it was established that children in lower-income families lose more of their educational attainment during the long summer vacation than children from higher-income families. Consequently, the effectiveness of summer school is important in our attempts to maintain equal opportunity. A recent meta-analysis of this subject by Harris Cooper and his colleagues collects the results of many studies and suggests that summer school can be effective in reducing the gap in achievement created by the long summer vacation.[1]

This summer loss in achievement also raises the question of whether some rearrangement of the school calendar might be more productive than depending on summer school.[2] For example, the year could be broken up into several periods of equal length with short vacations after each. Such a plan may be very difficult to implement and evaluate because it requires more agreement among the states and school districts than we ordinarily have in this country. On the other hand, similarly difficult challenges have been met in trials that randomly assigned entire schools to different schoolwide interventions.

The field of special education for handicapped or disabled students offers many opportunities for investigation. Recently, the trend has been to include the handicapped in regular classes as much as possible while also offering some special time for them alone. Various questions need to be addressed here: for example, is it appropriate to have multiple teachers in a class, are specially trained teachers required, and how many handicapped can be included in a class of given size?

We have had one large long-term investigation of the effect of class size on children's achievement. The STAR trial carried out in Tennessee suggests that reducing class size from about twenty-four to sixteen for the earliest years of schooling, kindergarten through grade 3, improved the scores of children.[3] This improvement occurred not only during the years that class size was reduced, but also in later years when class size was

1. Cooper and others (2000).
2. See Cooper and others (2000); Entwisle, Alexander, and Olson (2000).
3. Mosteller, Olson, and Youtz (1996).

restored to its previous level. Including a teacher's aide with class size did not seem to improve scholastic performance very much. What was it about smaller class size that improved scores in the beginning and later grades? To answer that question, it would be helpful to study how resources are reallocated in an environment of reduced class size and what the effects of reallocation are. For example, it might just be that less confusion in the classroom leads to more effective education, but we await more information on the cause of improvement.

Yet another topic of widespread interest is cooperative learning, which also appears to produce improvements in performance.[4] The basic idea here is to group students in a classroom into teams, and to give each team responsibility for making sure that all its members master the material in each lesson. In other words, members of a team work together to improve their performance. Extensive data and many investigations strongly suggest that this approach does produce improvements in performance.

Place-Based Trials

Many people do not realize that entire classrooms, schools, and districts have at times been randomly assigned to different interventions. Typically, the study's purpose is to estimate the relative effectiveness of a program that is deployed in many classrooms, schools, or districts. Tests of the Drug Abuse Resistance Education (DARE) program in Illinois, for instance, involved randomly allocating half the schools in twelve pairs of schools to DARE and half to a control condition. This study and similar randomized trials helped to show that, contrary to people's expectations of schoolwide DARE programs, the programs had no appreciable effect on substance abuse by the young.[5] The findings from this trial and earlier ones led to controversy and stiff opposition from DARE advocates. In 2001 DARE leaders decided to revise the program in ways that might enhance its effectiveness.

Other studies further illustrate the feasibility of such trials. Fifteen school districts in Minnesota and Wisconsin agreed to be randomly assigned to a specialized theory-driven schoolwide program to reduce under-age alcohol abuse and to a control condition in which ordinary education on the topic might or might not be provided.[6] Trialists have

4. See Slavin (1995).
5. Rosenbaum and Hansen (1998).
6. Wagenaar and others (1994).

randomly assigned classrooms to new sexual risk reduction programs to compare them to conventional handling of the topic in middle schools in California and elsewhere, to determine whether the new intervention did indeed reduce the risky youth behavior below ambient levels.

Still other trials have been mounted to test community-wide interventions (on smoking, for example), hospital-wide changes in handling certain illnesses, and AIDS risk reduction involving work sites as the units of allocation.[7] All of these examples can be counted as relevant here because they include education and information as program components, although they may not deal directly with youth in schools.

Such trials are institutionally complex because they demand the cooperation of different organizations and groups of people. The analysis of resultant data can also be complex, although statistical and methodological advances have made this exercise more tractable and orderly.[8] Nonetheless, they are extremely important where interventions with potential social benefits must be deployed at the institutional or community level. Theory, empirical evidence, and ordinary experience indicate that social norms influence human behavior. If these norms are changed at the institutional level through an intervention, then we may discern the effect of this on people's behavior through randomized trials that involve institutions as the units of allocation. The beneficial or harmful effects of schoolwide programs on children's education achievement can be discerned before the programs are adopted at the regional or state level.

These precedents are relevant to current debates about how to evaluate comprehensive school reforms, how to generate evidence about the effectiveness of various models of reform and effective practice, and how to enhance the well-being of children and youth. Evidence from randomized trials permits us to estimate the relative effect of the effort in the least ambiguous way possible and thus to engage in thoughtful debate about what ought to be done next.

Lists of the sort given here that direct attention to the topics in which more evaluation is needed will depend heavily on the people and the institutions that draw up the list. The choices for the list presented in this chapter, for example, were influenced by the people who advise the U.S. Department of Education, our own judgment, and the people who contributed to this volume. We can map the terrain of evidence on the effects

7. Boruch and Foley (2000).
8. See Murray (1998); and Donner and Klar (2000).

of interventions in other ways. One way is to generate good evidence on where the dry ground is: where educational interventions have been evaluated well. This involves searching for empirical evidence on where the sea is deep, where few or no interventions have been evaluated. And, of course, to map the evidential terrain we need to know where the swamps are, that is, where the evidence on the effectiveness of education interventions is ambiguous.

Collaborative Efforts

This kind of empirical mapping can be facilitated by international collaboration, such as the evolving Campbell Collaboration. This collaboration's main mission is to generate high-quality systematic reviews of studies of the effects of interventions, in other words, to find out what works, what does not work, and what is promising, according to good standards of evidence. The older sibling of the Campbell Collaboration is the Cochrane Collaboration in health care.[9]

The Campbell Collaboration's systematic reviews can be configured to provide a map of where research on the effects of interventions has and has not been done, and where such research may be sorely needed. This map will provide policymakers, practitioners, and researchers with an informed basis for delineating these areas. Since this is public information, people can add to it or offer constructive criticisms. To be useful for research policy, such mapping must be both prospective and retrospective in its orientation. Therefore it is essential to develop registries of evaluations that are just *beginning,* as well as collaborative systems for tracking their progress. These registries must also be updated continuously to keep track of studies that have been completed.

At present, the Campbell Collaboration is developing a Social, Psychological, Educational, and Criminological Trials Registry (C2-SPECTR) whose contents will be used to map studies in each of these arenas. C2-SPECTR is designed to be prospective and retrospective. In the educational arena, entries are coded along various dimensions, including the types of outcomes examined in each study (such as math achievement, dropout, or socioemotional development) and the kinds of interventions under study (such as tutoring or class size). This coding will make it possible to tailor the maps to the special interests of people who will be using them.

9. See www.campbell.gse.upenn.edu and www.cochrane.org.

Generating better evidence for better education is not an easy task. Unless researchers and practitioners work at it, they will, in Walter Lippmann's words "imperil the future by leaving great questions to be fought out between ignorant change on the one hand and ignorant opposition to change on the other."[10] The contributors to this volume give good advice on how to reduce our ignorance and generate better evidence. We trust that readers will take seriously what they have to say so as to enhance the education of children and youth.

References

Boruch, R., and E. Foley 2000. "The Honestly Experimental Society: Sites and Other Entities as the Units of Allocation and Analysis in Randomized Trials." In *Validity and Experimentation: Donald Campbell's Legacy,* edited by L. Bickman, 1:193–238. Thousand Oaks, Calif.: Sage Publications.

Cooper, H., K. Charleton, J. C. Valentine, and J. Muhlenburck. 2000. "Making the Most of Summer School: A Meta-Analytic and Narrative Review." *Monographs of the Society for Research in Child Development,* Serial 260, 65(1). Malden, Mass.: Blackwell.

Donner, A., and N. Klar. 2000. *Design and Analysis of Cluster Randomization Trials in Health Research.* Oxford University Press.

Entwisle, D. R., K. L. Alexander, and L. S. Olson. 2000. "Summer Learning and Home Environment." In *A Notion at Risk,* edited by Richard D. Kalenberg, 9–30. New York: Century Foundation Press.

Lippman, W. 1963. "The Savannah Speech." In *The Essential Lippmann,* edited by C. Rossiter and J. Lare. Random House. (Originally published in 1936.)

Mosteller, F., M. Olson, and C. Youtz. 1996. "Notes on Cooperative Learning, Center for Evaluation." *Initiatives for Children.* American Academy of Arts and Sciences (April 10): 1–7.

Murray, D. M. 1998. *Design and Analysis of Group Randomized Trials.* New York: Oxford University Press.

Rosenbaum, D. P., and G. S. Hanson. 1998. "Assessing the Effects of School-Based Education: A Six Year Multilevel Analysis of Project DARE." *Journal of Research in Crime and Delinquency* 35(4): 381–412.

Slavin, R. E. 1995. *Cooperative Learning.* 2d ed. Allyn & Bacon.

U.S. Department of Education. 2000. *Strategic Plan, 2001–2005.* Government Printing Office.

Waganeer, A. C., D. M. Murray, M. Wolfson, J. L. Forster, and J. R. Finnegan. 1994. "Communities Mobilizing for Change on Alcohol: Design of a Randomized Community Trial." *Journal of Community Psychology.* Monograph Series/CSAP (Special Issue): 79–101.

10. Lippmann (1963/1936, pp. 495–97).

CHAPTER TWO

The Politics of Random Assignment: Implementing Studies and Affecting Policy

JUDITH M. GUERON

AS THE ONLY nonacademic contributing to this volume, I see it as my charge to focus on the challenge of implementing random assignment in the field. I will not spend time arguing for the methodological strengths of social experiments or advocating more such field trials. Others have done so eloquently.[1] But I will make my biases clear. For twenty-five years, I and many of my colleagues at the Manpower Demonstration Research Corporation (MDRC) have fought to implement random assignment in diverse arenas and to show that this approach is feasible, ethical, uniquely convincing, and superior for answering certain questions. Our organization is widely credited with being one of the pioneers of this approach, and through its use producing results that are trusted across the political spectrum and that have made a powerful difference in social policy and research practice. So, I am a believer, but not, I hope, a blind one. I do not think that random assignment is a panacea or that it can address all the critical policy questions, or substitute for other types of analysis, or is always appropriate. But I do think that it offers unique power in answering the "Does it make a difference?" question. With random assignment, you can know something with much greater certainty and, as a result, can more confidently separate fact from advocacy.

This chapter focuses on implementing experiments. In laying out the ingredients of success, I argue that creative and flexible research design

1. See, for example, chapters 3 and 6 of this volume.

skills are essential, but that just as important are operational and political skills, applied both to marketing the experiment in the first place and to helping interpret and promote its findings down the line. Conducting a successful random assignment experiment in a complex, real-world context requires a continuing balancing of research ambition against operational realism. Lest this sound smug—because I am talking from an institutional track record of success in doing this—let me add that success remains an uphill battle. No one has ever welcomed random assignment. Moreover, this challenge has recently become more acute as research questions and programs become more complex, and the political and funding terrain more hostile.

My background theme is that this is a battle worth fighting. People who are active in public policy debates and who fund this type of research know the political and financial costs of evaluations that end in methodological disputes. Henry Aaron put this well in his influential book *Politics and the Professors*, which describes the relationship between scholarship and policy during the Great Society era and its aftermath. Pointing to the conservative effect on policymakers of disputes among experts, he asked: "What is an ordinary member of the tribe [that is, the public] to do when the witch doctors [the scientists and scholars] disagree?" Such conflict, he argued, not only paralyzes policy but also undercuts the "simple faiths" that often make action possible.[2]

Random assignment, because of its unique methodological strengths, can help avoid this kind of conflict—what Aaron called "self-canceling research." But random assignment studies must be used judiciously and interpreted carefully to ensure that they meet ethical norms and that their findings are correctly understood. It is also important that researchers not oversell this technique. Random assignment can answer the important "Does it make a difference?" and "For whom?" questions, but it must be combined with other approaches to get answers to the critical question of "Why?" and "Under what conditions?"

Background

Over the past twenty-five years, MDRC has conducted thirty major random assignment studies in more than 200 locations, involving close to

2. Aaron (1978, pp. 158–59).

300,000 people. Projects have ranged from the first multisite test of a real-world (that is, not researcher-run) employment program operated by community organizations (the National Supported Work Demonstration), to the first projects that moved social experiments out of the relatively contained conditions of specially funded programs into mainstream welfare and job training offices (the Work Incentive [WIN] Research Laboratory Project and the Demonstration of State Work/Welfare Initiatives), to what may have been the first efforts to use large-scale experiments to decompose the "black box" of an operating welfare reform program and determine the effects of its different components (the Demonstration of State Work/Welfare Initiatives and the more recent National Evaluation of Welfare-to-Work Strategies).[3] We have integrated random assignment into large bureaucracies (welfare offices, job training centers, courtrooms, public schools, and community colleges) and smaller settings (community-based organizations). The studies have targeted different populations, occurred in greatly varied funding and political contexts, and involved denying people access to services viewed as benefits (for example, job training to volunteers) or excluding them from conditions seen as onerous (such as time limits on welfare). We have been called names and have been turned down more times than accepted, but have so far managed to ward off legal challenges and avoid any undermining of the random assignment process. Although our experience shows ways to succeed, it also points to the vulnerability of this type of research and thus the need for caution in its use.

Because of this experience, I was asked to address two topics: What are the preconditions for successfully implementing a random assignment experiment? What are the preconditions for having an impact on policy? As I hinted earlier, I will argue that thinking solely in terms of "preconditions" is the wrong concept. True, there is soil that is more or less fertile and some that should be off-limits, but, to continue the metaphor, the key to success lies in how one tills the soil and does the hard work of planting and harvesting. One has to understand the context and clear away potential land mines.

3. See Hollister, Kemper, and Maynard (1984); Leiman, (1982); Gueron (1997); Gueron and Pauly (1991); and Hamilton and others (1997). The National Evaluation of Welfare-to-Work Strategies (NEWWS), formerly titled the Job Opportunities and Basic Skills Training (JOBS) Evaluation, was conceived and funded by the U.S. Department of Health and Human Services.

This chapter presents lessons from social experiments testing employment and training, welfare reform, and social service programs and systems. It lays out the challenges in implementing a random assignment study, strategies to promote success, and some guidelines on how staff should behave in the field. It then turns to the attributes of a successful experiment and the future challenges to using this approach.

First, a word about a number of terms used throughout this chapter. Any evaluation must differentiate between the test program's *outcomes* (for example, the number of people who get a job or graduate from school) and its *net impact* (the number who get a job or graduate who would not have done so without the program). The measure of net impact is the difference between what would have occurred anyway and what actually happened because of the program.

A random assignment study (also called a social experiment) uses a lottery-like process to allocate people to the two or more groups whose behaviors (outcomes) are subsequently compared to determine the program's net impact. People in one group are enrolled in the test program, and the others are enrolled in a control group intended to show what would have happened in the absence of the program, that is, to provide a benchmark, or counterfactual, against which to assess the program's accomplishments (to determine its value added). Less frequently, the experiment may be a *differential impact* study, wherein people are assigned to two or more test programs (or two programs and a control group), with the goal of determining both the net impact and the relative effectiveness of the two (or more) approaches.

It is the randomness of this process—producing a control group that provides a convincing and unbiased estimate of the counterfactual—that makes this approach so powerful. Other strategies to estimate net impacts face the challenge of identifying an alternative benchmark that can be defended as providing a reliable measure of what would have happened without the intervention.

Administrators often know and tout their program's outcomes, but they rarely know the program's net impacts. In addition to the perceived administrative and ethical burdens of implementing a random assignment study, one reason this approach is not always welcome is that outcomes tell a more positive story than impacts. As a result, the challenges in launching a random assignment study are not only explaining this difference between outcomes and impacts but also convincing administrators that they want to know about—and can sell their success on the basis of—net impacts.

Success in Implementing a Social Experiment

> *If someone is unreservedly enthusiastic about participating in the study, he or she doesn't understand it.* (MDRC field rep)

Successful implementation of a social experiment means overcoming a series of hurdles, including addressing the right question, meeting ethical and legal standards, convincing people that there is no easier way to get the answers and that the findings are "good enough," balancing research ambition against operational reality, implementing a truly random process and ensuring that enough people actually get the test service, following enough people for an adequate length of time to detect policy-relevant impacts, collecting reliable data on an adequate number of outcomes so one does not miss the story, and ensuring that people get the right treatment and enforcing this over time.

In this section, I discuss each of these obstacles in turn, focusing on the burden it places on operating programs.

This litany of challenges may sound unrelenting, leaving the reader wondering why any manager would want to be in such a study. The reasons unfold below, but key among these have been the opportunity to learn (from the study and other sites), the potential to contribute to national and state policy, pressure (from the federal government or state officials) to evaluate program achievements, special funding, and, critically, the fact that the burden on staff was much less than originally feared. These reasons may sound abstract, but they have been sufficient for many sites to participate in repeated random assignment studies, even when earlier findings were not positive.

Addressing the Right Question

The first challenge is to be sure that the evaluation addresses the most important questions. Is the key issue net impact, or feasibility, or replicability, or what explains success or failure, or cost-effectiveness? If it is net impact, is the question: (1) "Does the XYZ service achieve more than the services already available?" or (2) "Are services, such as XYZ, effective?" or (3) "Is one service more effective than another?" Once it is clear what question is to be answered, the next challenge is to determine whether one can design and enforce a social experiment to address it. The answer may be "no."

This "Compared to what?" issue may sound simple, but we have found it to be the most profound. The tendency in program evaluations is to focus on the treatment being assessed: make sure it is well implemented so that it gets a fair test. While this is critical, our experience suggests that it is as important to define the treatment for the control group, because it is the difference in experience that one is assessing.

The challenge arises from the fact that social programs do not occur in a laboratory, thus limiting the researchers' ability to structure both the test and the control environments. With adequate attention and realism, one can usually get the test treatment implemented, but, for legal, ethical, and practical reasons (see the next section), there are severe limits on how far the control environment can be structured. Specifically, one cannot exclude control group members from all services available in their community or school. This means that one can usually answer question 1 above: for example, "Does the test training program or school reform do better than the background of existing services (to the extent that they are normally available and used)?" If this is the right question, the evaluation will satisfy the policy audience. But if the policy question is "Are the services provided of value at all?" (question 2), and if people in the control group have access to some level of similar services, the evaluation will fall short.[4] The difficulty is that people often agree up front that question 1 is the right one, but then they interpret the findings as though they had answered question 2.

There is no simple formula for getting around this issue, but it helps if the program being assessed is new, scarce, or different enough from the background type and level of service (or the program with which it is being compared) so that there is likely to be a meaningful differential in service receipt. Otherwise, one risks spending a lot of energy and money to reach the unsurprising conclusion that the impact of no *additional* service is zero, despite the fact that the services themselves may be of great value.

4. Although this discussion focuses on this problem in social experiments, the same issue arises in many quasi-experimental, comparison-group designs.

Meeting Ethical and Legal Standards

You want to do what to whom for how long? (Question from the field)

Since all random assignment studies affect who gets what services, it is imperative to take ethical and legal concerns seriously. Inadequate attention to these issues can provoke the cancellation of a particular study and can poison the environment for future work. Experience suggests that social experiments should not deny people access to services to which they are entitled, not reduce service levels, address important unanswered questions, include adequate procedures to inform program participants and ensure data confidentiality, be used only if there is no less intrusive way to answer the questions adequately, and have a high probability of producing results that will be used.[5]

The first two points establish the threshold criteria. In some sense, randomly selecting who does and does not get into a program always involves the denial of service, but this issue is much less troubling when the study assesses a specially funded demonstration that provides enriched services that would not exist but for the research and where the number of applicants substantially exceeds the number of program slots. Under those circumstances, random assignment can be viewed as an objective way to allocate scarce opportunities. Since the control group retains eligibility for all other services in the community, the experiment increases services for one group without reducing services for controls. Thus when funds are limited and there will be no reduction in the level of service, random assignment can be presented as an ethical way to allocate scarce program slots, which at the same time will provide important answers as to whether the service is of value.[6]

It is more difficult to use a lottery to control access to existing services (for example, the regular job training system or a new welfare reform program). For certain individuals, such an evaluation will almost certainly lead to the denial of services that they would have received in the

5. For a discussion of ethical and legal issues in random assignment experiments, see Boruch (1997, chap. 3). Some of these are discussed in the following sections of this chapter.

6. Even when there was no research purpose, administrators have sometimes used a random assignment lottery as a fair way to ration scarce and valued program opportunities, for example, in special "magnet" schools or the subsidized summer jobs program for youth.

absence of the research. The key ethical demand in this case is to ensure that the study is conducted only in locations where there are more applicants (or potential applicants) than available slots, and where the study, therefore, will lead to no reduction in the aggregate number of people served but only a reallocation of services among eligible applicants.[7] It is particularly important to avoid any procedures that would deny people access to a service to which they are legally entitled (such as Medicaid or high school).

Suspicions about the ethics of researchers run deep, and despite attention to ethical and legal issues, MDRC staff have confronted numerous crises and, occasionally, horrific epithets. In one random assignment welfare reform study, county staff rejected participation, calling our staff "Nazis." In another state, a legislator accused our staff—and the state welfare agency funding the study—of using tactics similar to those in the infamous Tuskegee syphilis study, provoking extensive negative press (including a cartoon characterizing the state as an unethical scientist pulling the legs off spiders just to see what happens). To save that study, state agency and MDRC staff had to meet with individual state legislators to explain the treatment for people in both the program and the control groups. (Program group members were required to participate in welfare-to-work activities and were subject to sanctions for nonparticipation; control group members were subject to neither condition, but would continue to have access to all entitlements, that is, food stamps, welfare, and Medicaid.)[8] We also stated what would be learned through the study, that we did not know whether the test program would help or harm people, and that there were not adequate funds to provide the test program to all people on welfare in the state. This process culminated in a state legislative hearing and, ultimately, a positive vote to endorse the study and random assignment.

Another example comes from the ongoing NEWWS study, where, in three sites, welfare recipients were assigned to a control group or one of two different treatments: one that pushes rapid entry into the labor force and another that stresses gaining human capital (primarily via adult basic

7. For an extensive discussion of the challenges and their resolution in such a study, see Doolittle and Traeger (1990, chaps. 3, 4, and 6).

8. The fact that controls were excused from a mandatory program that could involve grant cuts (rather than being denied a clear benefit) helped in defending this against the argument of service denial.

education courses) before getting a job. Site staff were concerned that this random process would route people to services that did not meet their needs. The researchers responded that we were, in fact, undertaking the study because it was not clear which services were best for which people, an argument that ultimately proved persuasive.

In designing a social experiment, it is critical to determine how to inform people about the study and decide whether people can refuse to participate (the process of informed consent), to develop grievance procedures for controls, to protect the confidentiality of all data, and to limit the number of people in the control group. Most of these issues are straightforward, but that of informed consent is not. Researchers routinely use elaborate informed consent procedures in studies of voluntary employment and training or welfare reform programs that offer something of perceived value. At intake, individuals are told about the program, the intake lottery, and the data collection and confidentiality procedures and are offered the choice of participating in the study or not. Researchers have followed a different path in structuring evaluations of mandatory welfare reform programs, where the mandate was imposed by Congress or the state, not the evaluation. In this case, the research could not give people a choice of opting out of the program's requirements, because they were the law. Arrangements were worked out, however, to excuse a randomly selected group of controls from the new mandate, which might involve both services and financial penalties, including time limits on welfare. People in the program and control groups were informed that they would be in the study, told of the grievance procedures, and given a choice about participating in any surveys. The logic here was that (1) the study itself did not impose risks beyond those of daily life and (2) controls continued to receive current services and were excused from a more restrictive program.[9]

Finally, most large-scale field studies—whether or not they use random assignment—are expensive and are burdensome for program staff and participants. Funds spent on research may trade off against funds spent on services. Before launching such a study, the researchers should be

9. This was the case because, in the absence of the study, people in the experimental group could not refuse to be in the new program (since it was mandatory) and because some people would routinely be denied services (since funds were limited); thus controls were not unduly disadvantaged. Moreover, all people in the study would continue to receive all basic entitlements.

sure that there is a high probability of getting reliable findings, that there is no less intrusive and less expensive way to get equally reliable results, and that the study has a high probability of addressing important questions and of being used.

Convincing People That There Is No Easier Way to Get the Answers and That the Findings Are "Good Enough"

Over the past twenty-five years, as random assignment has proved feasible and research ambitions have grown, there has been a ratcheting up of study demands, making implementation increasingly challenging. Because of the service denial issue noted above, it was easier to promote participation in a small-scale test involving specially created programs than a random assignment evaluation of a large-scale ongoing program, especially one using a complex multigroup random assignment design. The ambitious, large-scale experimental tests of the Job Training Partnership Act (JTPA) and Job Opportunities and Basic Skills Training (JOBS) programs proved extremely difficult to launch, and many locations refused to participate.[10] One factor that helped enormously in promoting random assignment was evidence that the research community—not just the researchers conducting the study—had endorsed this approach as the most reliable way to determine net impacts. Of particular value were the findings of two national panels—the National Academy of Science's review of youth program evaluations and a U.S. Department of Labor (DOL) panel's assessment of job training studies—that random assignment was the most reliable approach to determining the net impact of employment and training initiatives.[11]

It takes courage for political appointees to favor independent studies that measure net impacts. Aside from the normal desire to control the story, the challenge comes from the fact that impacts are almost always smaller than outcomes. For example, a job training program may accurately claim that 50 percent of enrollees got jobs, only to have this deflated by an impact study showing that 45 percent of the control group also found work, meaning that the program actually produced only a modest 5 percentage point increase in employment. It is much easier to sell success based on the 50 percent than the 5 percent, and particularly

10. See, for example, Doolittle and Traeger (1990).

11. See Betsey, Hollister, and Papageorgiou (1985); and U.S. Department of Labor (1985).

bedeviling to state that a particular program produced a five percentage point gain when another one (spared the blessing of a quality impact study) continues to trumpet its 50 percent achievement. I remember well the poignant question of a welfare official whose program we were evaluating. The governor had sent her a press clipping, citing outcomes to praise Governor Michael Dukakis's achievements in moving people off welfare in Massachusetts, with a handwritten note saying, "Get me the same kind of results." She asked how our study could help, or compete.

Balancing Research Ambition against Operational Reality

Large-scale field research projects are rare opportunities. It is tempting to get very ambitious and seek to answer many important questions. Addressing some questions (for example, collecting more data on local economic conditions) adds no new burden on the operating program or study participants; addressing others clearly interferes with regular program processes. The challenge is to make sure that the research demands are reasonable, so that the program is not compromised to the point where it does not provide a fair test of the correct policy question or that the site is discouraged from participating in the study. Key decisions that can intrude on program processes include the degree of standardization versus local flexibility in multisite experiments, the extent to which sites must not change their program practices for the duration of the study, the point at which random assignment takes place, the duration of random assignment (and of special policies to serve experimentals and exclude controls), the intrusiveness of data collection, whether staff (as well as participants) are randomly assigned, and the use of multiple random assignment groups to get inside the "black box" of the program and determine which features explain program impacts.[12]

We have found that it is possible to implement random assignment, including large-scale studies in operating welfare offices, in ways that are not unduly burdensome. Among other steps, this has meant streamlining

12. The argument for randomly assigning staff arises in studies that compare two programs operating in the same offices or schools, in which staff or teacher quality may be a major explanation of program effectiveness. For an example of such a study, see Goldman (1981). For a discussion of the pros and cons of standardization, see Gueron (1984, pp. 295 ff.). For examples of welfare reform evaluations that changed the nature or order of program services for some participants as part of a differential impact study, see Hamilton and others (1997) and Miller and others (1997). And for a description of how the National JTPA Study took a different approach, see Doolittle and Traeger (1990).

the random assignment procedures so that they take about a minute per person assigned. (In one site, the random assignment process became so routine that the site continued it after the study ended, viewing it as the most efficient way to match the flow of people into the program with staff capacity.)

Implementing a Truly Random Process and Ensuring That Enough People Actually Get the Test Service

Program staff generally dislike random assignment. This is true in community-based programs, where, to do their jobs well, staff must believe that they are helping people improve their lives. It is also true in large agencies, where it is feared that random assignment will add another routine for already overloaded staff. While all of our studies concerned programs funded at levels where not everyone could be served (so that access had to be rationed)[13]—and usually assessed services of unproved value (which, in some cases, ultimately were shown to hurt participants)—program staff vastly preferred to use their own, often more arbitrary rationing strategies (for example, first-come/first-served, serving the more motivated or more employable people, allowing caseworker discretion, serving volunteers first, or limiting recruitment so that no one was actually rejected) than to use a random process whereby they had to personally turn away people whom they viewed as eligible.

Yet random assignment is an all-or-nothing process. It does not help to be a little bit random. Once the process is undercut, the study cannot recover. To implement the study successfully, it is critical to get administrative and line staff to buy into and own the process. Two factors are central to achieving this. The first was already noted: reducing the burden that random assignment places on staff. This is where skill and flexibility in experimental design come in. An experiment must be lodged in the complex program intake process in a way that minimizes disruption and maximizes intellectual yield. To do this, the researcher must understand the intricacies of recruitment and enrollment, the size of the eligible pool, and the likely statistical power of a sample under any particular design. One way to reduce the pain for staff is to place random assignment early in the process, before people reach the program office, for example, by

13. Arguably, this is not true for our studies of time-limited welfare, although even in those cases, there were often accompanying services that could not be extended to all who were eligible.

randomly assigning students using centralized Board of Education records and then telling school staff to recruit only among those assigned as potential participants. This helps on one goal—reducing the burden on program staff—but it hurts on another: The longer the route from the point of random assignment to actual enrollment in services, the lower the percentage of people assigned to the test program who actually receive the treatment. This may mean either that the study has to get unrealistically large (and expensive) in order to detect whether the program had a net impact or that the study may fail to detect program impacts, even if they actually occurred.

The second factor in persuading program staff to join a random assignment study is to show them that the study's success has real value for them or, ultimately, for the people they serve. Two examples demonstrate how this has been done. In 1982, when we were trying to persuade state welfare commissioners to participate in the first random assignment tests of state welfare reform initiatives, we argued that they would get answers to key questions they cared about, that they would be part of a network of states that would learn from each other and from the latest research findings, that the study could give them cover to avoid universal implementation of risky and untested policies, that they would get visibility for their state and have an impact on national policy, that they would get a partly subsidized study, that randomly excluding people from service was not unethical because they did not have enough money to serve everyone anyway, and, finally, that this technique had actually been used in a few local welfare offices without triggering political suicide.[14] Ultimately, eight states joined the study, which involved the random assignment of about 40,000 people in seventy locations and, in fact, delivered the benefits for the state commissioners that had been advertised.[15]

A few years later, MDRC launched a study that used random assignment to assess an education and training program for high school dropouts. To do this, we needed to find local providers who offered these services and persuade them to participate in the evaluation. One such program was operated by the Center for Employment Training (CET) in San Jose. CET leaders were dedicated to improving the well-being of Chicano migrant workers; the staff felt a tremendous sense of mission.

14. For a discussion of how this was done, see Gueron (1985).

15. For a discussion of the impact of this study—known as the Demonstration of State Work/Welfare Initiatives—on national policy, see Baum (1991); and Haskins (1991).

Turning away people at random was viewed as inconsistent with that mission, and managers felt that the decision to join such a study would have to be made by the program intake staff, the people who would actually have to confront potential participants. We met with these staff and told them what random assignment involved, why the results were uniquely reliable and believed, and how positive findings might lead the federal government to provide more money and opportunities for the disadvantaged youth they served, if not in San Jose, then elsewhere. They listened; they knew firsthand the climate of funding cuts; they asked for evidence that such studies had ever led to an increase in public funding; they sought details on how random assignment would work and what they could say to people in the control group. They agonized about the pain of turning away needy young people, and they talked about whether this would be justified if, as a result, other youth gained new opportunities. Then they asked us to leave the room, talked more, and voted. Shortly thereafter, we were ushered back in and told that random assignment had won. This was one of the most humbling experiences I have confronted in twenty-five years of similar research projects, and it left me with a sense of awesome responsibility to deliver the study and get the findings out. The happy ending is that the results for CET were positive, prompting the DOL to fund a fifteen-site expansion serving hundreds of disadvantaged youth.[16]

But even after getting site agreement on the rules, researchers should not be complacent. It is critical to design the actual random assignment process so that it cannot be gamed by intake staff. In our case, this has meant that we either directly controlled the intake process (that is, intake staff called MDRC and were given a computer-generated intake code telling them what to do, and we could later check that this was indeed followed), or we worked with the staff to ensure that the local computer system randomly created program statuses.[17]

Following Enough People Long Enough to Detect Policy-Relevant Impacts

In conducting a social experiment, it is important to ensure from the start that the sample is large enough and that the study will follow people long enough to yield a reliable conclusion on whether the program did or did not work. If a sample is too small, researchers might conclude that an

16. On the results for CET, see Cave and others (1993).
17. For a discussion of these procedures, see Gueron (1985).

effective program made no statistically significant difference; if a follow-up period is too short, they may miss impacts that emerge over time.[18]

This may sound easy, but estimating the needed sample size requires understanding factors ranging from the number of people in the community who are eligible and likely to be interested in the program to the recruitment strategy, rates and duration of participation by people in the program, what (if anything) the program staff offer controls, access to and participation by controls in other services, sample attrition (from the follow-up data), the temporal placement of random assignment, and the likely net impact and policy-relevant impact of the program. Some of these factors are research-based, but others require detailed negotiations with the program providers, and still others (for example, the flow of people or the cost of data collection) may be clear only after the project starts. The complexity of this interplay between sample size and program operations points to the advantage of retaining some flexibility in the research design and of continually reassessing the options as operational, research, and cost parameters become clear.[19]

The pattern of impacts over time can be key to conclusions on program success and cost-effectiveness.[20] While this may seem to be primarily a data and budget issue, it usually also involves very sensitive negotiations about the duration of services provided to the program group, the length of time that control group members must be prevented from enrolling in the test program, and the extent to which the program can provide any special support for controls.[21]

Collecting Reliable Data on Enough Outcomes to See the Story

A social experiment begins with some hypotheses about likely program effects. Researchers have ideas about these (usually based on some

18. See Boruch (1997).

19. For a discussion of this sequential design process in the National Supported Work Demonstration and National JTPA Evaluation, see Gueron (1984, p. 293) and Doolittle and Traeger (1990).

20. For example, our findings that different welfare-to-work programs have different time paths of impacts and that some produce taxpayer savings large enough to offset program costs depended on having data tracking people for several years after enrollment in the programs. See Gueron and Pauly (1991); Riccio, Friedlander, and Freedman (1994); Friedlander and Burtless (1995); and Hamilton and others (1997).

21. In many studies, there is strong site pressure to provide some services to controls.

model of how the program will work), as do program administrators, key political actors, advocates, and others. We have found that, to get the buy-in for a study that will protect it during the inevitable strains of multiyear implementation, it is important to bring a diverse group of local stakeholders together and solicit their thoughts on the key questions. If people own the questions—if they see the project as *their* study that addresses *their* questions—they are more likely to stay the course and help the researchers get the answers.

At MDRC, we learned this lesson in our first project that embedded random assignment in an operating social service agency: the WIN Research Laboratory Project of the 1970s. In proposing a partnership between staff in welfare offices and researchers, Merwin Hans (the DOL's WIN administrator) argued that local staff had undermined past studies because they did not care about the studies' success. To combat this, we asked program staff to develop the new approaches and then to work closely with researchers on the random assignment protocols and research questions. Because they cared deeply about answering the questions, they provided the data and cooperated fully with the random assignment procedures.[22]

Designing field studies involves balancing research ambition against budget constraints. There is usually good reason to address a wide range of questions: for example, did an employment program affect earnings, transfer payments, income, family formation, or children's success in school? In deciding whether all this is affordable, a key issue is which data will be used to track behavior over time. The earliest social experiments (the Negative Income Tax experiments) relied on special surveys and researcher-generated data to track outcomes. The data were expensive but covered a wide range of outcomes. One of the breakthroughs in the early 1980s was the use of existing computerized administrative databases to track behavior.[23] These were much less expensive (allowing for an enormous expansion in sample size and thus a reduction in the size of effects that could be detected), placed less burden on study participants, and did not have the same problem of sample attrition faced in surveys;

22. See Goldman (1981); and Leiman (1982).

23. Examples of computerized administrative data include welfare and Food Stamp payment records, unemployment insurance data (which track people's employment and earnings), and various types of school records. The low cost of these data allows large samples to be followed over long periods, providing both more refined estimates of the impacts for the full sample and, equally important, estimates for numerous subgroups.

but administrative databases covered a narrow range of outcomes and had other limitations.[24] Moreover, gaining access to these critical administrative data can often be difficult and sometimes impossible, as state agencies may see little advantage in cooperating with the study and must balance research needs against privacy concerns.

In our early welfare studies, we argued for the value of answering a few questions well—that is, tracking large samples using records data—even if this meant we could address only the most critical questions. This seemed appropriate for studies of relatively low-cost programs, where modest impacts were expected and we therefore needed very reliable estimates to find out whether the approach made a difference and whether it was cost-effective. However, where programs are more ambitious and can potentially affect a wide range of outcomes for participants and their families, there is a strong argument for combining records and survey data, or using only survey data, to address a broader group of questions.

Identifying the data source is important, but it is also critical to collect identical data on people in the program and control groups. Estimating net impact involves comparing the behavior of the two groups. While it is tempting to use rich data on the program participants (about whom you usually know a lot), the key is to use identical data for people in the two groups, so that data differences are not mistaken for program effects. Further, in all stages of the study, researchers need to be vigilant about data quality and comprehensiveness (thereby minimizing sample attrition).

Ensuring That People Get the Right Treatment over Time

Random assignment is the gateway to placement in the different study groups. But a process that starts out random may yield a useless study if it is not policed. This means that, for the duration of the study, members of each research group must be treated appropriately; that is, they must be offered or denied the correct services. This is relatively easy if the test program is simple and controlled by the researchers. It is much more difficult if the program provides multidimensional services or is ongoing and operated in many sites, or if there is a differential impact study in which two or more program treatments are provided by staff in the same office.

24. For a discussion of the relative merits of administrative records and surveys, see Kornfeld and Bloom (1999). While records data are relatively inexpensive to process, the up-front cost and time needed to gain access to these data can be high.

To ensure appropriate treatments and reduce crossovers (that is, people from one study group receiving services appropriate for the other group), staff need clear procedures on how to handle people in the different groups, adequate training, reliable systems to track people's research status over time, and incentives to follow the procedures. One needs to be sure, for example, that if people return to a program (at the same or another office), they are placed in the same research status and offered the intended services. Obviously, the longer the treatment and the control embargo, the more costly, burdensome, and politically difficult is the enforcement of such procedures.[25] All these challenges are multiplied in a differential impact study, especially when two or more treatments are implemented in the same program office or school. In that case, it is particularly difficult to ensure that staff or teachers stick to the appropriate procedures and that the treatments do not blend together, thus undermining the service distinction.

Strategies That Promote Success

The above discussion suggests some threshold "preconditions" that should be met to conduct a random assignment study: not denying people access to services or benefits to which they are entitled; not having enough funds to provide the test services for all people eligible; no decrease in the overall level of service, but rather a reallocation among eligible people; and, for programs involving volunteers, a careful process of informed consent.

Even if these conditions are met, successfully enlisting sites in a random assignment study is an art. As a neophyte to social experiments in the 1970s, I had thought that, to overcome the obstacles, it was critical that researchers have sufficient funding and clout to induce and discipline compliance with the requirements of the evaluation.[26] This surely helps, but as operating funds subsequently became scarce even while social experiments flourished, we learned that other factors could substitute. As noted earlier, key points were convincing the agency that the study would advance its mission; provide the most reliable answers to questions the agency cared about; satisfy political concerns (for example, provide a way to avoid immediate large-scale implementation of an untested approach);

25. For a discussion of these issues, see Gueron (1985, pp. 9–10).
26. See Gueron (1980, p. 93).

get national visibility for the local program and its staff; follow ethical procedures, including, where appropriate, informed consent, full explanations of procedures, and a grievance process; and satisfy federal or state research requirements or open up opportunities for special funding.

This last point has been particularly important. Obviously, states and sites would be more likely to participate in random assignment studies if this participation was a condition of their ability to innovate or get funds. This was one of several factors that explain the unusually large number of reliable, random assignment evaluations of welfare reform and job training programs. Key among these were that such studies were shown to be feasible and uniquely convincing, that staff at MDRC and other research organizations promoted such studies, and that staff in both the U.S. Department of Health and Human Services (HHS) and the DOL favored this approach.[27] Early studies (for example, the National Supported Work Demonstration and the WIN Research Laboratory Project) showed that random assignment could be used in real-world employment programs and in welfare offices. In the job training field, this success prompted the two review panels cited above to conclude that random assignment was superior to alternative evaluation strategies, leading DOL staff to fund both a large number of demonstrations that provided special funding to sites that would participate in such a study and a large-scale random assignment evaluation of the nation's job training system.[28]

In the welfare field, HHS staff similarly became convinced of the value of random assignment and the vulnerability of other approaches. HHS staff were assisted in translating this preference into action by the requirement that Congress had put into Section 1115 of the Social Security Act, which allowed states to waive provisions of the Aid to Families with Dependent Children (AFDC) law in order to test new welfare reform approaches, but only if they assessed these initiatives. Since the early 1980s, through Republican and Democratic administrations, HHS staff have taken this language seriously and required states to conduct rigorous net impact studies.[29] In some states, there was also legislative pressure for such studies. The 1996 welfare reform legislation—the Personal

27. In particular, Howard Rolston at HHS and Raymond Uhalde at DOL remained vigilant in promoting high-quality, rigorous evaluations.

28. See Betsey, Hollister, and Papageorgiou (1985); and U.S. Department of Labor (1985, 1995).

29. For summaries of these studies, see Gueron and Pauly (1991); Greenberg and Wiseman (1992); Bloom (1997); Greenberg and Shroder (1997); and Gueron (1997).

Responsibility and Work Opportunity Reconciliation Act (PRWORA)—substituted block grants for the welfare entitlement and ended the waiver process and evaluation requirements. No large-scale welfare evaluation using random assignment has been started under the new law.[30] Other key points included showing that the study would not undermine the program's ability to meet operational performance measures, reduce the number of people they served, overburden hard-pressed line staff, deny control group members access to basic entitlements or otherwise violate state laws and regulations, or likely lead to a political and public relations disaster.[31]

Finally, a number of other factors can make it more difficult to promote participation in a random assignment study, beginning with political concerns. For high-profile issues like welfare reform, public officials may prefer to control the data (using what they know about program outcomes) rather than risk more modest results from a high-quality independent evaluation. Other influential factors are the perceived value of the services denied controls and the clout of members of the control group or their families, the intrusiveness of the research design (including the duration of any special procedures and the extent of interference with normal operations), and the difficulty of isolating controls from the program (for example, from its message or similar services), which can limit the questions addressed in the study.

Lessons on How to Behave in the Field

I have argued that discovering which factors will induce participation and negotiating the design of an experiment that is politically and ethically feasible involve a balance of research and political/operational skills. To make this artistry less abstract, I now present some very basic operating guidelines that three senior MDRC staff members (Fred Doolittle, Darlene Hasselbring, and Linda Traeger) prepared for their colleagues to use as a starting point for more refined discussions.[32] As is clear from the tone, these were directed at staff seeking to enlist sites in a particularly challenging random assignment study of an ongoing operating program.

30. However, between 1996 and mid-1999, when this essay was completed, a number of small-scale, one-state studies were started.

31. For an example of how these factors worked to bring states into the 1980s welfare experiments, see Gueron (1985).

32. Doolittle, Hasselbring, and Traeger (1990); see also Doolittle and Traeger (1990).

In many studies, the site recruitment task is simpler, and this level of promotion is not needed.

General Rules

1. *The right frame of mind is critical. Remember, you want them more than they want you.* Even if they are eager initially, they will eventually figure out how much is involved and realize they are doing you a service if they say "yes." *Do not say "no" to their suggestions unless they deal with a central element of the study (for example, no random assignment).* You may well need to come back later with a modified design (for example, a different intake procedure) when the pickings of sites look slim. *Remember to be friendly and not defensive.* They really cannot know for sure what they are getting into, and their saying "yes" will be much more likely if they think you are a reasonable person they can work with over time.

2. *Turn what is still uncertain into an advantage.* When potential site partners raise a question about an issue that is not yet sorted out, tell them they have raised an issue also of concern to you and they can be part of the process of figuring out how to address it.

3. *Make sure you understand their perspective.* As much as possible, try to "think like them" so you will understand their concerns.

4. *Never intimate some aspect of the research is too complex to get into.* This implies they are not smart enough to understand it. Work out ways to explain complicated things about random assignment using straightforward, very concrete examples rather than research terms.

5. *Be sensitive about the language and examples you use.* Occasionally you will run into someone who has a research background and may want to use the jargon, but most people tend to be put off by terms that are everyday, shorthand expressions to researchers. For example, many people find the terms "experiment," "experimental," "control group," "service embargo," and even "random assignment" offensive. Use more familiar, longer ways of saying these, *even if they are less precise or even technically wrong.* Site staff often react negatively to discussions of how random assignment is often used in medical research, probably because they are only familiar with outrageous examples.

6. *If some issues are sure to come up (ethics, operational issues, site burden), raise them yourself.* This shows that you understand the implications of random assignment, have grappled with them yourself, and think they can be addressed.

7. *If pressed on an awkward issue about random assignment, do not give an evasive answer.* For example, if site people forcefully ask if you really mean they will have to deny services to those in the control group, say "yes." Then, explain the reasons for the rule, and address the underlying concerns that led them to raise the question.

8. *If someone is unreservedly enthusiastic about the study, he or she does not understand it.* While it might sound nice to let them cruise along happily, if their continued support matters, you must make sure they understand what they are getting into.

9. *Make sure you highlight the benefits of participating.* Usually, the key one is site-specific findings. Do not mislead them or allow them to think they will get more than you can deliver. Often, they want a lot of "inside-the-black-box" results.

10. *Negative momentum can occur and must be countered.* If things start going badly in many sites, regroup and rethink the model and the arrangements you are offering before things get out of hand.

Learning about the Program

1. *Ask as many people as possible how the program works.* Different perspectives are vital. You need to know things at a micro level that only local people can know.

2. *Do not rely too much on their estimate of participation rates.* Unless they have an extraordinary management information system, most program operators have never had a reason to ask the type of client-flow questions needed to decide the details of a random assignment design.

Developing the Details of the Model and Closing the Deal

1. *Operational issues are your problem, and you have to get site partners to buy into the study before they become their problem.* You know you have made progress when they start helping you figure out how to address the problems.

2. *Do not be surprised by the level of "detail" you will have to address.* Something that seems like a minor point from a research perspective may turn out to be a crucial operational barrier to putting the model in place. Try to learn the vocabulary about the "details" so they will realize you understand and take their issues seriously.

3. *Recognize that in working out procedures you will be dealing with people representing very different perspectives.* Program directors worry

about different things than managers or the line staff. Be sensitive to the differences in perspective, and recognize that a good director may give the managers who represent the line staff a veto over participation if you cannot address their concerns. Support by an outside board or director removed from program operations is not enough, although it is a start and will open the door. Administrative managers must be on board.

4. *Protect the core of the study and figure out where you can be flexible.* Do not lose sites over something not central. Depending on the study, noncentral items might include who controls lists of people referred for random assignment, exclusion of certain groups of people from random assignment, temporary changes in the random assignment ratio to ensure an adequate flow of program participants, length of the service embargo for controls, and limited services after random assignment for controls.

5. *Sometimes the best response to a question about how a procedure would work is to ask a question.* The goal is to develop procedures for the study that disrupt the program as little as possible. When the staff raise a tough operational issue, the starting point is what they normally would do if the study were not in place. So ask them, and then go from there. Often, this will suggest minor changes that everyone can live with.

6. *Recognize that model development is an iterative process.* New issues come up over time that will need to be addressed. Expect a continued balancing between research preferences and operational constraints.

7. *Develop a memorandum of agreement both parties can live with.* Do not push or even allow a site to sign an agreement you think its staff cannot fulfill. A key factor to be realistic about is sample size. Do not set targets they cannot meet.

8. *Money can often fix some problems, but do not get into a position where it looks as though you are trying to bribe them into betraying their ethics.* Operational issues relating to staffing can often be helped by financial support. Serious ethical concerns cannot be addressed in this way.

Community Relations

1. *No news is good news.* Imagine yourself as a reporter. Would you rather write about the human interest side of the study ("Poor used as human guinea pigs") or the abstract policy and research issues that motivate the study? You should expect most local news stories done before findings are available to be negative if the reporter understands what random assignment is.

2. *Make sure the site knows you will take the bullets for it.* Persuade the site that it has a compatriot who will join the battle if things get rough.

3. *There are pros and cons to your initially playing a prominent role in explaining the study.* Ideally, the site should take the lead in building support for the study, because this shows the staff understand and really do support it. However, site staff can easily be surprised by local opposition or may not be able to explain the reasons for the study or its procedures as well as you can. If there is doubt how a meeting will go, fight for a role without implying that the local people do not understand the study or know the local situation.

4. *Be available to brief agencies affected by the study and advocates, but do not expect them to be won over instantly.* Persuading someone that this type of research is okay is a long process. Make sure site staff understand the pros and cons of outreach to other groups versus a low profile. Then let the site staff decide how to handle this.

5. *Prepare a press kit, and leave it up to the sites to decide what to do with it.* This should be viewed as a defensive rather than an offensive weapon, to be used if called for.

6. *Develop a thick skin, and do not get defensive when speaking with the press or community groups.* There is one exception: If your personal integrity is attacked, fight back. You are not a "Nazi."

7. *Never say something is too complex to discuss or refuse to acknowledge key issues as legitimate.* Ultimately, participation involves trust. Random assignment is not business as usual, and site staff have to know you are leveling with them.

Training Local Staff on Study Procedures

1. *Taking the time to write a good manual, with examples, is time well spent.* A detailed manual describing the study rationale and the intricacies of program intake and random assignment, and providing scripts for site staff, will serve as a valuable training tool and future reference for site staff.

2. *Recognize that the training may be the first time many have heard much about the study and that you must win them over.* At the beginning of training, explain the reason for the study and random assignment and your common concern about people in the study. Try to get the site directors to lay the groundwork for the study and to show up at the training to indicate their support.

Setting the Right Tone for Study Implementation

1. *Program managers should understand that it is better to tell you about issues early, before they get serious and can threaten the study.* Try to convince people that you might be a source of possible solutions, since you can draw on MDRC's past experience.

2. *Make sure they understand you will show as much flexibility as possible on procedures.* Sites that decide to participate sometimes come to view the initial procedures as holy writ. They may nearly kill themselves trying to follow them without realizing you might be able to make a change that will not matter to the research but that will make their lives much easier. They probably will have trouble distinguishing between rules central to the study and those that can be adjusted at the margins.

From Research to Policy: Lessons from MDRC's Experience

Up to now, I have discussed the challenge of implementing a random assignment study and the field techniques that promote success. But the ultimate goal of policy research is to inform and affect public policy. MDRC's studies have been credited with having an unusual effect on public policy, particularly welfare policy.[33] Looking back primarily at our welfare studies, I draw the following lessons about running a successful social experiment.[34]

Lesson 1: Correctly diagnose the problem. The life cycle of a major experiment or evaluation is often five or more years. To be successful, the study must be rooted in issues that matter—concerns that will outlive the tenure of an assistant secretary or a state commissioner and will still be of interest when the results are in—and about which there are important unanswered questions.

Lesson 2: Have a reasonable treatment. An experiment should test an approach that looks feasible operationally and politically—where, for example, it is likely that the relevant delivery systems will cooperate, that people will participate enough for the intervention to make a difference, and that the costs will not be so high as to rule out replication.

33. See, for example, Baum (1991); Haskins (1991); Greenberg and Mandell (1991); Szanton (1991); and Wiseman (1991).

34. This section is based on a discussion in Gueron (1997, pp. 88–91).

Lesson 3: Design a real-world test. The program should be tested fairly (if possible, after the program start-up period) and, if feasible, in multiple sites. The results will be all the more powerful if they are comparable in Little Rock, San Diego, and Baltimore. Replicating success in diverse environments is highly persuasive to Congress and state officials.[35]

Lesson 4: Address the key questions that people care about. Does the approach work? For whom? Under what conditions? Why? Can it be replicated? How do benefits compare with costs? It is important not only to get the hard numbers but also to build on the social experiment to address some of the qualitative concerns that underlie public attitudes or that explain which features of the program or its implementation account for success or failure.

Lesson 5: Have a reliable way to find out whether the program works. This is the unique strength of a social experiment. Policymakers flee from technical debates among experts. They do not want to take a stand and then find that the evidence has evaporated in the course of obscure debates about methodology. The key in large-scale projects is to answer a few questions well. Failure lies not in learning that something does not work but in getting to the end of a large project and saying, "I don't know." The cost of the witch doctors' disagreeing is indeed paralysis that, ultimately, threatens to discredit social policy research.

The social experiments of the past twenty-five years have shown that it is possible to produce a database widely accepted by congressional staff, federal agencies, the Congressional Budget Office, the General Accounting Office, state agencies, and state legislatures. When MDRC started its welfare studies, the uncertainty about the cost, impacts, and feasibility of welfare-to-work programs was the size of a football field. Twenty-five years of work have shortened this field dramatically.

Random assignment alone does not ensure success, however. As I discussed earlier, one needs large samples, adequate follow-up, high-quality data collection, and a way to isolate the control group from the spillover effects of the treatment. One also needs to pay attention to ethical issues and site burden. Finally, rigor has its drawbacks. Peter Rossi once formulated several laws about policy research, one of which was: the better the study, the smaller the likely net impact.[36] High-quality policy research

35. This point is stressed in Baum (1991).
36. Cited in Baum (1991).

must continuously compete with the claims of greater success based on weaker evidence.

Lesson 6: Contextualize the results. To have an impact on policy, it is usually not enough to carry out a good project and report the lessons. Researchers need to help the audience assess the relative value of the approach tested versus others. To do this, they should lodge the results of the experiment in the broader context of what is known about what works and what does not.

Lesson 7: Simplify. If an advanced degree is needed to understand the lessons, they are unlikely to reach policymakers. One of the beauties of random assignment is that anyone can understand what you did and what you learned. One strategy we used was to develop a standard way to present results and stick to it. This meant that people learned to read these studies and understand the results. As social experiments become more complex—involving multiple treatment groups and multiple points of random assignment—they put this overwhelming advantage at risk.

Lesson 8: Actively disseminate your results. Design the project so that it will have intermediate products, and share the results with federal and state officials, congressional staff and Congress, public interest groups, advocates, academics, and the press. At the same time, resist pressure to produce results so early that you risk later having to reverse your conclusions.

Lesson 9: Do not confuse dissemination with advocacy. The key to long-term successful communication is trust. If you overstate your findings or distort them to fit an agenda, people will know it and will reject what you have to say.

Lesson 10: Be honest about failures. Although many of our studies have produced positive findings, the results are often mixed and, at times, clearly negative. State officials and program administrators share the human fondness for good news. To their credit, however, most have sought to learn from disappointing results, which often prove as valuable as successful ones for shaping policy.

Lesson 11: You do not need dramatic results to have an impact on policy. Many people have said that the 1988 welfare reform law, the Family Support Act, was based and passed on the strength of research—and the research was about modest changes. When we have reliable results, it usually suggests that social programs (at least the relatively modest ones tested in this country) are not panaceas but that they nonetheless can make improvements. One of the lessons I draw from our experience is that modest changes have often been enough to make a program cost-effective and can also be enough to persuade policymakers to act. However, while this was true in the mid-1980s, it was certainly not true in the mid-1990s. In the last round of federal welfare reform, modest improvements were often cast as failures.

Lesson 12: Get partners and buy in from the beginning. In conceptualizing and launching a project, try to make the major delivery systems, public interest groups, and advocates claim a stake in it so that they will own the project and its lessons. If you can do that, you will not have to communicate your results forcefully; others will do it for you.

One reason our research has had an impact is the change in the scale, structure, and funding of social experiments that occurred in the 1980s. The Supported Work and Negative Income Tax experiments of the 1970s were relatively small-scale tests conducted outside the mainstream delivery systems (in laboratory-like or controlled environments) and supported with generous federal funds. This changed dramatically in 1981, with the virtual elimination of federal funds to operate field tests of new initiatives. Most social experiments that we have conducted since then have used the regular, mainstream delivery systems to operate the program. There has been very little special funding.

This new mode has a clear downside: the boldness of what can be tested is limited. One has to build on what can be funded through the normal channels, which may partly explain the modest nature of the program impacts. The upside has been immediate state or local ownership, or both, since by definition one is evaluating real-world state or local initiatives, not projects made in Washington or at a think tank. If you want to randomly assign 10,000 people in welfare or job training offices in a large urban area, state or county employees have to have a reason to cooperate. When you are relying on state welfare and unemployment insurance earnings records to track outcomes, people have to have a reason to give you these data. The reason we offered was that these were *their* studies, addressing *their* questions, and were usually conducted under state contracts. They owned the studies, they were paying some of the freight, and thus they had a commitment to making the research succeed. In the welfare case, their commitment was aided by the fact that such evaluations also could satisfy the Section 1115 research requirements imposed by HHS.

Through this process, we converted state and local welfare and job training demonstrations and programs into social experiments, involving the key institutions as partners from the beginning. For the major actors and funding streams, the relevance was clear from the outset. This buy-in was critical. This partnership also had a positive effect on the researchers, forcing us to pay attention to our audience and their questions. In this process, during the 1980s and 1990s, social experiments moved out of the laboratory and into welfare and job training offices. Studies no longer involved a thousand, but tens of thousands of people. You did not have to convince policymakers and program administrators that the findings were relevant; the tests were not the prelude to a large-scale test but instead told states directly what the major legislation was delivering.[37] Because of the studies' methodological rigor, the results were widely believed. But the limited funding narrowed both the outcomes that could be measured and the boldness of what was tested.

Five years ago, I might have argued that these twelve "lessons" explained why these studies had such a large impact on state and federal welfare policy. But that was clearly not the case in 1996. In contrast to the 1988 Family Support Act, which drew heavily on the research record, block grants and time limits are very much a leap into the unknown. While not necessarily pleasant, it is always useful for researchers to remember that their work is only one ingredient in the policy process and that, when the stakes are high enough, politics usually trumps research.

Future Challenges

Over the past two decades, random assignment studies have been used to build a solid foundation of evidence about the effectiveness of welfare reform and job training programs. In the early 1970s, it was not known whether this approach could be used to test real-world operating programs. We now know that it can be, and that the results are convincing. Although participation in random assignment studies involves clear burdens, administrators and staff in many programs have found the overall experience worthwhile and, as a result, have often joined multiple studies.

Yet the climate for such evaluations, at least in the welfare and job training fields, has grown chillier. Several factors explain this. One is the growing complexity of the research questions. Twenty-five years ago, the evaluation questions were very basic—Do employment and training

37. See Baum (1991); and Greenberg and Mandell (1991).

programs make a difference? For whom?—and so were the random assignment designs. Thus in the first random assignment test of such a program, the National Supported Work Demonstration, special funds were provided to small community programs to implement a clearly defined treatment; volunteer applicants were randomly accepted in the program or placed in a control group that got no special services. The study worked; the answers were clear.

Subsequently, the research questions have become more complex—What works best? What duration and intensity of the "treatment" produce what results? Which elements of a program explain its success or failure? Consequently, the operational demands have also grown in complexity, at the very time when there has been a reduction in special program funding. Random assignment moved out of small community programs into regular welfare and job training offices; tests covered not only special new programs but regular, ongoing services; studies involved not just one test treatment and a control group but multiple tests and more than one point of random assignment.

The result has been a major increase both in what is learned and—even more quickly—in what people want to learn. Random assignment has greatly increased the reliability of estimates of program impacts, but we have not progressed at the same rate in linking this to our understanding of program implementation. For example, most impact studies show substantial variation across locations, but they are not able to explain the extent to which this results from factors such as local labor market conditions or different aspects of program implementation. This limits researchers' ability to generalize the findings to other locations and also to get inside the "black box" of the program. Differential impact studies (comparing several approaches) are a major breakthrough, but realistically they can isolate the effects of only a few aspects of the treatment or can compare only a few multidimensional approaches. They cannot provide an experimental test of the many separate dimensions of the program model and its implementation; yet this is the concern of people increasingly interested in understanding why initiatives produce the results they do and what should be done differently. More work in this area is critical if we are to increase the potential of evaluations to feed into the design of more effective programs.

A further complexity arises from the interest and need to assess saturation initiatives, for example, the end of the basic welfare entitlement or the launching of a comprehensive community-wide initiative. Random assignment has proved feasible in some cases, but not in others.[38]

In addition, funders and consumers of research are concerned that random assignment social experiments are intrinsically conservative, because the control group receives services regularly available in the community. In some studies, particularly of voluntary programs, the actual service differential may not be large. The resulting finding of a modest net impact leaves unanswered the question of whether the services themselves (received in varying forms and intensity by people in both groups) have a more substantial impact.[39] Yet that may be the question uppermost in people's minds. The fact that this dilemma is not unique to random assignment studies, but is inevitable in any evaluation involving a comparison group, has not reduced the frustration. But it does mean that there is a hunger for a methodological breakthrough that would allow people to measure "total" not "net" impacts.

Finally, in the welfare field, the 1996 law, with its combination of block grants and the end of the Section 1115 waiver process, dramatically changed the funding and incentive structure that supported random assignment studies in the past. While block grants create pressure on states to figure out what works, the politicization of the welfare debate pushes in the opposite direction.[40] At a time when the stakes have never been higher for figuring out how to move people from welfare to work and out of poverty, the outlook for large-scale random assignment tests is unclear.

Postscript: The Implications for Education

This chapter summarizes the practical lessons from random assignment studies of welfare reform and employment and training programs, but it is part of a series of essays addressing random assignment in education. Without straying from my topic unduly, some of the lessons suggest clear

38. For example, MDRC randomly assigned public housing communities in the Jobs-Plus Demonstration (see Bloom, 1999; Riccio, 1999) but took a different approach in evaluating the effects of the 1996 welfare reform law in urban areas (see Quint and others, 1999). See also Connell and others (1995).

39. See, for example, the discussion of the New Chance Demonstration in Quint, Bos, and Polit (1997).

40. See Gueron (1997).

challenges for school-based random assignment studies. These include the following:

—Control services will be even more extensive, which has implications for the questions that can be addressed and the likely magnitude of impact.

—Controls will often be served in the same schools as experimentals, increasing the risk of the treatment's spreading from experimental to control classrooms.

—Treatments may extend over many years, making it harder to ensure that people get the services defined in the research protocols.

—Schools are dynamic institutions, with many simultaneous innovations that can affect all students in the study.

—The unit of random assignment may have to be the school or the classroom.

—Teachers may be a key dimension of the treatment, raising the issue of teacher random assignment.

—Parents may pressure school principals to circumvent random assignment.

—The multidimensional experimental and control treatments will be more difficult to define and standardize across locations.

—The decentralized funding structure will both reduce the pressure for evaluation and increase the difficulty in disseminating research results.

—The involvement of children will make the implementation of informed consent and related procedures more demanding.

While this list is long, it should be remembered that random assignment has a successful track record in very diverse environments. In part building on this, researchers have recently begun an important expansion of random assignment studies in education.[41] At a time of growing pressure to improve the performance of the nation's schools, these studies promise to bring new rigor to our understanding of the effectiveness of alternative reform strategies. It is essential to push forward on this front.

41. See, for example, Pauly and Thompson (1993); Kemple (1998); Cook (1999); Nave, Miech, and Mosteller (1998); Mosteller (1999); and Kemple and Snipes (2000).

References

Aaron, Henry J. 1978. *Politics and the Professors: The Great Society in Perspective.* Brookings.

Baum, Erica B. 1991. "When the Witch Doctors Agree: The Family Support Act and Social Science Research." *Journal of Policy Analysis and Management* 10 (4): 603–15.

Betsey, Charles L., Robinson G. Hollister, and Mary R. Papageorgiou. 1985. *Youth Employment and Training Programs: The YEDPA Years.* Washington: National Academy Press.

Bloom, Dan. 1997. *After AFDC: Welfare-to-Work Choices and Challenges for States.* New York: Manpower Demonstration Research Corporation.

Bloom, Howard S. 1999. *Building a Convincing Test of a Public Housing Employment Program Using Non-Experimental Methods: Planning for the Jobs-Plus Demonstration.* New York: Manpower Demonstration Research Corporation.

Boruch, Robert F. 1997. *Randomized Experiments for Planning and Evaluation.* Thousand Oaks, Calif.: Sage.

Cave, George, Fred Doolittle, Hans Bos, and Cyril Toussaint. 1993. *JOBSTART: Final Report on a Program for School Dropouts.* New York: Manpower Demonstration Research Corporation.

Connell, James, Anne Kubisch, Lisbeth Schorr, and Carol Weiss, eds. 1995. *New Approaches to Evaluating Community Initiatives: Concepts, Methods, and Contexts.* Roundtable on Comprehensive Community. Washington: Aspen Institute.

Doolittle, Fred, Darlene Hasselbring, and Linda Traeger. 1990. "Lessons on Site Relations from the JTPA Team: Test Pilots for Random Assignment." Internal paper. New York: Manpower Demonstration Research Corporation.

Doolittle, Fred, and Linda Traeger. 1990. *Implementing the National JTPA Study.* New York: Manpower Demonstration Research Corporation.

Friedlander, Daniel, and Gary Burtless. 1995. *Five Years After: The Long-Term Effects of Welfare-to-Work Programs.* New York: Russell Sage Foundation.

Goldman, Barbara. 1981. *Impacts of the Immediate Job Search Assistance Experiment: Louisville WIN Research Laboratory Project.* New York: Manpower Demonstration Research Corporation.

Greenberg, David H., and Marvin B. Mandell. 1991. "Research Utilization in Policymaking: A Tale of Two Series (of Social Experiments)." *Journal of Policy Analysis and Management* 10 (4): 633–56.

Greenberg, David, and Mark Shroder. 1997. *The Digest of Social Experiments.* 2d ed. Washington: Urban Institute.

Greenberg, David, and Michael Wiseman. 1992. "What Did the OBRA Demonstrations Do?" In *Evaluating Employment and Training Programs*, edited by Charles Manski and Irwin Garfinkel. Cambridge, Mass.: Harvard University Press.

Gueron, Judith M. 1980. "The Supported Work Experiment." In *Employing the Unemployed,* edited by Eli Ginzberg. Basic Books.

———. 1984. "Lessons from Managing the Supported Work Demonstration." In *The National Supported Work Demonstration,* edited by Robinson G. Hollister Jr., Peter Kemper, and Rebecca A. Maynard. University of Wisconsin Press.

——— 1985. "The Demonstration of State Work/Welfare Initiatives." In *Randomization and Field Experimentation,* special issue of *New Directions for Program Evaluation* 28 (December 1985): 5–14, edited by Robert F. Boruch and Werner Wothke. San Francisco: Jossey-Bass.

———. 1997. "Learning about Welfare Reform: Lessons from State-Based Evaluations." *New Directions for Evaluation* 76 (Winter): 79–94.

Gueron, Judith M., and Edward Pauly. 1991. *From Welfare to Work.* New York: Russell Sage Foundation.

Hamilton, Gayle, Thomas Brock, Mary Farrell, Daniel Friedlander, and Kristen Harknett. 1997. *National Evaluation of Welfare-to-Work Strategies: Evaluating Two Welfare-to-Work Program Approaches: Two-Year Findings on the Labor Force Attachment and Human Capital Development Programs in Three Sites.* Washington: U.S. Department of Health and Human Services and U.S. Department of Education.

Haskins, Ron. 1991. "Congress Writes a Law: Research and Welfare Reform." *Journal of Policy Analysis and Management* 10 (4): 616–32.

Hollister, Robinson G., Jr., Peter Kemper, and Rebecca A. Maynard, eds. 1984. *The National Supported Work Demonstration.* University of Wisconsin Press.

Kemple, James J. 1998. "Using Random Assignment Field Experiments to Measure the Effects of School-Based Education Interventions." Paper prepared for the annual conference of the Association for Public Policy Analysis and Management, New York, October.

Kemple, James J., and Jason C. Snipes. 2000. *Career Academies: Impacts on Students' Engagement and Performance in High School.* New York: Manpower Demonstration Research Corporation.

Kornfeld, R., and Howard Bloom. 1999. "Measuring the Impacts of Social Programs on the Earnings and Employment of Low-Income Persons: Do UI Wage Records and Surveys Agree?" *Journal of Labor Economics* 17 (1).

Leiman, Joan M. 1982. *The WIN Labs: A Federal/Local Partnership in Social Research.* New York: Manpower Demonstration Research Corporation.

Miller, Cynthia, Virginia Knox, Patricia Auspos, Jo Anna Hunter-Manns, and Alan Orenstein. 1997. *Making Welfare Work and Work Pay: Implementation and 18-Month Impacts of the Minnesota Family Investment Program.* New York: Manpower Demonstration Research Corporation.

Mosteller, Frederick. 1999. Forum: "The Case for Smaller Classes." *Harvard Magazine* (May–June).

Nave, Bill, Edward J. Miech, and Frederick Mosteller. 1998. "A Rare Design: The Role of Field Trials in Evaluating School Practices." Paper presented at meeting of the American Academy of Arts and Sciences, Harvard University.

Pauly, Edward, and Deborah E. Thompson. 1993. "Assisting Schools and Disadvantaged Children by Getting and Using Better Evidence on What Works in Chapter 1: The Opportunities and Limitations of Field Tests Using Random Assignment." New York: Manpower Demonstration Research Corporation.

Quint, Janet, Johannes M. Bos, and Denise F. Polit. 1997. *New Chance: Final Report on a Comprehensive Program for Young Mothers in Poverty and Their Children.* New York: Manpower Demonstration Research Corporation.

Quint, Janet, Kathryn Edin, Maria L. Buck, Barbara Fink, Yolanda C. Padilla, Olis Simmons-Hewitt, and Mary Eustace Valmont. 1999. *Big Cities and Welfare Reform: Early Implementation and Ethnographic Findings from the Project on Devolution and Urban Change.* New York: Manpower Demonstration Research Corporation.

Riccio, James. 1999. *Mobilizing Public Housing Communities for Work: Origins and Early Accomplishments of the Jobs-Plus Demonstration.* New York: Manpower Demonstration Research Corporation.

Riccio, James, Daniel Friedlander, and Stephen Freedman. 1994. *GAIN: Benefits, Costs, and Three-Year Impacts of a Welfare-to-Work Program.* New York: Manpower Demonstration Research Corporation.

Szanton, Peter L. 1991. "The Remarkable 'Quango': Knowledge, Politics, and Welfare Reform." *Journal of Policy Analysis and Management* 10 (4): 590–602.

U.S. Department of Labor. 1985. *Recommendations of the Job Training Longitudinal Survey Research Advisory Panel.* Washington.

———. 1995. *What's Working (and What's Not): A Summary of Research on the Economic Impacts of Employment and Training Programs.* Washington.

Wiseman, Michael. 1991. "Research and Policy: An Afterword for the Symposium on the Family Support Act of 1988." *Journal of Policy Analysis and Management* 10 (4): 657–66.

CHAPTER THREE

The Importance of Randomized Field Trials in Education and Related Areas

ROBERT BORUCH

DOROTHY DE MOYA

BROOKE SNYDER

IN 50 A.D. St. Paul wrote to the Thessalonians advising them to "try all things, and hold fast to that which is good." Trying all things is ambitious. Holding onto activities that prove good is also no easy matter. To judge from Paul's written record, he skipped a step in providing no counsel to the Thessalonians, or anyone else, on how to generate evidence so as to discern what is good.

The topic of evidence has occupied the attention of distinguished thinkers apart from Paul, of course. In the fourteenth century, the Arab polymath Ibn Khaldun, in his *Muqadimmah,* tried to understand the effects of changes in imperial regimes at the national and subnational level and discussed the difficulty of discerning such effects on the basis of the evidence at hand. Five hundred years later, Florence Nightingale complained that England's Parliament neglected to consider seriously the consequences of changing statutory programs, charging that without an inquiry after results, past or present, it is all experiment, see-saw, doctrinaire, a shuttlecock between two battledores. In the 1930s, Walter Lippmann worried about disguised presidential doctrines and their need for better evidence. He criticized President Franklin D. Roosevelt for failing

Research on this topic has been supported by the Smith Richardson Foundation, the National Science Foundation, the U.S. Department of Education, the Rockefeller Foundation, and the Swedish Social Research Council. Some of the information given here is adopted from earlier work in a special issue of *Crime and Delinquency* (volume 46, no. 2).

to be "honestly experimental" in leading the nation out of the depression and enhancing societal welfare. In the 1990s, the U.S. General Accounting Office reviewed evidence on the effects of employment and training programs and put the matter more bluntly than Nightingale did, stating that most federal agencies do not know if their programs are working.[1]

The problem of estimating the relative effects of new programs or variations on existing programs is the subject of this chapter. These programs may be dedicated to preventing or ameliorating people's problems or to enhancing their well-being or performance. We make two major assumptions in what follows: (1) any new programs can be mounted on a trial basis before being adopted at the national level, and (2) new variations on current approaches can be implemented on a trial basis so as to periodically learn whether they work.

We discuss a particular approach to generating good evidence about the effect of interventions in education, civil and criminal justice, social welfare, and employment and training: randomized field trials (RFTs). In trials of this kind, eligible individuals or entities are randomly allocated to each of two or more treatment conditions. These treatment conditions may be a program group and a no-program control group. The treatments may be two or more different programs with the same objective, or two or more variations on the same program. The groups delineated by random allocation do not differ systematically, though they may differ on account of chance. This arrangement permits one to make a fair comparison of programs because the groups are statistically equivalent. It also allows one to make a statistically legitimate statement about one's confidence in the results because chance differences can be taken into account.

We have two justifications for choosing randomized field trials as a theme. First, during 1995 and thereafter, numerous national and multinational conferences focused on producing better evidence on the effectiveness of new programs in delinquency and crime prevention, education, and other fields. These discussions often concentrated on RFTs because in many situations they provide the best possible evidence about relative program effects.

A second justification for choosing RFTs as a theme is that we need to understand the importance of such trials in relation to different standards

1. U.S. General Accounting Office (1995).

or frames of reference. Randomized trials are irrelevant or useless in relation to some standards. They are extremely useful in relation to other standards.

Standards for Judging the Importance of Randomized Field Trials

At least five kinds of standards may be used to understand whether and when RFTs are important. First, government policy on the evaluation of educational and other projects can be used as a standard. The best of such policies treat basic questions about societal problems and the effectiveness of purported solutions. The value of RFTs can be judged by whether they produce evidence that addresses the basic questions.

Second, RFTs can be judged by their history. The relevant evidence includes milestones in the use of randomized trials and the increased number of trials undertaken to assess the effects of programs in education, welfare, crime and justice, and other fields.

Third, ethical standards circumscribe the import of RFTs. The Federal Judicial Center's (1981) counsel is used here to help decide when RFTs ought to be considered seriously, or when they should be rejected, on ethical grounds.

Fourth, it seems sensible to determine how often RFTs are used by researchers and evaluators, in comparison with other approaches that might be used to estimate the relative effects of new programs. Here, we depend on evidence from recent reviews of evaluations of programs in criminal justice, education, and other fields.

The fifth standard is scientific. It focuses on whether and when the estimates of a program's effect based on a randomized trial differ from the estimates based on a nonrandomized study. Though placed at the end of our list, this standard is of fundamental importance.

The Policy Context

The first frame of reference for judging the importance of randomized field trials is how such trials fit into the broad context of evaluation policy and research policy. No nation has a uniform policy that drives the evaluation of all government-sponsored programs. Nonetheless, particular government agencies (and private foundations) in the United States,

Sweden, Israel, Mexico, the United Kingdom, and elsewhere have supported efforts to evaluate the effects of particular education interventions.

Evaluation and research efforts fall under a wide variety of rubrics. Phrases such as "summative evaluation," "formative evaluation," "performance measurement," "illuminative evaluations," "responsive evaluation," and "applied research" have become part of the vernacular. Looking beneath these labels, one finds that evaluations usually address four basic questions.

The first question is: What is the nature and severity of the problem and how do we know this? National probability sample surveys or administrative records are usually employed to determine the rates of delinquency, illiteracy, educational achievement, and so on in a jurisdiction or nation, which are then used to answer the question. Case studies and ethnographic research might also provide information on the local dynamics of the problem. In the United States, reports such as *Indicators of School Crime and Safety* (1998) and the various school supplements to the *National Crime Victimization Survey* typify one way of addressing the question.[2]

Generally, randomized trials are run at the subnational level. They depend on prior evidence from good surveys indicating that a problem is severe enough at the local level to justify a trial on whether a new program works. National surveys on the problem's severity are usually not a part of RFTs. Good local surveys, at times, are an important by-product of an RFT.

A second question that underlies evaluation activity is: What programs have been deployed to resolve the problem and how do we know they have been deployed? Laws may be enacted but not enforced. Resources may be allocated but not distributed to their proper targets. School reform plans that were supposed to enhance children's achievement may not be put into place.

Policy researchers, practitioners, and other people often want to know how well a new program is implemented regardless of the program's effects. For instance, case studies of twelve U.S. communities that received federal teenage crime prevention grants under Title V were undertaken to understand whether, how, and how well the monetary resources were

2. See Bilchik (1998); Kaufman and others (1998).

used. Teams of researchers studied the sites to document how communities, public agencies, and community organizations rearranged their resources and collaborated with one another to prevent delinquency.[3]

The best of contemporary RFTs address not only this program implementation question but also a question about relative program effects. RFTs usually address both because it is not safe to assume that a program is delivered as advertised. In one study designed to determine whether a particular theory-based program for violent youthful offenders had been deployed well in four cities, the resulting evidence showed that the program had indeed been implemented, and this helped to justify further attempts to estimate the program's effects on delinquency in a randomized trial.[4]

The third question that underlies many evaluation policies is: What is the relative effectiveness of different programs and how do we know? To assess impact, one must first answer questions about the severity of problems and the deployment of programs. Because these earlier questions are themselves difficult to answer, the frequency of impact studies in general and RFTs in particular is understandably limited. Even so, researchers have mounted randomized trials to investigate a vast array of topics, some of which are highly controversial.[5] The following are a few that fall into that category:

—The impact of mandatory arrest versus conventional police handling of misdemeanor domestic assault on offenders' recidivism.[6]

—The impact of education "choice" (vouchers, scholarships) versus conventional public school education on children's academic achievement.[7]

—The relationship between foster care versus "family preservation" and the incidence of child abuse and neglect.

—The effect of special employment programs for recipients of social security disability insurance versus ordinary disability insurance.[8]

In less volatile arenas, trialists have also had to surmount political, managerial, and other obstacles to generating good evidence about what works

3. Bilchik (1998).
4. Fagan and Forst (1996).
5. See Boruch (1997).
6. See Garner and others (1995).
7. See Peterson and others (1998).
8. See Kornfeld and Rupp (2000).

and what does not. For instance, the U.S. Department of Labor has sponsored RFTs to understand the relative effects of new employment and training programs on employment and wage rates.[9] The U.S. Department of Health and Human Services has supported RFTs on the effect of health risk reduction programs on the behavior of adults, adolescents, and middle school children and on changes in welfare regulations. And the National Institute of Justice, a unit of the U.S. Department of Justice, invested in RFTs to learn whether various approaches to preventing crime or reducing delinquency actually accomplish what they purport to do.[10]

The U.S. Department of Education's Planning and Evaluation Service has also sponsored important randomized field trials.[11] These trials produced evidence about the effectiveness of Upward Bound, among other programs.[12] The evidence suggests that some popular programs have few discernible effects. Revealing this takes fortitude.

Many private foundations in the United States have no explicit policy on the evaluation of projects that they sponsor. As a consequence, relatively few foundations have funded RFTs that generate evidence about whether programs actually work. Nonetheless, a few have taken the commendable step of subsidizing field tests that (a) a national, state, or local government is unable or unwilling to mount, and that (b) build on government-sponsored RFTs to generate new knowledge. In the education, training, and welfare arena, the Rockefeller Foundation's support of randomized trials on the Jobs Plus Program and of developing the program itself is noteworthy. The William T. Grant Foundation has supported trials on mentoring, nurse visitation programs, and New Chance, a teen-parent demonstration program. The Smith Richardson Foundation has supported RFTs on voucher-based school choice and reanalyses of data from the Tennessee Class Size trials.[13]

Typically, individuals have been randomly assigned to "treatments" in RFTs. Nonetheless, it is easy to uncover trials that randomly assigned numerous communities, schools, factories, hospitals, organizations, or

9. Greenberg and Shroder (1997).

10. University of Maryland (1997).

11. See USDE (1999).

12. See Myers and Schirm (1997).

13. On voucher-based school choice, see Peterson and others (1998); on class size trials in Tennessee, see Krueger (1999).

police hot spots to different programs so as to discern relative program effects.[14]

A fourth question underlying evaluative activity in some governments and foundations is: What is the cost/effectiveness ratio for the alternative approaches and how do we calculate it? Here, the economist's knowledge and empirical evidence are brought to bear on the question. For instance, it seems important to understand whether children's academic achievement can be increased at a lower cost using one approach as against another. Economists specializing in education have generated helpful cost-effectiveness analyses and production functions based on randomized trials and on other kinds of studies.[15]

What we have said so far about evaluation policy and the role of RFTs is based on illustration. What particular federal evaluation agencies do is more general. Consider, for example, the Planning and Evaluation Service (PES) of the U.S. Department of Education's Office of the Under Secretary. PES supports evaluations of education programs in states, municipalities, and school districts. It does so through contracts, rather than grants, worth about $30 million in fiscal year 1999. PES's ambit includes all education programs supported by the U.S. Department of Education; the department's budget was about $38 billion in 1999.

The PES's evaluation portfolio is given in the *Biennial Report*.[16] Appendix A to this report is summarized here in table 3-1, which shows that PES awarded 144 contracts for evaluation studies during 1995–97. Almost 25 percent of the 144 contracts that were awarded by PES for evaluation addressed questions about the severity of a problem and the educational state of the nation. Some of this PES support was for the analysis of data from surveys such as the National Assessment of Educational Progress. Along with the National Center for Education Statistics, PES then informed the public about the academic achievement of children and about the differences in performance of various ethnic groups and decreases in these differences over the last decade.

About 67 percent of the PES contracts entailed studies of the implementation of federal programs. One of their objectives was to develop

14. See Boruch and Foley (1999). For a recent study that randomized schools to the Comer comprehensive school reform program versus control conditions, see Cook and others (1999).

15. For analyses of this issue in education, see Krueger (1999); and Levin (1991). For a study in a related area, delinquency, see Greenwood and others (1996).

16. USDE (1997).

Table 3-1. *Evaluation Contracts Awarded by the USDE's Planning and Evaluation Service: The Portfolio for Fiscal 1995–97*[a]

Primary purpose	*Percentage of 144 contracts with one or more primary purposes*
Surveys of need or status	24
Program implementation/monitoring studies	67
Impact evaluations	37
Randomized field trials (5 of 51 contracts for impact evaluations)	10 (of the impact evaluations)

Source: USDE (1997).

a. Any given main category of contracts can involve multiple primary objectives. For instance, 37 percent of the 144 total contracts had impact evaluation as a primary objective. Some of these contracts also included program implementation as a main objective. Consequently, the percentages add up to more than 100.

performance indicators on programs such as Chapter I/Title I compensatory education.

Over a third of the contracts (51 of the 144 projects) evaluated the impact of federally sponsored programs. Just under 10 percent of these contracts—5 of the 51 contracts—involved randomized field trials. These 5 focused on California's GAIN trial database, Upward Bound programs, the Even Start Family Literacy program, the School Drop-out Demonstration Assistance Program, and a plan to evaluate adult basic literacy programs.[17]

Just under 3 percent of all the evaluation contracts made by PES were for randomized trials. This rate may seem small. Understanding the importance of RFTs in relation to monetary outlays, rather than to their frequency seems important, however.

In 1996, for instance, the total amount awarded in contracts by PES was about $18.6 million. In the same year, about $1.4 million was awarded for work on randomized studies of Upward Bound and other programs. The relative amount invested in RFTs, 5 percent or so in a given year, may seem small. However, one must recognize that these RFTs are multiyear trials and that financial commitments had been made in earlier years. For instance, the total commitment over 1991–95 to the School Drop-out Demonstration Assistance Program, involving a randomized trial in each of sixteen sites, was $7.3 million. For the Upward Bound Trials, which involved RFTs in each of sixty-seven sites, the commitments exceeded $5.4 million over the period of 1992–96.

17. On the first four listed, see Riccio, Friedlander, and Freedman (1994); Myers and Shirm (1997); St. Pierre and others (1996); and Dynarski and others (1998), respectively.

Table 3-2. *Program Evaluations and Studies Identified in the U.S. Department of Education's Annual Plan for Fiscal 2000*[a]

Primary purpose	*Number of projects with this purpose at least*	*Percentage with this primary purpose at least*
Surveys of need or status	51	61
Program implementation/ monitoring studies	49	58
Impact evaluations	16	19
Total	116	
Randomized field trials	1	

Source: USDE (2000), which lists 84 studies.
a. Any given study can have more than one primary purpose. There are then 116 projects with one, two, or three primary purposes. For instance, 51 of the projects (61 percent of 116) have needs surveys as their primary objective.

We can use a second resource for understanding specific U.S. investments in education evaluations—the U.S. Department of Education's Annual Plan for fiscal 2000. Appendix B of this plan, summarized in table 3-2, covers "program evaluations and other studies" that are expected to generate evidence about achieving the plan's objectives.

The department's plan identified eighty-four studies. Many of these focused on at least two broad evaluation policy questions. For instance, about fifty-one of the eight-four studies aimed to assess the severity of problems or the educational state of the population. About forty-nine of the eighty-four studies focused mainly on the implementation of various programs, including developing indicators of implementation. Both kinds of studies respond to the 1993 Government Performance and Results Act.

About sixteen of the eighty-four studies in the department's plan direct attention to the relative effect of federal programs. Of these, only one study involved a randomized field trial. This particular study was massive. It consisted of nearly seventy independent and coordinated trials designed to estimate the relative effect of the TRIO-Upward Bound program.[18] Upward Bound focuses on encouraging disadvantaged students to achieve higher education levels. Of course, other studies in the USDE's 1999 Annual Plan depend on the randomized field trials that were conducted earlier and identified in the 1997 Biennial Report. The Even Start trial is among them.[19]

18. Myers and Shirm (1997).
19. St. Pierre and others (1996).

Pedigree and History as a Standard

Evaluation policy, as we have described it, is a contemporary standard for judging the importance of RFTs. Our second standard is historical. In what follows, we outline the pedigree of such trials and the growth of RFTs.

Between 1850 and 1880, a number of psychologists who specialized in visual perception appear to have used random allocation in laboratory experiments.[20] Late in the nineteenth century, Denmark tested a diphtheria serum in randomized clinical trials.[21] H. F. Gosnell's dissertation research at the University of Chicago in the late 1920s appears to have employed random assignment to assess alternative strategies for enhancing voter registration rates in Chicago neighborhoods.[22] A decade later, Sir Ronald Fisher laid out a mathematical rationale for randomization, along with formal statistical tests of hypotheses.[23] This work is exploited routinely nowadays in agricultural, animal research, and some genetic work. Fisher did little to foster randomized trials in social and other sectors.[24]

In medicine, the watershed period for randomized trials occurred during the 1940s and 1950s in the United Kingdom and the United States. The streptomycin trials on treating tuberculosis led by Bradford Hill and the Salk vaccine trials to prevent poliomyelitis set precedents in health care.[25] The Edinburgh College of Physicians has a website on controlled trials that covers these and other early efforts (www.rcpe.ac.uk).

In the 1960s the U.S. government's requirements for the evaluation of the Head Start Preschool program provided an opportunity to design high-quality impact research. During this period, the Ypsilanti Preschool Demonstration Project (High/Scope) was distinctive in using a randomized trial to estimate the High/Scope's effect on children's achievement.[26] Few other preschool programs were evaluated using RFTs in the 1960s, however. The Cochrane Collaboration (2000) database lists only a half dozen trials.

20. See Stigler (1986, pp. 242–45).
21. See Hrobjartsson and others (1998).
22. Gosnell (1927).
23. See the work of Fisher (1935).
24. Marks (1997).
25. See Yoshioka (1998); and Meier (1972), respectively.
26. Schweinhart and others (1993).

One of the less well-known milestones in the 1960s is a randomized field trial of a program for girls who are at risk of delinquency, pregnancy, and school truancy in New York. This vocational high school program involved case management, group therapy, and the engagement of parents. It was undertaken in collaboration with New York's Youth Consultation Service, a nonsectarian youth agency. The trial was designed, executed, and reported by a remarkable team of researchers and social service providers.[27]

During the late 1960s and 1970s, economists developed large-scale RFTs to assess the effects of graduated work incentive tax plans in New Jersey, Wisconsin, Denver, and Washington.[28] In the 1980s and thereafter, RFTs were used at times to inform civil, criminal, and administrative justice policy. The Spouse Assault Replication Program, for example, depended on randomized trials to evaluate the effects of mandatory arrest for misdemeanor assaults. Triggered partly by debates over the Minneapolis Domestic Violence Experiment, RFTs were mounted by five city police departments.[29] In the administrative arena, residents of the United States who were subject to a random audit by the U.S. Internal Revenue Service have been a part of a sizable and invisible series of trials.[30] They were designed to learn how to get people to pay a "proper" tax.[31]

RFTs were used during the middle 1980s through the late 1990s to estimate the effect of welfare reform incentives on school-related behavior of children and youth. The examples include New Chance, Ohio's LEAP, Wisconsin's Learnfare, and the Teenage Parent Demonstration Project in New Jersey and Illinois.[32] A major RFT in education during this period was Tennessee's evaluation of the effects of reducing class size.[33] The more recent RFTs on school voucher programs are also noteworthy.[34]

An increase in the number of trials over time might reasonably be interpreted as a reflection of the importance that people attach to making

27. Meyer, Borgotta, and Jones (1965).

28. For abstracts of reports on these RFTs, see Riecken and others (1974); and Greenberg and Shroder (1997). For further discussion, see Ferber and Hirsch (1982); and Rossi, Freeman, and Lipsey (1998).

29. On the debates, see Sherman and Berk (1984); on the RFTs, see Garner and others (1995).

30. Garner and others (1995).

31. Roth and Sholtz (1989).

32. Granger and Cytron (1999).

33. See Finn and Achilles (1990); Mosteller (1995); and Krueger (1999).

34. See Peterson, Greene, and Noyes (1996); and Peterson, Myers, and Howell (1998).

Figure 3-1. *Incidence of Randomized Field Trials over Time, 1945–75*

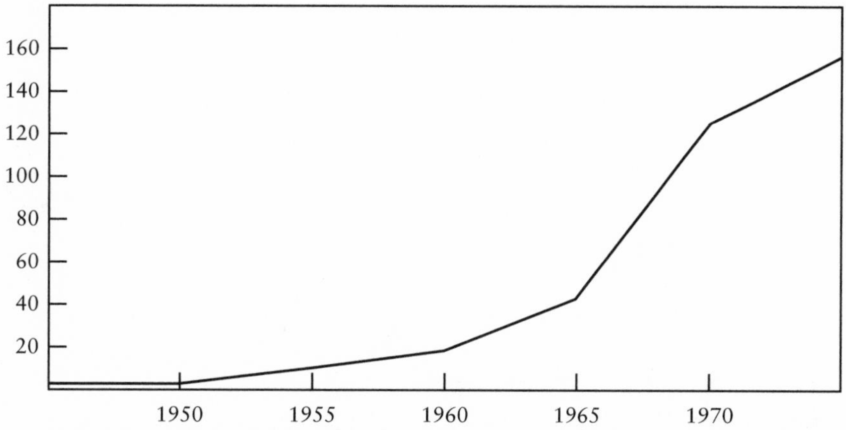

Source: Boruch, McSweeny, and Soderstrom (1978).

a fair comparison of programs' effects. As evidence, consider first a bibliography published in 1978 on all the randomized trials on educational, behavioral, criminological, and social interventions undertaken between 1920 and 1975 that the authors were able to uncover.[35] Figure 3-1 gives the simple count of the number of trials, indexed by one publication on each trial, plotted against the year of the publication. The frequency has increased greatly.

Next, consider Michael Dennis's dissertation research on the conduct of randomized experiments in civil and criminal justice. His evidence, summarized in figure 3-2, suggests that the frequency of publications on such trials increased considerably between 1950 and1985.[36] More recent and thorough work suggests a similar increase.[37]

Greenberg and Shroder compiled abstracts of randomized trials on economic programs, including employment and training programs, and welfare interventions that relate to the education of children in poor families.[38] Figure 3-3 summarizes the incidence of trials based on the contents

35. See Boruch, McSweeny, and Soderstrom (1978).
36. See Dennis (1988).
37. For other evidence of a similar increase, see Petrosino (forthcoming).
38. See Greenberg and Shroder (1997).

Figure 3-2. *Incidence of Publications on Randomized Field Trials in Criminal and Civil Justice, 1955–1987*

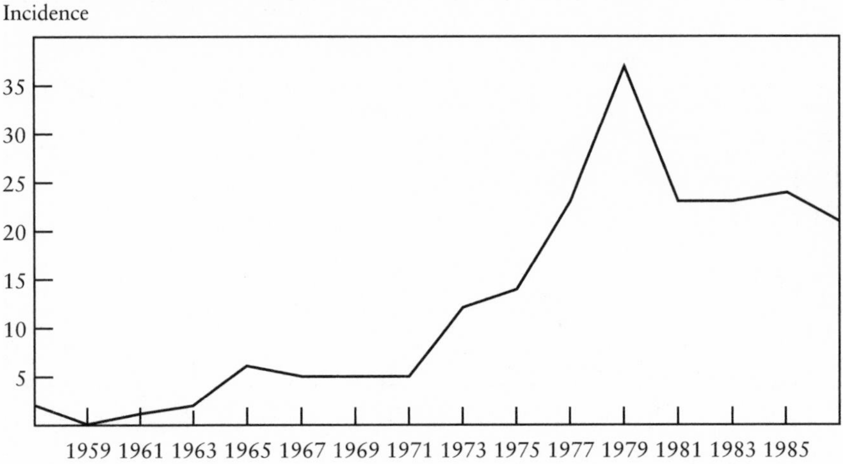

Source: Dennis (1998).

of their book: the frequency of such trials clearly increased over the period 1975–95.

During the periods covered in figures 3-1, 3-2, and 3-3, the U.S. government's federal funding for evaluative research is likely to have varied appreciably. An increase in the frequency of RFTs may be a consequence or correlate of an increase in funding levels. Or the increase may have occurred despite no increase in the budget for evaluative research. The topic deserves some study.

Figure 3-4 shows the increase in the number of articles on randomized and *possibly* randomized experiments that have appeared in about 100 peer-reviewed journals and in other places since 1950. The figure is based on the Campbell Collaboration Social, Psychological, Educational, and Criminological Trials Registry (C2-SPECTR) that is being developed in a continuing effort to identify all RFTs.[39] C2-SPECTR contains about 10,000 entries. Although this number may seem large, it is small in comparison with a similar registry on trials in health care literature, which contains over 250,000 entries.[40]

39. See Petrosino and others (2000).
40. See Cochrane Collaboration (www.cochrane.co.uk).

Figure 3-3. *The Incidence of Randomized Economic Experiments Plotted over Time, 1965–95*

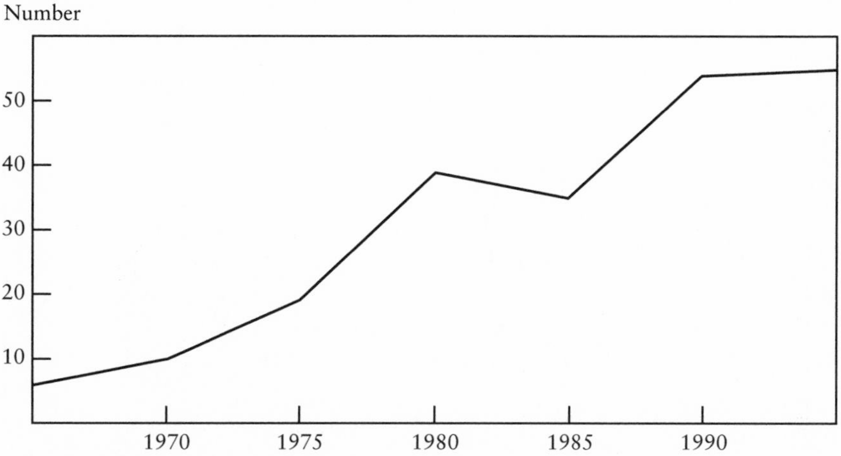

Source: Greenberg and Shroder (1997).

Figure 3-4. *SPECTR-Cumulative Totals of Reports of Trials Identified, 1950–97*

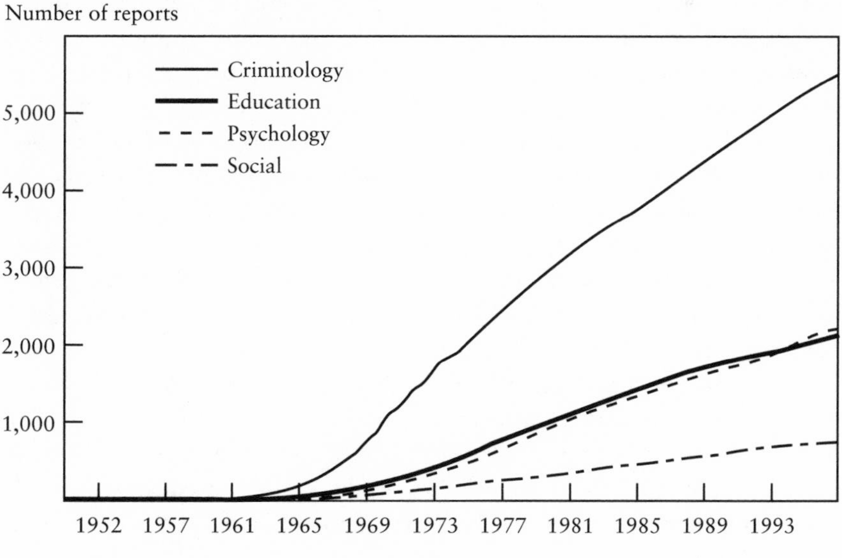

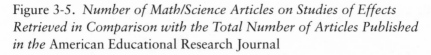

Figure 3-5. *Number of Math/Science Articles on Studies of Effects Retrieved in Comparison with the Total Number of Articles Published in the* American Educational Research Journal

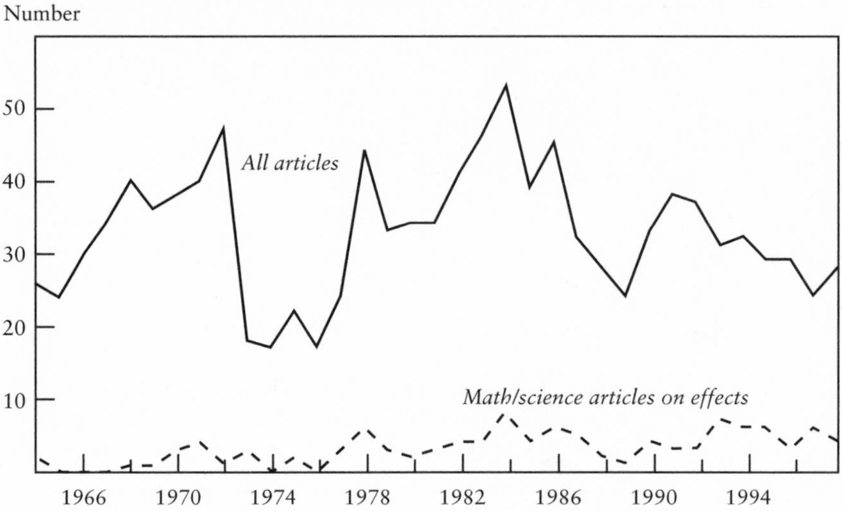

Source: Loew and Boruch (1999).

To complicate matters, the entries in C2-SPECTR include very small bench studies and trials that are possibly randomized. So, for instance, the incidence of education trials is arguably inflated because the search for entries was inclusive (rather than exclusive). It includes studies that are described in abstracts, titles, and key words such as "experiments" and "random sample," but that may not have involved any random allocation of individuals or groups to different regimens. Further screening is essential to determine which studies were randomized and which were based on some alternative research design.

Evidence that runs counter to the idea that RFTs have uniformly increased is given in figure 3-5, which summarizes the results of a hand search of every article in every issue of the *American Educational Research Journal* since the journal's inception in 1964. The figure shows the incidence of articles each year and the incidence of articles that report on the effectiveness of interventions in mathematics and science education. Of about 1,200 articles, only 35 concern randomized trials in math and science education; there is no obvious increase in their number over the period 1964–98.[41] Similarly, the Education Group for Guidelines on Evaluation (1999) has encouraged the use of RFTs in medical education, but such trials are scarce.[42]

This evidence on the increasing frequency of randomized field trials is fresh. Presenting such evidence this way is not original, however, and can be traced to the period between 1916 and 1951.[43] These studies were not necessarily randomized trials.

The general implication of the evidence presented in this section is that RFTs have a fine pedigree and they are being used more frequently. Standards other than historical ones are important, of course. We discuss standards of ethics next.

Randomized Field Trials in Relation to Ethical Standards

In 1981 the Federal Judicial Center (FJC), which is the research arm of the U.S. federal courts, promulgated five ethical conditions that ought to be met before undertaking a randomized field trial on justice-related programs. These conditions, which pertain also to trials in areas such as housing, mental health, and education, delimit the importance of RFTs.

The FJC's first condition for seriously considering a randomized trial is that the social problem at issue is serious. If the problem is serious, then RFTs may be ethical. If it is not, then RFTs may be unethical. For example, the state of Wisconsin mounted a large randomized field trial to evaluate a program that some people would argue was unnecessary. This RFT was designed to assess the effect of special welfare rules on the school attendance rates of children from poor families: welfare payments would be reduced if the child's daily attendance rate at school was not satisfactory. In fact, the ambient daily attendance rates of children in lower grades were very high. This suggests that some of the rules laid on by the state's legislature were unnecessary in the first place. One could then argue that a randomized field trial of the program was unnecessary.

The FJC's second standard for deciding when an RFT is warranted hinges on the question "Is the purported solution to the serious problem known to be effective?" For instance, if a new "conflict resolution" program for school children is known to work, on the basis of good evidence

41. See Leow and Boruch (2000).
42. Eitel and others (2000).
43. See Boring (1954).

in a set of schools, then one might deploy the new program in other schools. New randomized trials to estimate the effect of the program in the same area might be unnecessary. On the other hand, if there is a disagreement about the conflict resolution program's effectiveness, or if good evidence on the program's effects does not exist, then an RFT may be warranted.

In the United States, debates about the evidence on the effects of certain programs have preceded many of the government-sponsored randomized field trials. Such arguments led the Tennessee State Legislature to support a randomized trial so as to determine whether reducing class sizes in elementary schools would enhance children's achievement.[44] Political and scientific debates about the quality of evidence preceded large-scale RFTs on welfare training, and work initiatives, education "choice" programs, police approaches to handling misdemeanor domestic violence, and court-related procedures in civil and criminal justice, among others.[45]

The FJC suggested that a third standard be used to assess when an RFT is warranted. This standard involves deciding whether research designs other than randomized field trials produce satisfactory evidence about the program's effectiveness. If other study designs yield satisfactory evidence, a randomized trial would be unnecessary. If not, then an RFT ought to be considered seriously.

For instance, some U.S. communities have instituted curfew laws that require school-aged children to be off the streets by a certain time of night.[46] Many local evaluations of the effect of such curfew laws have involved simple "before-after" comparisons of juvenile arrest rates. These evaluations often concluded that curfews lead to a reduction in juvenile arrest rates. Surprisingly, these local evaluations ignored extraneous factors, particularly the fact that the juvenile arrest rate has declined for the nation as a whole.[47] It is because of this ambiguity in evidence that the Office of Juvenile Justice and Delinquency Prevention properly phrased the title of its 1996 report on the effectiveness of curfew laws as a question: "Curfew: An Answer to Juvenile Delinquency and Victimization?" More to the point, if one wanted to understand the effect of curfews on

44. Ritter and Boruch (1999).

45. On welfare and work debates, see Gueron (1985, 1999); on education choice, Peterson and others (1998); on misdemeanor domestic violence, Sherman and Berk (1984); and on civil and criminal justice, Goldman (1985) and Lind (1985).

46. Office of Juvenile Justice and Delinquency Prevention (1996).

47. Snyder (1998).

juvenile crime and thought it important to do, one might mount an RFT that involves thirty or fifty jurisdictions to produce better evidence.

The fourth FJC condition is that the results of the RFT will be used to inform policy decisions. If the results are likely to be used, then investing in a randomized field trial is ethical. If the results of an RFT will not be used, then such a study might be unjustified.

It is clear that the results of *some* randomized trials have been used. As governmental and professional awareness about the Tennessee class size trials grew, about eighteen states initiated efforts to reduce class size. Complicating matters is the fact that a study's results may or may not be used, or it may take time to use. For instance, although the first reports on the Tennessee study appeared in the late 1980s, policymakers made little effort to exploit the results until the late 1990s.[48] Similarly, a series of trials during the 1990s and earlier showed that the school-based DARE programs failed to produce discernible reductions in drug-related behavior of youth. It was not until 2001 that DARE leadership agreed to try to modify the program.

The FJC's last condition for judging when a randomized experiment is ethically warranted (and important) is that the rights of the research participant in a randomized field trial can be protected. To ensure that the rights of people who participate in RFTs and other studies are protected, the United States and some other countries have created an elaborate system of institutional review boards (IRBs). Under current U.S. laws, these IRBs examine all research undertaken by universities and research institutes to assess their ethical propriety. All of the randomized field trials cited in this chapter have passed muster in IRBs that include laypersons, lawyers, researchers, and practitioners. It is equally important to note that the design of any randomized field trial can be tailored to ensure that human rights are recognized.[49]

These FJC conditions and the examples given here have at least three implications. First, the frequency with which a randomized trial is employed will be constrained by ethical values, broadly defined. Second, the frequency with which RFTs are employed must depend on debates about evidence. Third, RFTs can be tailored to ensure that the standards of human ethics and of scientific evidence can be met simultaneously.

48. Ritter and Boruch (1999).

49. For specific design tactics in medicine, see Zelen (1990); for tactics in the social sciences and education, see Boruch (1997).

Practice: A Normative Standard

The increased use of RFTs in some arenas (see figures 3-3 to 3-4) reflects their importance in relation to a historical standard. In this section, we provide evidence about their importance in comparison with a contemporary normative standard, that is, how often RFTs are done in contrast to nonrandomized trials.[50]

Consider first the evidence from the University of Maryland's 1997 Report to Congress on the effectiveness of programs in criminal justice. This report identified 149 impact evaluations of school-based crime prevention programs, including RFTs.[51] Of these evaluations, 14—that is, less than 10 percent—were carried out as RFTs. When examined by type of program evaluated, about 16 of the large-scale impact studies looked at gang prevention programs, 4 of which were randomized trials. No RFT was among the 3 major studies of "after-school" programs for children who are at risk of perpetrating crime or being victims. Three nonrandomized studies of the effects of "gun buy-back" programs have been mounted, but there have been no RFTs.

Further information on the incidence of RFTs comes from studies of the effects of class size in public schools in the United States. Glass and Smith located seventy-eight such studies.[52] Of these, eight of the studies considered well designed were all nonrandomized experiments. More recently, the Tennessee work has received considerable attention because (a) it was based on a well-designed randomized field trial, and (b) it showed striking effects of reduced class size on children's achievement and involved many schools, teachers, and students in the state.[53]

Another sixteen studies examined the effects of grouping students in middle schools by ability and the students' mathematics achievement.[54] Of these, two were RFTs, each mounted before 1975; five were matched control studies, and the remaining nine were correlational studies. The estimated size of effects varied a great deal.

50. Understanding how to structure a nonrandomized study and to analyze the resultant data is important for obvious reasons. Scholars who have tried to arrange our thinking about how to do so include Campbell and Stanley (1963); Rosenbaum (1995); Cochran (1983); and Shadish, Cook, and Campbell (1979). Nothing said here should be interpreted as a denigration of these efforts.

51. Gottfredson (1997, chap. 5).

52. See Glass and Smith (1979).

53. See Finn and Achilles (1990); Mosteller (1995); and Krueger (1999).

54. Slavin (1993).

The normative importance of RFTs can also be seen in a recent report on the effectiveness of schoolwide reforms.[55] This report reviewed all studies that were done on twenty-four "whole school," "comprehensive," or "schoolwide" approaches to school reform that had become popular in the United States up to 1999. The team responsible for the report made deliberate efforts to determine (a) whether any evidence on effectiveness of the reforms had been produced and (b) what the quality of the evidence was.

The team found that about 25 percent of these high-visibility comprehensive school reform programs had nothing beyond anecdotal evidence and personal testimonials to support claims of their effectiveness. That is, the evidence available on five of twenty-four comprehensive school reform efforts was not defensible or was nonexistent when held up against basic scientific standards.

About 116 studies of the effects of reform programs were undertaken on the remaining nineteen reform approaches.[56] Any given reform approach was subject to between 1 and 18 independent studies. The High/Scope Perry Preschool randomized trial, for instance, is counted as *one* study of program effect.[57] As far as we can determine, at least 1, but no more than 4 of these studies involved a randomized trial.

The implication of this evidence is as follows. Relative to contemporary practice in evaluating delinquency prevention programs, randomized trials are in a minority. In research on class size and ability grouping of students in schools, RFTs are also infrequent compared with nonrandomized experiments. Contemporary practice in evaluating schoolwide education reforms shows RFTs in a small minority. The reasons *why* randomized field trials might not be used more frequently in education, delinquency research, and so on, are a matter of debate (see chapters 2, 6, and 7).

Alternative Approaches to Estimating a Program's Effect: A Scientific Standard

A well-run randomized field trial produces an unbiased estimate of the relative effectiveness of the programs or program variations that are

55. Herman and others (1999).
56. For a review of these studies, see Herman and others (1999).
57. Schweinhart and others (1993).

compared. The alternatives to randomized trials include before-after comparisons and time-series analyses, statistical selection models, instrumental variable methods, propensity scoring, and structural equation modeling, among others. These alternative approaches may or may not produce an estimate of a program effect that is statistically unbiased compared with the estimate produced in a well-run randomized experiment. That is, results of the RFT and nonrandomized trial may differ. The mathematical conditions (assumptions) under which an RFT and a nonrandomized quasi experiment will differ are reasonably well understood.[58]

Not so clear are the *empirical* conditions under which this difference occurs. In particular, what would we find if we compared the results of randomized field trials on an intervention with the results of analyses of data that are generated in nonrandomized trials on the same intervention? Following are some examples from medical and social research.

In the Salk polio vaccine studies of the 1950s, the randomized trials that were mounted in some U.S. states produced sizable estimates of the effectiveness of the vaccine. These estimates were appreciably greater than the estimates based on a parallel series of *nonrandomized* trials that had been mounted in other states.[59] The factors that might have led to this difference in estimates, including assumptions and statistical models in the nonrandomized trials, are still not well understood.

After the Salk trials, controversy erupted over the use of oxygen enrichment for premature infants. Early nonrandomized studies suggested that the infant death rate was appreciably reduced by the oxygen-enriched therapy. Subsequent randomized clinical trials helped to reveal that enriched oxygen environments for premature infants caused blindness (retrolental fibroplasia) and did not decrease infant mortality.[60] These findings were provocative because they contradicted the results of earlier nonrandomized trials.

More recent meta-analyses of over 500 randomized controlled trials and nonrandomized trials in the medical arena produced two interesting conclusions.[61] First, the results of the nonrandomized and randomized trials differ at times, in either a positive direction or a negative direction, and at times they do not differ. Second, the differences are not predictable.

58. See, for example, Cochran (1983); and Rubin (1974, 1991).
59. Meier (1972).
60. Silverman (1985).
61. Kunz and Oxman (1998).

Table 3-3. *Effect Sizes (ES) of an Employment and Training Program on High-Risk Males Based on a Randomized Field Trial and a Nonrandomized Trial*[a]

Randomized trial	*Nonrandomized trial*
ES 1977 = +$313 (NS)	ES 1977 = –$ 688 (S)
ES 1978 = –$ 28 (NS)	ES 1978 = –$1191 (S)
ES 1979 = –$ 18 (NS)	ES 1979 = –$1179 (S)

a. The entries for ES is the difference in average wages earned by males at high risk who were engaged in the employment program minus the wages earned by males at high risk who did not participate in the program. The results for the randomized trials suggest no statistically significant difference (NS). The results from the nonrandomized trial suggest a significant difference (S) in relation to chance.

In educational research, it is hard to find systematic efforts to run RFTs in parallel with nonrandomized trials. Only two examples that permit comparison of results come easily to hand. One consists of evaluations of the effects of a national employment and training program designed for male school dropouts and poor youth (table 3-3). In a large-scale randomized field trial, the program's impact on their earnings appeared negligible. That is, individuals who were assigned randomly to the program earned no more than did individuals who had been randomly assigned to a control group.

A nonrandomized parallel study of the same employment and training program, targeted toward young males, had also been mounted. Estimates of program effect were based on passive survey data and econometric models that were thought to simulate the results of a randomized trial. The results of this parallel study, also given in table 3-3, suggested a *negative* program effect. Program participants appeared to earn less, as a consequence of the employment and training program, than they would have earned in the absence of the program. The program was made to appear harmful, rather than merely useless.

This comparison of the results of the randomized trial against a parallel nonrandomized study is disturbing.[62] That is also the case for related work comparing RFT and non-RFT results in estimating another training program's effects.[63] The differences are large at times, small at times, and generally unpredictable.

The second example comes from an evaluation of the Even Start Family Literacy Program.[64] One part of this study used an RFT to estimate the

62. See Lalonde (1986); Fraker and Maynard (1987).

63. Bell and others (1995).

64. St. Pierre and others (1996).

program effects: families were randomly assigned to either Even Start or to a control condition in five sites. A separate evaluation estimated the program's effects on the basis of a national information system on many more sites. No randomization was involved in this system. Statistical controls involved linear models that employed pretest scores and other covariates.

Analyses of data based on the Even Start RFTs and on the national Even Start information system suggest that program effect in each case is in the same direction for the first year or so. That is, the effects in both cases are positive. But the magnitudes appear to differ appreciably. The reasons for the accord in direction and discord in magnitude in these findings are not clear.

A Broad Implication: The Campbell Collaboration

People want to know about the effectiveness of new programs in education, social services, crime and justice, and other areas. Their interest in program effectiveness and in the quality of evidence on program effects will continue. The use of randomized field trials will increase in frequency in the social sector, including education, as they have in the health sciences, partly because of people's interest in good evidence.

How might we encourage high-quality studies in education and also ensure that the cumulative evidence they generate is accessible and can be exploited well? One option is offered by the international Campbell Collaboration.[65] Formally inaugurated in 2000 at a meeting of eighty people from twelve countries, the collaboration's objective is to prepare, maintain, and make accessible systematic reviews of studies of the effectiveness of interventions. The collaborators formed review groups on a large array of social and behavioral topics, including many connected with education. Methods groups were formed to handle cross-cutting evidential issues. This collaboration's first concern is randomized field trials; the second is nonrandomized trials, or quasi experiments.

The precedent for the Campbell Collaboration is the international Cochrane Collaboration in health care. Since 1993, the Cochrane Collaboration has produced systematic reviews on over 1,000 interventions in health. Most of the evaluations reviewed by Cochrane's project teams are randomized controlled trials (RCTs), which are analogous to the RFTs discussed in this chapter.

65. See Campbell Collaboration (www.campbell.gse.upenn.edu).

There are obvious benefits to the evolving Campbell Collaboration, some of which are related to standards for judging the importance of randomized field trials. First, the collaboration and its registries of trials can help identify RFTs and determine which interventions have been evaluated well using RFTs or other defensible research designs, which interventions have not been evaluated at all, and which have been the subject of studies that yield ambiguous results. Second, systematic reviews, a major collaboration product, provide a vehicle for cumulating results of RFTs. Periodic reviews of the resulting knowledge can be construed as an index of the substantive productivity of RFTs.

Third, the Campbell Collaboration transcends academic disciplinary boundaries. This permits us to construct systematic reviews of trials on delinquency and welfare programs in which education outcomes are the subject of attention. This makes it possible to mine the new knowledge that often lies at the interstices of existing disciplines.

Fourth, the collaboration transcends geopolitical jurisdictions. It permits us to track the use of experiments in many countries and the resultant increases in new knowledge. Finally, the collaboration provides an empirical basis for research on how the results of RFTs and systematic reviews are used by people. The use of the results is, of course, another important standard for judging the importance of particular trials, and more interestingly, the collection of studies that is embodied in a systematic review.

Summary

There are at least five ways to judge the value of randomized field trials in education research. First, we need to understand the RFT's import in a broad context of evaluation policy. RFTs are less common than other evaluative studies, the aims of which differ from those of the RFTs. Surveys of people's needs, for instance, must often precede RFTs that are designed to discern whether purported approaches to the need actually work. Randomized trials must be in a minority simply because other work—such as surveys of public need or of program implementation—must be done before such trials on program effects can be mounted sensibly.

Second, the importance of RFTs can be judged by their pedigree and recent history. Part of the pedigree lies with randomized trials in medicine, such as tests of the Salk vaccine and streptomycin. They also have a good pedigree in the social sector, to judge from the Negative Income Tax

Experiments, the Spouse Assault Replication project, and others. Since the 1960s, RFTs have been used with obviously increasing frequency to test programs in criminology, employment and training, and some other areas. Their use may not have increased in certain other arenas, such as mathematics and science education.

The importance of RFTs depends on a third standard: ethics. Many trials that meet good ethical standards have been undertaken. Doubtless, many other trials have not been undertaken because they cannot meet a reasonable ethical standard. This means that RFTs must be in the minority of studies. Nevertheless, trials can often be designed so as to meet ethical standards.

The fourth standard for judging the importance of RFTs is normative. Most studies on the effects of social and educational programs are not based on RFTs. This norm suggests that randomized trials are less important than nonrandomized studies. On the other hand, a single RFT can help to clarify the effect of a particular intervention against a backdrop of many nonrandomized trials. Tennessee's randomized trials on reducing class size did so.

The fifth standard is a scientific one. Randomized field trials are a sturdy device for generating defensible evidence about relative effectiveness. Nonrandomized trials can do so at times. But the conditions under which they produce the same results as randomized trials depend heavily on assumptions that may or not be plausible and empirically testable. It is then crucial to keep account of whether nonrandomized trials approximate the results of RFTs and to learn why they do or do not. This invites attention to new efforts to accumulate knowledge that is based on field trials and that can inform the way one thinks about randomized and nonrandomized studies. The Campbell Collaboration is one vehicle for tracking trials in the social and behavioral sector, in the same way that the Cochrane Collaboration has been in health care research.

At bottom, many people try to hold fast to that which is good, as St. Paul suggested. To advance our collective understanding of what is good in this sector, we must try to make comparisons transparently fair and verifiable. RFTs do this. They have been used frequently and to good effect in learning about what works and what does not in medicine. Their use is also increasing in studies of the impact of social and behavioral interventions. In education research they will lead to better evidence about how to enhance children's achievement and well-being.

References

Bell, Steve H., Larry L. Orr, J. D. Blomquist, and Glen G. Cain. 1995. *Program Applicants as a Comparison Group in Evaluating Training Programs: A Theory and a Test.* Kalamazoo, Mich.: W. E. Upjohn Institute.

Bilchik, Shay. 1998. *1998 Report to Congress: Juvenile Mentoring Program (JUMP).* Washington: U.S. Department of Justice, Office of Juvenile Justice and Delinquency Prevention.

Boring, Edward G. 1954. "The Nature and History of Experimental Controls." *American Journal of Psychology* 67: 573–89.

Boruch, Robert F. 1997. *Randomized Experiments for Planning and Evaluation: A Practical Guide.* Thousand Oaks, Calif.: Sage Publications.

Boruch, Robert F., and Ellen Foley. 2000. "The Honestly Experimental Society: Sites and Other Entities as the Units of Allocation and Analysis in Randomized Experiments." In *Validity and Social Experimentation: Donald T. Campbell's Legacy,* edited by L. Bickman, 193–238. Thousand Oaks, Calif.: Sage Publications.

Boruch, Robert F., A. John McSweeny, and Jon Soderstrom. 1978. "Randomized Field Experiments for Program Planning, Development and Evaluation: An Illustrative Bibliography." *Evaluation Quarterly* 2 (4): 655–95.

Cochran, William. 1983. *Planning and Analysis of Observational Studies,* edited by L. Moses and Frederick Mosteller. John Wiley and Sons.

Cook, Thomas D., F. Habib, M. Phillips, R. A. Settersten, S. C. Shagle, and S. M. Degirmencioglu. 1999. "Comer's School Development Program in Prince George's County, Maryland: A Theory-Based Evaluation." *American Educational Research Journal* 36 (3): 543–97.

Dennis, Michael L. 1988. "Implementing Randomized Field Experiments: An Analysis of Criminal and Civil Justice Research." Ph.D. dissertation, Northwestern University.

Dynarski, Mark, P. Gleason, A. Rangarajan, and R. Wood. 1998. "Impacts of Drop-out Prevention Programs: Final Report." Contract LC91015001. Princeton, N.J.: Mathematica Policy Research.

Education Group for Guidelines on Evaluation. 1999. "Education and Debate: Guidelines for Evaluating Papers on Educational Interventions." *British Medical Journal* 318: 1265–67.

Eitel, F., K. G. Kanz, and A. Tesche. 2000. "Training and Certification of Teachers and Trainers: The Professionalization of Medical Education." *Medical Teacher: An International Journal of Education in the Health Sciences* 22 (5): 517–26.

Fagan, Jeffrey, and Michael Forst. 1996. "Risks, Fixers, and Zeal: Implementing Experimental Treatments for Violent Juvenile Offenders." *Prison Journal* 76 (1): 22–59.

Federal Judicial Center. 1981. *Social Experimentation and the Law.* Washington.

Finn, Jeremy, and Charles Achilles. 1990. "Answers and Questions about Class Size: A Statewide Experiment." *American Educational Research Journal* 27: 557–77.

Ferber, Robert, and Werner Z. Hirsch. 1982. *Social Experimentation and Economic Policy*. Cambridge University Press.

Fisher, Ronald A. 1935. *The Design of Experiments*. Edinburgh: Oliver and Boyd.

Fraker, Thomas, and Rebecca Maynard. 1987. "Evaluating Comparison Group Designs with Employment Related Programs." *Journal of Human Resources* 22: 195–227.

Garner, Joel, Jeffrey Fagan, and C. Maxwell. 1995. "Published Findings from the Spouse Assault Replication Program." *Journal of Quantitative Criminology* 11 (1): 3–28.

Glass, Gene, and May Ann Smith. 1979. "Meta-Analysis of Research on Class Size Achievement." *Educational Evaluation and Policy Analysis* 1: 2–16.

Goldman, J. 1985. "Negotiated Solutions to Overcoming Impediments in a Law-Related Experiment." In *New Directions of Program Evaluation,* 28, edited by Robert F. Boruch and W. Wothke, 63–72.

Gosnell, H. F. 1927. "Getting Out the Vote." Ph.D. dissertation, University of Chicago.

Gottfredson, Denise C. 1997. "School-Based Crime Prevention." In *Preventing Crime: What Works, What Doesn't, What's Promising,* 5-1–5-74. Report to the U.S. Congress, prepared for the National Institute of Justice.

Granger, Robert C., and R. Cytron. 1999. "Teenage Parent Programs: A Synthesis of the Long-Term Effects of the New Chance Demonstration, Ohio's Learning, Earning and Parenting Program, and the Teenage Parent Demonstration." *Evaluation Review*, 23 (2): 107–45.

Greenberg, David, and Mark Shroder. 1997. *The Digest of Social Experiments.* 2d ed. Washington: Urban Institute Press.

Greenwood, Peter W., K. E. Model, C. P. Rydell, and J. Chiesa. 1996. *Diverting Children from a Life of Crime: Measuring Costs and Benefits*. Santa Monica, Calif.: Rand Corporation.

Gueron, Judith M. 1985. "The Demonstration of Work/Welfare Initiatives." In *New Directions for Program Evaluation,* 28, edited by Robert F. Boruch and W. Wothke, 5–14.

———. 1999. "The Politics of Random Assignment Report." New York: Manpower Demonstration Research Corporation.

Herman, Rebecca, Daniel Aladjem, Patricia McMahon, Erik Masem, Ivor Mulligan, Amy S. O'Malley, Sherri Quinones, Alison Reeve, and Darren Woodruff. 1999. *An Educator's Guide to School-wide Reform.* Arlington, Va.: Educational Research Service.

Hrobjartsson, A., P. C. Gotzche, and C. Gluud. 1998. "The Controlled Clinical Trial Turns 100: Fibieger's Trial of Serum Treatment of Diphtheria." *British Medical Journal* 317: 1243–45.

Kaufman, P., X. Chen, S. P. Choy, K. A. Chandler, C. D. Chapman, M. R. Rand, and C. Ringel. 1998. *Indicators of School Crime and Safety, 1998*. Washington: National Center for Education Statistics.

Kornfeld, R., and Kalman Rupp. 2000. "The Net Effects of the Project NetWork Return to Work Case Management Experiment on Participant Earnings, Benefit Receipt, and Other Outcomes." *Social Security Bulletin* 63 (1): 12 –33.

Krueger, Alan B. 1999. "Experimental Estimates of Education Production Functions." *Quarterly Journal of Economics* 114: 497 –532.

Kunz, R., and A. D. Oxman. 1998. "The Unpredictability Paradox: Review of Empirical Comparisons of Randomised and Nonrandomised Clinical Trials." *British Medical Journal* (7167): 1185–90.

LaLonde, Robert J. 1986. "Evaluating the Econometric Evaluations of Training Programs with Experimental Data." *American Economic Review* 76 (4): 604–19.

Leow, Christine, and Robert F. Boruch. 2000. "Randomized Experiments on Mathematics and Science Education: Results of a Hand Search and a Machine-Based Search." Report of the Campbell Collaboration and the Third International Mathematics and Science Study. University of Pennsylvania.

Levin, Henry M. 1991. "Cost Effectiveness at the Quarter Century." In *Evaluation and Education at the Quarter Century: Ninetieth Yearbook of the National Society for the Study of Education,* edited by M. W. McLaughlin and D. C. Phillips, 189–209. University of Chicago Press.

Lind, Alan E. 1985. "Randomized Experiments in the Federal Courts." In *New Directions for Program Evaluation,* 28, edited by Robert F. Boruch and W. Wothke, 73–80.

Marks, H. M. 1997. *The Progress of Experiment: Science and Therapeutic Reform in the United States, 1900–1990.* Cambridge University Press.

Meier, Paul. 1972. "The Biggest Public Health Experiment Ever: The 1954 Field Trial of the Salk Poliomyelitis Vaccine." In *Statistics: A Guide to the Unknown,* edited by J. M. Tanur, Frederick Mosteller, W. H. Kruskal, R. F. Link, R. S. Pieters, and G. Rising, 2–13. San Francisco: Holden Day.

Meyer, H. J., E. F. Borgotta, and W. C. Jones, with E. P. Anderson, H. Grunwald, and D. Headley. 1965. *Girls at Vocational High: An Experiment in Social Work Intervention.* New York: Russell Sage Foundation.

Mosteller, Frederick. 1995. "The Tennessee Study of Class Size in the Early School Grades." *The Future of Children* 5: 113–27.

Myers, David, and A. Schirm. 1997. *The Short-Term Impacts of Upward Bound: An Interim Report.* Princeton, N. J.: Mathematica Policy Research.

Office of Juvenile Justice and Prevention Programs. 1996. "Curfew: An Answer to Juvenile Delinquency and Victimization?" *Juvenile Justice Bulletin* (April). Washington.

Peterson, Paul E., J. P. Greene, and C. Noyes. 1996. "School Choice in Milwaukee." *Public Interest* 125: 38–56.

Peterson, Paul E., David Myers, and W. G. Howell. 1998. *An Evaluation of the New York City School Choice Scholarships Program: The First Year.* Research Report. Harvard University, Education Policy and Governance Program.

Petrosino, Anthony J. Forthcoming. *What Works to Reduce Offending: A Systematic Review of Randomized Field Evaluations.* Oxford University Press.

Petrosino, Anthony J., Robert F. Boruch, Cath Rounding, Steve McDonald, and Iain Chalmers. 2000. "The Campbell Collaboration Social, Psychological, Educational, and Criminological Trials Register (C2-SPECTR) to Facilitate the Preparation and Maintenance of Systematic Reviews of Social and

Educational Interventions." *Evaluation and Research in Education* (UK) 14 (3, 4): 206–19.
Riccio, James, D. Friedlander, and S. Freedman. 1994. *GAIN: Benefits, Costs, and Three-Year Impacts of a Welfare to Work Program*. New York: Manpower Demonstration Research Corporation.
Riecken, Henry W., Robert F. Boruch, Donald T. Campbell, Nathan Caplan, Thomas K. Glennan, John W. Pratt, Al Rees, and Walter W. Williams. 1974. *Social Experimentation: A Method for Planning and Evaluating Social Intervention*. Academic Press.
Ritter, Gary, and Robert F. Boruch. 1999. "The Political and Institutional Origins of a Randomized Trial on Elementary School Class Size: Tennessee's Project STAR." *Educational Evaluation and Policy Analysis* 21 (2): 111–25.
Rossi, Peter, Howard Freeman, and Mark Lipsey. 1998. *Evaluation*. 6th ed. Thousand Oaks, Calif.: Sage Publications.
Roth, Jeffrey A., and John T. Scholz, eds. 1989. *Taxpayer Compliance*. Vol. 2: *Social Science Perspectives*. University of Pennsylvania Press.
Rubin, Donald B. 1974. "Estimating Causal Effects of Treatments in Randomized and Non-Randomized Studies." *Journal of Educational Psychology* 66: 688–701.
———. 1991. "Practical Implications of Modes of Statistical Inference for Causal Effects and the Critical Role of the Assignment Mechanism." *Biometrics* 47: 1213–34.
Schweinhart, Lawrence J., H. V. Barnes, and David P. Weikart, with W. S. Barnett and A. S. Epstein. 1993. *Significant Benefits: The High/Scope Perry Preschool Study through Age 27*. Ypsilanti, Mich.: High/Scope Press.
Shadish, William R., Thomas D. Cook, and Donald T. Campbell. 2002. *Experimental and Quasi-Experimental Designs for Generalized Causal Analysis*. Houghton Mifflin.
Sherman, Lawrence W., and Richard A. Berk. 1984. "The Specific Deterrent Effects of Arrest for Domestic Assault." *American Sociological Review* 49: 262–72.
———. 1985. "The Randomization of Arrest." In *New Directions for Program Evaluation*, 28, edited by Robert F. Boruch and W. Wothke, 15–26.
Silverman, W. A. 1985. *Human Experimentation: A Guided Step into the Unknown*. Oxford University Press.
Slavin, Robert E. 1993. "Ability Grouping in the Middle Grades: Achievement Effects and Alternatives." *Elementary School Journal* 93 (5): 535–52.
Snyder, H. N. 1998. "Juvenile Arrests, 1997." *Juvenile Justice Bulletin* (December). Washington: Office of Juvenile Justice and Delinquency Programs, U.S. Department of Justice.
St. Pierre, Robert G., J. P. Swartz, S. Murray, and D. Deck. 1996. *Improving Family Literacy: Findings from the National Even Start Evaluation*. Cambridge, Mass.: Abt Associates.
Stigler, Steven M. 1986. *The History of Statistics: The Measurement of Uncertainty before 1900*. Harvard University/Belnap Press.

U.S. Department of Education, Planning and Evaluation Service (USDE). 1997. *Biennial Report: 1997 Appendix*. Washington: USDE, Office of the Under Secretary, Planning and Evaluation Service.

———. 1999. *Annual Plan: FY 2000, Appendix B: Descriptions of Program Evaluations and Other Studies*. USDE 1/15/99. Washington.

U.S. General Accounting Office. 1995. *Multiple Employment and Training Programs*. GAO/T-HEHS-95-93. Washington.

University of Maryland, Department of Criminology and Criminal Justice. 1997. *Preventing Crime: What Works, What Doesn't, What's Promising*. Report to the United States Congress, prepared for the National Institute of Justice.

Yoshioka, A. 1998. "Use of Randomization in the Medical Research Council's Clinical Trial of Streptomycin in Pulmonary Tuberculosis in the 1940's." *British Medical Journal* 317: 1220–24.

Zelen, Marvin. 1990. "Randomized Consent Designs for Clinical Trials: An Update." *Statistics in Medicine* 9: 645–56.

CHAPTER FOUR

Resources, Instruction, and Research

DAVID K. COHEN
STEPHEN W. RAUDENBUSH
DEBORAH LOEWENBERG BALL

FOR MOST OF AMERICA'S history, educators, parents, and policymakers assumed that familiar educational resources, such as money, curriculum materials, and facilities, and their regulation, directly influenced student outcomes. Many still do, writing about the "effects" of class size or expenditures on learning. This view implies that resources carry "capacity," such that schools produce better learning by virtue of having more books or teachers with more degrees. Regulation has been thought to work by steering resources and thus capacity within and among educational organizations. These assumptions made school improvement efforts seem relatively straightforward: allocate more resources or regulate schools' allocation. But several decades of research suggest that relationships between resources and outcomes are not that direct. Researchers report that schools and teachers with the same resources do different things, with different results for students' learning. Resources are not self-enacting, and differences in their effects depend on

We thank Anthony Bryk, Jeremy Finn, Fred Gofree, Henry Levin, Richard Murnane, Will Onk, and Alan Ruby for helpful comments. We are also grateful for grants from the Pew Charitable Trusts and the Carnegie Corporation of New York to Michigan State University and the University of Michigan, from the Office of Educational Research and Improvement (U.S. Department of Education) to the Consortium for Policy Research in Education (CPRE) and the Center for the Study of Teaching and Policy, and from the Atlantic Philanthropies to CPRE. None of these agencies is responsible for any of the views discussed.

differences in their use. That makes school improvement a much more complex enterprise, one that depends as much on what is done with resources as what resources are available. This complexity arises at a time when policymakers are more concerned than ever about how to improve schools, and when efforts to do so have risen to the top of many state and local agendas.

We reconsider the role of resources in instruction. We briefly highlight some critical developments in recent research on the impact of resources. We use that to sketch a theoretical perspective on instruction, including resource use. We argue that resources have no direct effects, but that their effects depend on their use. If so, research on resources' effects requires designs that take use into account. We then discuss such designs.

Relating Resources to Outcomes

Resources have conventionally been conceived as either money or the things that money buys, including everything from books and bricks to libraries and the formal qualifications of teachers. For decades now, studies have focused on the allocation of such conventional resources and their relation to student learning. Until quite recently, education policy at all levels of government focused chiefly on the allocation of such resources. There is a great deal of data on such resources partly because it is required for official reporting. But thirty years of research on their effects on student learning raised fundamental questions about how schools worked and what education policy should do to help them work better. The questions began four decades ago, with Project Talent, James Coleman's *Equality of Educational Opportunity Survey,* and *Inequality* by Christopher Jencks and others.[1] Much to the astonishment of Coleman and others, the studies revealed that conventional resources seemed to be weakly related to student performance. Differences among school libraries, teachers' experience and education, expenditures, science labs, and other facilities had weak or no associations with differences among school average student achievement. Despite large differences in average achievement among schools, and especially troubling achievement differences between schools that enrolled the children of affluent and poor parents, differences in the educational resources that most people thought

1. Coleman (1966); Jencks and others (1972).

significant were weakly related to student performance differences among schools. The most powerful predictors of student performance were parents' educational and social backgrounds. In contrast, school resources had trivial effects. Schools with more conventional resources did not have substantially higher performance, once students' social and economic background was accounted for.

This research was often taken to mean that schools did not "make a difference," an idea that many conservatives embraced to support arguments against liberal social policy, and that liberals rejected in an effort to retain such policies. But the research dealt only with schools' differential effectiveness. The researchers' question was not whether schools made a difference, but whether some were better at boosting learning than others, given knowledge of students' social and educational backgrounds. Researchers found that, on average, differences in schools' effects on aggregate measures of achievement were not related to differences in their aggregate conventional resources.

Most studies of such resources since then, prominently including the meta-analyses of Eric Hanushek, supported Coleman and Jencks.[2] But a few researchers recently revived claims for conventional resources that Coleman and Jencks had reported to be ineffective. Larry Hedges and his colleagues reanalyzed scores of studies and found that money did make a modest difference to student performance.[3] The Tennessee class size experiment showed that some students' learning benefited from dramatic class size reductions.[4] These reports seem to diverge both from the research of Coleman and Jencks and from the studies summarized above, but it is not clear what accounted for the divergence. Researchers who have analyzed the STAR data from Tennessee disagree about why class size made a difference, and no convincing theoretical frame has been offered in the published discussions.

Research by Coleman and Jencks marked a watershed in educational thought. Public debate about schools previously had focused much more on access to and allocation of resources than on results, even though the latter often were tacitly assumed to be implied in the former. The new work ruptured the supposed connection between resources and results, and, by the mid-1970s, adding resources could no longer be assumed to affect student performance.

2. Hanushek (1981, 1989).

3. Hedges and others (1994).

4. Finn and Achilles (1990). See also Mosteller (1995).

New Understandings about What Makes Instruction Work

In response to that shift, and often in deliberate opposition to the work of Coleman, Jencks, and Hanushek, several new lines of research focused more closely on what might make instruction work. These studies probed instructional processes and, deliberately or by implication, the resources used therein. Although the researchers did not necessarily say that they were studying resources, their work nonetheless offers clues to how resources are related to educational outcomes. Though most of the work just mentioned appeared to focus on direct relationships between resources and learning, subsequent studies suggested a less direct relationship.

In the 1970s and 1980s, researchers sought to figure out whether some teaching was more effective and, if so, why. In one summary of the evidence, the practice of unusually effective teachers, as judged by students' gains on standardized tests, seemed significantly different from that of their less effective peers. More effective teachers planned lessons carefully, selected appropriate materials, made their goals clear to students, maintained a brisk pace in lessons, checked student work regularly, and taught material again when students had trouble learning.[5] They also made good use of the time they spent on instructional tasks.[6] Such teachers seemed to have coherent strategies for instruction and deployed lessons, books, and other resources in ways that were consistent with the strategies. They believed that their students could learn and that they themselves had a large responsibility to help. These teachers could be seen as deploying resources that were consequential for student learning, but they were not the sort of resources that could be captured well in measures of teachers' formal qualifications, their schools' expenditures, or other such things.

Some researchers during the same decades brought a similar perspective to bear on schools. They sought to distinguish more and less effective schools and to identify the causes, and probed connections between schools' collective characteristics and student performance. These characteristics could be seen as resources, evident in some schools and not in others. Faculty in unusually effective schools appeared to share a vision of the purposes of instruction.[7] They agreed that the purpose of schools was

5. Brophy and Good (1986).
6. That was first reported by Cooley and Leinhardt (1978).
7. See Edmonds (1984); Rutter and others (1979); and Rosenholtz (1985).

to promote students' learning, that they were responsible for helping students to learn, and that all students had real capacity to learn. Teachers in such schools had a strong commitment to students' academic success, and their principals helped to create and sustain these beliefs and practices.[8] A comprehensive and sophisticated study in this line, focusing especially on Catholic high schools, found that teachers in more effective high schools were more likely to have a shared commitment to their students' academic success, have strong collegial relations, and believe that they were obliged to help students learn.[9] Similar conclusions were reached in a study of "restructuring" schools.[10] And in an extensive program of research on teachers' academic community in high school departments, strong relationships were observed between teachers' community and sense of collective responsibility for students' work, on the one hand, and students' academic performance, on the other.[11]

A third line of inquiry probed interactions between teachers and students around specific content and provided finer clues to the role resources play in instruction. Those who tried to map and unpack the domains that lay between such gross influences as the time that teachers and students spent, on the one hand, and what students learned, on the other, found that instructional time itself was not consequential.[12] Only when the nature of academic tasks was taken into account were effects on learning observed. The researchers then focused on teachers' task definitions and students' approaches to learning. They defined several of those domains, including teachers' task definition, their task enactment, and students' performance of instructional tasks.[13] From detailed measures of each, they were able to show that students' performance of instructional tasks mediated between teachers' task setting and students' learning. One could see this work as an effort to track the paths by which a variety of resources were turned into instructional actions that had the potential to affect learning.

A major study of practices (termed "strategy instruction") that seemed to distinguish more from less effective readers also produced important

8. Edmonds (1984, 1979).
9. Bryk and others (1993).
10. Newman and Wehlage (1995).
11. McLaughlin and Talbert (forthcoming).
12. Cooley and Leinhardt (1978).
13. Leinhardt, Zigmond, and Cooley (1981).

results.[14] When the practices were taught to teachers, who in turn taught them to students, they had positive effects on students' adoption, and students who used the practices performed better in reading.[15]

Related work showed that learners' attributions about intelligence and learning may also play a key role in their classroom practices and learning.[16] Children who viewed intelligence as fixed tended to avoid intellectual challenges that might publicly reveal wrong answers, while children who viewed intelligence as expandable through effort sought out and used those challenges. These experiments also showed that children could be taught to change their attributions for negative feedback from teachers, and that when they did, their effort increased, and they made better use of differentiated feedback from teachers. The children learned how to study better, in part, by learning to think differently about the academic efficacy that they brought to the available instructional resources.

New Conceptions of Resources

The studies sketched here and others suggest that some scholars' interest has moved away from conventional conceptions of resources—such as money, teachers' qualifications, and school facilities—toward particular instructional practices and organizational arrangements, and the actions, strategies, knowledge, skill, and culture that they entail. They also show that practice-embedded knowledge and actions can have significant effects on learning. Teachers' knowledge, skills, and strategic actions can be seen as resources, as can students' experiences, knowledge, norms, and approaches to learning. These resources attach to the agents of instruction and appear to mediate their use of such conventional resources as time and material. Such studies shed considerable light on the organizations and cultures in which teachers and students work—including administrators' leadership, the collective will to take responsibility for students' learning, schools' academic organization, the collective embrace of academic goals, and the nature of collegial relations—as potential resources in the environment of instruction.

14. Palincsar and Brown (1984).

15. In the same line, Carol Sue Englert conducted several experiments in which students were taught to understand the processes of writing (including outlining, drafting, revising, editing), to monitor those processes as they wrote, and to develop strategies to push the process along. Englert taught learners how to be more effective students, boosting learning by improving their academic practices (see Englert and others 1991).

16. Dweck (1986, 1988).

These studies imply that teachers' and students' practices mediate between the conventional resources that schools and school systems deploy, on the one hand, and learning accomplishments, on the other. Many researchers treat teaching as though it directly provoked learning, but in the work summarized here effective teaching encouraged and closely supported what students did during instruction, and students' work then helped—or did not help—them to learn. Teaching is portrayed as a set of activities that enabled students to use materials, tasks, and other resources, more or less well. According to these studies, the effectiveness of resources depends on their use in instruction. What students and teachers do with resources is no less consequential than the resources that schools deploy. Moreover, a great deal of instruction that researchers had associated with individual teachers' work turned out to have collective features; it was shaped and supported by teachers' work together, by educational leaders, and by the organizations and cultures in which students and teachers worked.

If these things are true, instructional quality cannot be created simply by collecting a stock of conventional resources such as books or formal qualifications or money. Nor does quality arise simply from attributes of teachers, curricula, or facilities. Instructional quality instead appears to depend on the mobilization of a complex collection of knowledge and practices, collective actions, and the conventional resources on which those actions and practices draw. This implies that there are several kinds of resources, and that their use is crucial in understanding their effects on learning and teaching. For example, well-educated teachers spending time on academic lessons would not be enough; only if they use the time in academically productive ways does student learning seem to benefit. Such benefits also depend on students knowing how to apprehend and use the tasks and materials that teachers deploy, and on school leaders focusing, encouraging, and supporting the practices with which teachers and students make use of each other and materials. This, in turn, suggests a complex and interactive picture of the processes by which conventional resources become effective for teaching and learning. It also suggests that schools cannot be improved simply by intervening either on individuals' stocks of knowledge or on schools' stocks of conventional resources. Improvement would instead depend on the way in which students, teachers, and school leaders use resources; the knowledge and skill applied in using resources for instruction; the usability of resources; and the conditions that enable resource use.

These ideas offer a major challenge to research. The studies we just discussed used increasingly direct and complex methods to measure teachers' knowledge, skill, and strategic actions; the time devoted to academic work; norms of professional conduct; and students' use of instruction. Such evidence is difficult to come by in part because it requires the observation and measurement of complex social and intellectual processes, which is expensive even on a small scale. Evidence on such matters is included in no official reports, for it does not fit well with the disciplines that have dealt most extensively with policymaking, or with the interests of those who make policy. One reason is that any ensuing advice for policymakers would be complex and may even seem beyond the reach of government. In contrast, studies of conventional resources are relatively easy to carry out and affordable because the resources with which they deal are familiar and easy to observe. Such work also accords with the intellectual orientation of the fields—economics, sociology, and policy analysis—that have dealt most extensively with policymaking. And it fits well with the interests of those who make policy because the influences observed and measured are those that decisionmakers can most easily manipulate.

Thus the research that promises better understanding of the operation and effects of specific resources and more salient advice for the education professionals who manage and deliver instruction is difficult to do, expensive to support, and complex to use. In contrast, the research that is less likely to deepen understanding of resources and assist educators is more straightforward, relatively affordable, and easy to use. One challenge for educational research will be to link these traditions. In the next section we begin to sketch a theoretical frame that links the two sorts of work, and outline an approach to research that would expand those links.

Toward a Theory of Instructional Resources

The research summarized in the preceding section suggests that conventional resources are used or not used depending on the actions of teachers, students, and the organizations in which they work. Researchers wishing to adequately model the effects of resources need a theory of instruction, because it is in instruction that resources are used or not used in ways that could influence learning.

Figure 4-1. *Instruction as Interaction of Teachers, Students, and Content, in Environments*

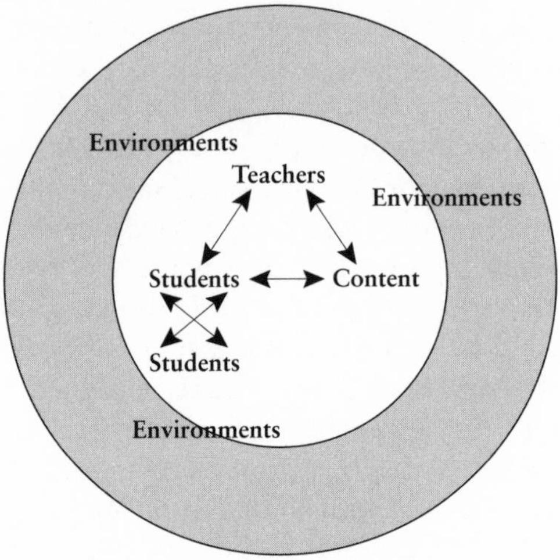

Resources within Instruction

Instruction consists of interactions (see figure 4-1) among teachers, students, and content in various environments. The interactions occur in distance learning, small groups in classrooms, informal groups, tutorials, and large lectures. "Interaction" does not refer to a particular form of discourse but to the connected work of teachers and students on content, in environments. Although this depiction of instructional relationships has adherents going back to John Dewey, some researchers and practitioners still refer to teaching as though it was something done by teachers to learners.

The interactions extend through time: over minutes, days, weeks, and months.[17] Instruction evolves as tasks develop and lead to others, as students' engagement and understanding waxes and wanes, and as organization changes. Instruction is a stream, not an event. That stream flows in instructional environments and draws on their elements, including other

17. Lampert (2001).

teachers and students, school leaders, parents, professions, local districts, state agencies, test and text publishers, and more.

To illustrate, imagine a classroom in which second-graders are working on mathematics. Their school district made mathematics a priority for improvement and recently adopted a new mathematics curriculum. Every teacher received a complete set of the materials. To support the initiative, the district math coordinator organized ten professional development sessions for teachers. In several of the elementary schools, principals devoted faculty meeting time to work on instructional and curricular issues in math. A district committee also developed a map, indexing the goals and benchmarks of the new textbook and the state proficiency test, to help teachers connect the two in instruction. The school board, however, was divided on issues related to the mathematics program and recently cut the district mathematics coordinator position from full to three-quarters time in order to fund additional computer support at the middle school. A few teachers considered applying for state funds available for mathematics curriculum development.

At the end of the previous class, the teacher had posted this problem on the board:

> Suppose you have pennies and nickels in your pocket. If you pull out two coins, how much money might you have in your hand?[18]

She asked the children to copy the problem into their home-school notebooks and to try to find some possible answers to this question for homework. The teacher opens class on this day by asking who had come up with some possibilities for the problem. Danya announces, confidently, "You would have six cents. Me and my mom figured it out." The teacher pauses, and then asks the other students, "Do others agree?" Several hands shoot up. "That's what I got, too!" exclaims Timmy. Darien raises his hand hesitantly. "It could be two cents. If you pulled a penny and another penny. Danya got a nickel and a penny, but you could also pull out a penny and a penny." Several children nod. "What do you think, Danya?" asks the teacher. Danya nods. "Mmm-hmm. I agree."

The teacher asks whether there are other possibilities. "Ten cents," suggests Kim. "How did you get that?" asks the teacher. "She used two

18. This is a variant on a problem in the National Council of Teachers of Mathematics *Curriculum and Evaluation Standards for School Mathematics* (1989, p. 28).

nickels," Louis calls out. "Are there other possibilities?" The teacher looks at the children waiting, and sees that Ruben is slumping down in his seat. "What do you think, Ruben?" she asks. "I didn't do it," he says softly. "This is stupid. This isn't math. My dad told me I should be doing math, and so he told me not to do it."

The teacher puts a new problem up on the board:

> Suppose you have pennies, nickels, and dimes in your pocket. Now if you pull out three coins, how much money might you have in your hand?

"I want you to work alone on this for a few minutes, and this time try to find all the possible amounts of money you can have." She pulls out trays of coins and asks a few children to help distribute them. While the children start copying the problem onto their regular notepads, she stoops down beside Ruben to help him get started. She knows that his father is quite upset with the new math program and is worried that this is affecting Ruben's work.

She helps him read the new problem and works with him to get one solution. He lights up. "I could get three dimes!" he exclaims. The teacher smiles and asks Ruben how much money he would have. "Thirty cents!" he replies, happily, "And that is the most money I could get." Pleased, the teacher tells him to see whether he can figure out others. "What is the smallest amount of money you might pull out?" she asks.

The teacher notices the school principal standing at the door and beckons her to come in. She enters the room and watches the children at work. When she sees Ruben, she asks the teacher how he is doing. The principal says that Ruben's father had called her to complain that his son was not getting enough math skill practice. The teacher suggests meeting with the father to show him some of the work they are doing. "Or perhaps we should plan a meeting for more parents, since he is not the only one," muses the principal. They agree to discuss this later.

In this brief example, what we casually call teaching is not what teachers do and say and think, which is what many researchers have studied and many innovators have tried to change. Teaching is what teachers do, say, and think with learners, concerning content, in a particular organization of instruction, in environments, over time. What we often mistakenly refer to as the practice of teaching is a collection of practices, including pedagogy, learning, instructional design, and managing instructional organization.[19] There are more instructional practitioners than teachers, and more practices than pedagogy. Moreover, the environments in which teaching and learning are situated are often implicated in teachers' and students' interactions.

The effects of resources in teaching and learning depend on how teachers, students, and others solve four central problems: how to use resources, coordinate instruction, mobilize incentives for performance, and manage environments.

Use Resources

Our interactive view of teaching and learning implies that resources only become active in instruction if they are used by students or teachers.[20] Even the best curriculum materials are of little consequence if teachers cannot turn them to advantage in framing tasks for students, or if students cannot understand or engage them. Ample school budgets will have little constructive effect on learning if they are not used to hire good teachers and enable them to work effectively. Independent observers might report that such classrooms and schools had rich resources, but their potential to affect instruction would be unrealized.

One crucial set of influences on teachers and students' use of resources is their instructional knowledge and skill. Teachers who know a good deal about a subject and how to make it available to learners will be more likely to frame productive tasks from the available materials and to turn students' work and ideas to fruitful use. For instance, our teacher used knowledge of combinatorics and mathematical problem solving to exploit the task she framed for the class and Ruben. Discovering that Ruben was alienated from the work and stuck, she used the material to bring him into the task, drawing on her knowledge to help him see how to use the task to learn. She helped him get one solution to the problem and then built on his own mathematical observation of the largest possible amount of money. She was able to see what was obstructing his engagement with the work and to use her knowledge to help him make good use of the task. Her mathematical insight was critical, for she was able to exploit the arithmetic and problem-solving dimensions of the

19. For convenience, we often refer in what follows to "instruction," in which we include this clump of practices, rather than either teaching alone or the more clumsy "teaching and learning with materials."

20. Allan Odden's extensive research on school finance and school improvement develops a version of this view. See, for example, Odden and Busch (1998).

problem without sacrificing either. Had she seen this as only a matter of getting answers or of strategies, her interaction with students and their work would have unfolded quite differently. Teachers with a superficial knowledge of subject matter would be less effective in working with students like Ruben, to connect their understanding to instructional tasks.

Similarly, students who have learned to reflect on their ideas, listen carefully, and express themselves clearly are likely to be better users of materials, teachers, and other students' contributions. They also are likely to make it easier for other students and teachers to use their ideas. How students and teachers organize their interactions also shapes resource use. Students and teachers whose classroom cultures support the respectful expression, explanation, and scrutiny of ideas are likely to generate more usable material for instruction, and thus to have more resources to use than classrooms in which conventional lecture and recitation are the rule.

Realizing the potential of resources also depends on the settings in which teachers and students work. The classroom in our example is a place where children volunteer their ideas and conjectures and where the teacher listens attentively and teaches the children to use each other's ideas. But there are many schools in which principals would discourage such work in favor of more conventional drill on facts and procedures.

Quality in instruction thus does not inhere in teachers' formal qualifications or the caliber of materials, but in how the knowledge and skill is deployed to frame tasks and use instructional resources. Teacher quality is determined less by a teacher's formal qualifications and more by that teacher's ability to make pedagogically fruitful use of materials, students' work, and their own subject matter knowledge. Similarly, the quality of materials depends both on how accessible and engaging they are for learners and on how well they enable teachers to make sense of and use them.

One important implication of this view is that students' ability depends in part on how well teachers probe, understand, and use their work. Even the strengths or disadvantages that students are said to "bring" to instruction are partly a matter of what their teachers can see and hear in students' work and how skillfully they recognize and respond to them. Students' ability is in part interactively determined. In another classroom, perceived and questioned by a teacher who knew or could use mathematical knowledge less well, Ruben might have been seen as "not ready" and given a simpler assignment. What reformers and researchers term "instructional capacity" is not a fixed attribute of teachers or students or materials, but a variable feature of interaction among them.

Variation in resource use also stems in part from the versions of knowledge, teaching, and learning at play in instruction. If knowledge is treated as fixed, teachers' and students' use of materials will focus on facts, algorithms, and formulas. But if it is treated as something learners reinvent, students will use materials to frame interpretations, discover relationships, and apply knowledge in new situations. The latter is more complex and opens up more uncertainty, while the former enables teachers to simply use materials as they appear, as scripts or assignments.

Similarly, if learning is treated as assimilation, resource use for teachers can be restricted to extracting formulas, algorithms, and lists for presentation to learners. But if it is treated as reinvention or discovery, teachers must use materials to devise tasks that enable reinvention and discovery. Creating materials that are usable in the second sense is more complex and demanding than creating materials that are usable in the first sense. Using the second sort of materials also is more complex and opens up much more uncertainty for teachers and learners than using materials of the first sort. When learning is treated as discovery, teachers find it more complex to know if they have made good use of their knowledge or students' work.

Coordinate Instruction

Using resources well also depends on solving problems of coordination. If instruction consists of interactions among teachers, learners, and content, there will be many opportunities for lack of coordination because these interactions can be extremely complex and easily disorganized. One focus for coordination is teachers, students, and content. The teacher in our example was trying to work on the coin problem, but some students may have been fiddling with their pencils, passing notes, or drawing. When she began class, a couple of her students may have forgotten their homework, and those who were absent the day before may not know what is being discussed. A new student may be pulled out for testing. In the midst of class, the principal may enter and raise an issue about parental support for the mathematics curriculum. Even if everyone works on the task and knows what to do, some teachers might address it algorithmically while the curriculum developers intended to support the development of mathematical ideas. Teachers may address the task as the text does but not probe students' ideas and so remain unaware of how they understand it. Teachers may agree on the task with half the class without knowing that the other half remains in the dark.

Instruction occurs over time, and that opens up another fundamental problem of coordination. How, for instance, do these coin problems connect with each student's work tomorrow and whatever happens two weeks later? How do students and teachers make the small bits of lesson work develop into learning over time, despite absences and lapses of memory?[21] Other dimensions of coordination exist among subjects within classrooms, among classrooms within grades, from one grade to the next, and between home and school.

Each dimension of coordination presents a set of potential problems. If students and teachers are not focused on the same task, learning is likely to suffer. If students' learning is not paced to maintain appropriate cognitive demand, students may be either overwhelmed or bored, and learning will suffer. The fewer steps that are taken to ensure coordination of these and other sorts, the more diffuse and less effective instruction is likely to be.[22] If our teacher merely assigned the task and later collected and graded papers, as has been typical, the lesson would have been far different. What she did enabled her to coordinate in many ways, including her trouble-shooting work with Ruben, her use of the home-school notebooks, and her staging of increasing difficulty from the two-coin to the three-coin version.

The difficulty of coordination varies with the conceptions of knowledge, teaching, and learning that are in play. Knowledge can be treated as fixed or constructed. In the first case it is a given, while in the second it is partly a matter of invention and interpretation. Teachers' efforts to coordinate their work with students' in the latter case is more difficult than in the former, for invention and interpretation are more complex. Learning also can be treated quite differently, as a process either of assimilation, on the one hand, or of discovery or reinvention, on the other. Coordination is much easier in the first case because teachers need only check to see whether students remember the proper formulas, algorithms, or procedures and can work them satisfactorily. To learn is to have mastered such

21. For a discussion of coordination problems, see Lampert (2001).

22. There also are structural features of coordination, including the ways in which time and instruction are organized in periods, days, school years, vacations. Student mobility within and between schools also bears on coordination.

things and to produce them on demand. Teachers can determine whether students are learning what they are teaching with a quick check of recitation or homework. But if learning has students uncovering the material through their work, it is much more difficult for teachers to ascertain what students learn. Such teaching is much less direct. As in our example, teachers set general tasks or problems and invite students to work them out. There often are many solution paths, and while some may be more efficient, others may be more inventive. It is much more difficult for teachers and students to know if students are on a productive track when they manage much more complex and ambiguous tasks.

Mobilize Incentives

It takes effort to teach and learn, and incentives are required to mobilize the effort. Mobilizing such incentives within instruction is a third sort of instructional problem, one that is complicated by conflict about effort. Teachers have incentives to press for ambitious work and exert themselves, for their professional success depends on learners' success—or on explaining why learners could not succeed. Learners also have reasons to work hard, for it can satisfy their curiosity and wish to learn, enhance their sense of competence, and enable them to meet teachers' and parents' hopes. But teachers and learners also have incentives to do less ambitious work, for effort increases as learners encounter more difficulty, uncertainty, risk of failure, and more chances to disappoint themselves and others. The coin problems our teacher used are of this latter sort, for the tasks entail ambiguous and challenging work for second-graders. Teachers who frame such work are more likely to encounter learners' resistance, frustration, and failure, even if greater success beckons. Learners and teachers who do less ambitious work reduce these problems and increase the chance of some success. Teachers and students thus face a dilemma. Should they aim low, accepting modest results in return for some success, or aim high, risking difficulty, resistance, and failure in the hope of greater improvement for learners and impressive accomplishments for teachers? Incentive conflict is internal to teaching and learning, and to teach and learn is to manage the conflict.

In our example, the teacher posed a challenging task when she asked her students to find all the solutions to a combinations problem. Her decision to introduce the task as a homework problem allowed students to get started and build confidence. Her choice to leave one last step open stimulated interest. She also offered students support as an incentive to persist.

The difficulty of mobilizing incentives for ambitious performance depends in part on the conceptions of knowledge, teaching, and learning in play. If knowledge is treated as fixed and learning as assimilation, students need only focus on facts, algorithms, and formulas. But if knowledge is constructed and learning is reinvention, students' tasks are much more complex, as frame interpretations, discover relationships, and apply existing ideas in new situations. The first conception of knowledge and learning is less engaging for some, but more secure and less troublesome for others, because it is less complex and entails less uncertainty, invention, and cognitive demand. Had our teacher passed out a basic facts drill sheet, the work would have been more constrained, and what it took to complete the task would have been clearer. The conceptions of knowledge and learning embedded in the coin problem require more of teachers, for they must hold knowledge in more complex and flexible form, consider more complex and uncertain work from students, and cope with greater difficulty, risk, and resistance.

Managing Environments

Instruction cannot be separated from seemingly external influences, including other teachers, school leaders, parents, district policies, state requirements, professional education, and much more.[23] To teach and learn is to notice or ignore, enact or reject, and thus in a sense to manage elements of the environment. When teachers and students solve problems of coordination, resource use, and incentives, they do so in and with elements of their environments.

For example, teachers and students are more likely to want to do quality work in schools that are linked to institutions of higher education or to firms that offer strong incentives for ambitious performance than in institutions that do not offer such incentives. Teachers and students who work in schools whose principals urge ambitious performance will be more likely to do such work themselves and to press each other for it, while equally able colleagues in schools whose principals prefer less ambitious performance will have more difficulty mobilizing incentives for demanding work. While some U.S. schools, families, principals, firms,

23. This problem is not practically distinct from those of coordination, incentives, and resource use, but it is so important that we treat it as distinct.

and institutions of higher education encourage demanding schoolwork, many more do not.

Similarly, coordinating teaching and learning is less difficult in environments with coherent organization and guidance for instruction, and more difficult in those that lack such coherence. The United States presents distinctively incoherent organization and guidance for instruction. These environments do exist outside of instruction, but they also are implicated in interactions among teachers and students. As our teacher tried to develop mathematical concepts and skills, she also sought to deal with parents' questions about the district's new emphases in math. She suspected that Ruben and perhaps others were doing less well than they might partly because their parents disparaged the assignments. She also was aware of many signals about instruction, including the upper-grade teachers' expectations, her principal's exhortations to make sure all students develop basic skills, the district's investment in the new curriculum focusing on concepts, and the new state assessment that tests speed and accuracy. Fragmented organization within and among an extraordinary number of education agencies produces profuse, uncoordinated guidance for instruction and impedes collective action. Lacking strong and focused leadership at the school and district level, students and teachers find it difficult to fashion coherent instruction.[24]

Resource use also depends on instructional environments. Other things being equal, teachers who work in schools that focus on students' work and offer opportunities for teachers to learn how to interpret it will be better able to make sense of students' ideas. Principals who structure school budgets to support instruction help to bring resources to bear on teaching and learning, and make the resources more usable. Professional education that focuses on knowledge of the content teachers teach, and how to make it pedagogically usable, are more likely to enable teachers and learners to be artful users of materials and each other. But most U.S. teachers do not have such professional education, nor do they work in schools in which resources are focused on instruction and teachers' learning. In our example, the district cut the mathematics coordinator position

24. State standards-based reform has sought to order the confusion, but in most cases it has not reduced the proliferation of guidance and in some cases has increased it. New guidance that calls for coherence has been laid on many earlier layers of less coherent guidance. Or new conventional guidance was added in response to the more ambitious guidance of standards-based reform. This reform also never offered a way to reduce the variety of organizations that act on schools and the guidance they direct at classrooms.

just as it made mathematics instruction a priority, reducing the resources available for teacher support as it increased the need for such support. Since resources traditionally have been seen as a matter of mere provision, not as a matter of use, those working in the environments of U.S. schools have had little reason to strongly support effective resource use.

Though teachers and students shape environmental influences by what they notice and how they respond, action in the environment can affect their attention and response. When school and district leaders place a high priority on improving teachers' work with disadvantaged students by raising the incentives for such work—rather than ignoring the matter or arguing that nothing can be done—the chances are greater that teachers will try to overcome students' disadvantages. If school and district leaders go further, and coordinate efforts to solve the problem by engaging the teachers and offering them opportunities to learn how to improve, the chances that teachers will constructively deal with student disadvantage increase further. Managing environments depends on clarity and authority in environmental priorities, on teachers' and learners' attention, and on their will and skill to respond.

From a conventional perspective, environments and practice seem separate. Since teachers practice on and with learners and cannot work without them, it seems sensible to think of teachers and learners as doing technical work inside practice, and of environments as outside influences. Many researchers and educators portray economic and social differences among families as causes of differences in student performance. But these environmental differences become active inside instruction, as learners import elements of the environment. Ruben's father tells his son that the work in school is not worthwhile, and so Ruben does not do his homework and is less ready to use the day's instruction. National debates about the goals and means of mathematics education thought to be external to the classroom enter the transactions between Ruben and his teacher, affecting his learning and her teaching. Teachers pick up many signals about instruction that influence their decisions about how to use instructional materials and what to emphasize with students. Both the messages and their reception shape incentives for teacher and students to work in particular ways, toward particular goals.

Students are delegates from environments beyond the technical and professional worlds, yet students are essential to work in those worlds.

The same thing can be said of teachers and materials.[25] Teaching and learning cannot be conceived simply as internal technical work that is influenced by external environments, for as teachers and learners work together they work with and on elements of the world conventionally thought to lie beyond practice. The outside is in certain respects inside, and work inside is, in certain respects, work with and on elements of the outside. Teachers and learners work on a boundary, where they habitually manage often difficult relations between the inner and outer worlds of practice.

Our discussion has highlighted four problems that teachers and learners must face: using resources, coordinating instruction, mobilizing incentives, and managing environments.[26] We call them problems because teaching and learning are practical activities, and many practitioners attentively deal with them as problems. But these problems often are solved inattentively, implicitly, in the course of practice. In either case, they make visible several key domains of instructional practice.

Types of Resources

Our analysis implies different sorts of instructional resources: conventional, personal, and environmental. Conventional resources include teachers' formal qualifications, books, facilities, expenditures, class size, time, libraries and laboratories, and more. Each can be consequential. Students in classes of thirty-five or forty are less likely to have access to teachers' time and expertise than students in classes of fifteen. Students who study in schools with ancient texts may have access to less substantial and engaging content than those who work with more up-to-date materials. And students in less-developed nations who work with uneducated teachers and no books have access to many fewer resources than those in wealthy and industrialized nations who attend modern schools with better-educated teachers and contemporary materials. But these resources only make a difference to teaching or learning as they enter

25. Materials often frame content so as to manage the boundary between instruction and its environments—as in the case of U.S. textbooks intended for sale in southern states, which fail to mention evolution.

26. We use "solve" in the sense of manage, or cope with, and imply no satisfactory solution. Nor do we suppose that all teachers and students address these problems attentively. The problems are a rhetorical device used to define the terrain of teaching and learning.

instructional interactions. They cannot make a difference unless they are noticed, seen as resources, and used by teachers and students.

They enter by way of teachers' and students' personal resources: their knowledge, skill, and will affect the perception and use of conventional resources. There could not be much school learning without schools, books, and other materials, but only teachers and students can use them, and what they know and are able to do influences what they use, and how. Even a single learner working alone needs tasks or materials, the knowledge and skill to use them, and norms of learning. Teachers' knowledge of the subjects they teach, the will to improve learners' work, the skill to elicit students' ideas, and the knowledge to understand them—all affect what they notice and use.

Environmental resources, such as leadership, academic norms, and institutional structures, also influence whether and how teachers and students notice and use conventional resources. The social organization of teachers' and students' work, such as arrangements for coordination within schools, can affect the resources that they notice and use. The building principal in our example sought to influence teachers' and students' engagement with mathematics by attending to substantive issues of mathematics instruction herself—such as parental understanding of the math curriculum—and by making mathematics a focus of professional conversation in the school. School and district leaders can support or inhibit effective teaching, as can state and federal policy—for example, by offering teachers opportunities to learn through professional development. Since teachers' and students' use of resources is central to their influence on instruction, one crucial means by which actors in the environment can influence teaching and learning is by shaping what teachers and students notice, and their knowledge, skill, and will to use various resources.

These three kinds of resources interact. Conventional resources make a difference, for most teachers could not do well without schools, or books, or quiet places to work, and most students could not do well without books and teachers. But these resources only bear on instruction when teachers and learners notice and use them. How well teachers and learners use them depends on the particular mix of personal and environmental resources. There is no *primum mobile*—no one resource that causes all others. Rather, they are interdependent. Since teachers and students are the agents of instruction, they play a central role in what gets noticed and used, but agents in their environment influence what they notice and use.

Class size is a conventional resource that could affect learning only as teachers and students use it. Suppose that teachers in a particular state used to have fifty students in each class and taught in didactic fashion. In 1990 the legislature reduced class size to twenty-five, while ensuring that teacher quality remained constant over the expanded labor force. In this scenario, we would expect learning to improve only in classrooms in which teachers and learners used existing personal resources to make good use of smaller classes. Teachers in these classes might spend more time with each student or take more time to read students' work, probe students' thinking, or offer comments on students' work. Students might make better use of their teachers or instructional materials. These teachers and students would notice the opportunity to improve practice, and use it.

Class size reduction also could enable some teachers and students to learn new knowledge and skills on their own, which would improve teaching and learning. Such improvements would occur if those in the classroom saw the new conditions—such as greater student access to teachers or more time for teachers to probe students' work—as an opportunity to learn how to do better work. Such teachers and students would use what they already knew to learn more.[27]

Students would not learn more if they and their teachers did not use existing personal resources more intensively. Teachers given a smaller class might not spend more time with each student; instead they might assign more seat work, have students correct their own worksheets, and do other tasks themselves. Students might not make better use of their teachers because they chose not to, did not know how, or were discouraged from doing so by their teachers or other students. These teachers and students would not notice this opportunity to improve practice, or they would notice but not take it. This might be because they did not believe improvement was possible, because they did not have the required knowledge and skills, or because they did not care to make the effort. Opportunities to improve practice are not always accompanied by

27. This analysis implies that, were new studies done on class size, it would be useful to collect evidence that would allow researchers to learn three sorts of things: (a) the content and dynamics of teachers' responses, including those sketched above; (b) the patterns of student learning growth that were associated with those responses; and (c) the attributes of students and instructional environments that were associated with differences in teachers' response and the growth of student learning.

incentives to act. These classrooms might improve only if agents in the school, district, or elsewhere help teachers take advantage of the greater exposure to students' work and ideas and provide incentives to act.[28] Principals or district leaders could organize efforts to help teachers learn how to make more efficient use of time or how to elicit and interpret students' work. They might help teachers learn how to teach students to be more effective users of materials and tasks. And they might make clear to students and teachers that taking advantage of improved conditions would be rewarded, while failure to do so would be noticed and perhaps penalized. In some fraction of these cases, teachers and students would learn how to use the added resource more effectively, and learning would improve.

On this account, students' and teachers' resources mediate between class size and learning, as they would mediate the effects of any other conventional resource. Any mix of personal and environmental resources opens some possibilities for, and contains some limits on, the use of any conventional resource. Given any particular configuration of personal and environmental resources, research could show that added conventional resources appeared to independently affect learners' accomplishments, other things being equal. But that apparent independent effect actually would express an interaction among personal, environmental, and conventional resources. The instructional effects of conventional resources depend on their usability, their use by those who work in instruction, and the environments in which they work.

When added conventional resources appear to affect learning accomplishments, it is because they were usable, because teachers and students knew how to use them effectively, and because environments enabled or did not impede use by these particular teachers and students. The effects of conventional resource increments are in reality an average computed over the classes in which the resources are available and, within classes, over the students enrolled. In the case of class size, we know that teachers vary in their capacity to use this resource, that students vary both in their exposure to the resource and in their capacity to use it, and that environmental resources vary over both. Hence the potential effect of

28. Giving teachers access to the improved student work that would likely follow from teachers' learning to make use of reduced class size would become such an incentive, since such knowledge would capitalize on teachers' success through students' success.

something like the Tennessee class size experiment will be greater than this average, perhaps much greater, if teachers and students who make weak spontaneous use are taught to do better. The experiment offers an estimate of the average effects of the use of one conventional resource, but only further analysis could weigh the effects in classrooms that made good, poor, or no use of that resource.

This discussion also implies that when added resources lie outside the range of teachers' and students' practices, knowledge, norms, and incentives, they will have no discernible effect on learning. For instance, our hypothetical legislature might instead have mandated that teachers use innovative academic content standards to engage learners in creative discussion of more demanding academic content. The legislature might have provided money to write and disseminate the standards and to support discussion of them. We expect that research on the effects of such a policy would show that the new resources had no average positive effects on students' learning, for the policy would have required most teachers and students to work well beyond their skills, knowledge, and will, without providing opportunities and incentives for them to learn much more.[29]

When researchers fail to find effects for particular conventional resources, it should not be seen as evidence that such resources are ineffective until several other explanations are ruled out. One possibility is that teachers and learners did not know how to use a given resource, and ruling that explanation out would require research on the effects of teaching teachers and students to use it. Another possibility is that the change in conventional resources was not enough to enable significantly better

29. The same sort of argument can be made about research showing that teachers who have higher test scores, or who know more about a subject, have students with higher test scores. See Coleman (1966); Jencks and others (1972); Ferguson (1991). If we think of teachers as people who stand and deliver, teachers who know more about a subject have more to deliver. But the very words are deceptive, because knowledge is not self-enacting. If students benefit from teachers' greater stock of knowledge, it probably is not only because they can use greater knowledge to better advantage in teaching. The connection between students' scores and teachers' knowledge must have something to do with teachers' use of their knowledge. Many teachers who know plenty of mathematics can barely use it for purposes of teaching. Teachers who know more of a subject probably are, on average, able to make better use of texts, to set better problems, and to better understand students' work, class comments, and the like. Knowledge of the subject would have been a necessary condition of such use—teachers cannot use knowledge they do not have—but it would not have been sufficient.

use of existing practices, knowledge, and norms. The evidence on class size suggests that only large reductions permit changes in teaching and learning, given teachers' and students' extant knowledge and motivation. A third possible explanation is that some conventional resources simply are not salient to the learning in question, or to learning in general. Science laboratories might bear on learning in science, but it would be surprising if they were relevant to learning literature or history. Building two gymnasiums, three pairs of bathrooms, and a larger playground for every school could have many good effects, but they may not be academic effects.

Our formulation does not deny the significance of instructional materials, facilities, teachers' qualifications, and other conventional resources. Nor does recent research that focuses on students' and teachers' practices and personal resources "refute" the work of James Coleman or Christopher Jencks, who found that averages of such resources had little effect on variance in students' performance from one school to another.[30] Both lines of work could be accommodated in research that posits interdependent relationships between resources and users.

Instructional Interaction and Research

That interdependence poses a major challenge for investigators of resource effects. For when teachers and learners use resources, they make judgments about which to use, how to use them, with whom, and to what end. They base these judgments on what they know and believe about themselves, one another, and the content. Though some teachers judge with great care and seek evidence with which they might revise, others are less careful. In either event, teachers calibrate instruction to their views of their capacities and their students' abilities and will to learn. Teachers and students work in organizations that formalize such calibration in ability groups, grade retention or promotion, and related practices. These groups and practices allocate resources within classes and schools, and even within the same student across subjects, on the basis of judgments about students' capabilities, aspirations, motivation, and so forth.

30. For example, Brophy and Good (1986) argue that their research has "refuted" the earlier work of Coleman and Jencks (1986). But their work talked past the earlier studies: Brophy and Good made large strides toward defining a new class of educational resources, which Coleman and Jencks had not been able to investigate owing to the sorts of data collected in Coleman's study.

Students make judgments about instruction and use resources on the basis of estimates of teachers' and parents' wishes and their own preferences and expectations. Ruben, the student in our example, navigated between his father's disdain for the school's math program and his teacher's instructional interventions. His father did not help with his homework, and Ruben was less prepared for class. He was also less interested since his father told him that the work was not worth doing. Ruben's teacher had to act as though she believed he could do the work; she had to convince him that this work was worth doing; and she had to help him use what he knew and could learn. In the end, Ruben's work and willingness reflected features of his school environment.

One cannot imagine instruction without such calibration—even computer-based instruction entails versions of it. But if teachers adjust instruction within and among students on the basis of their estimates of students' will and ability to learn, there will be significant differences in the resources that teachers use with individual students among subjects, among students within classes, and among classes within schools. If this is so, how can researchers identify, observe, and measure the resources that are used in instruction? If teachers adjust the tasks they assign and the materials they use, correct estimates of resource allocation and effects would depend on valid evidence of variable use. The evidence also would depend on teachers knowing and articulating what they did and having the time and inclination to do so, or on researchers' valid observation of teachers' reports and practices, or both. Such evidence would not be easy to define or collect, especially since teachers often adjust their own knowledge, skill, and will as they apply them. How can teachers be aware of such things? If they are, how can researchers learn about such extensive and continuing variation in resource use? Lacking valid and reliable evidence on such matters, how could we make valid inferences about the effects of resources on learning? Nonexperimental studies of resource effects on student outcomes that fail to take account of how teachers adjust instruction in light of their judgments about students will likely "mis-estimate" and confound the resources used, those merely present, and their effects.

Recent research on "dynamic treatment regimes" in medicine and psychotherapy illuminates this matter.[31] In such treatment regimes, the dose,

31. Robins, Greenland, and Hu (1999).

or treatment, is calibrated to the current status of the patient treated, on the basis of some assessment of that patient's condition. The regime consists of one set of rules for assessing those to be treated and another set for assigning interventions to them. One can arrive at strong causal inferences about the effects of any such regime, if those treated are randomly assigned to alternative regimes. Weaker causal inferences can be based on quasi-experimental comparisons of regimes. However, within a given treatment regime—which is where nonexperimental research often operates—it appears impossible to make a meaningful causal inference about the association between dose and response. This is because in continuing adjustment processes the dose is as much a consequence of the patient's current condition as it is the cause of his or her subsequent condition.[32] Research in medicine and psychotherapy shows that a regression of responses on doses, controlling initial status, will not give a reasonable estimate of a treatment effect.[33] It also suggests that the effects of interactive treatment regimes can only be accurately evaluated if: (a) there are different regimes that (b) consist of well-explicated rules for assigning doses, given particular statuses, and (c) the regimes vary across patients treated.

By extension, if teachers calibrate instruction to their views of student ability, one could make accurate causal inferences about instructional effects only by reconceiving and then redesigning instruction as a "regime" and comparing it with different regimes. That idea is consistent with the interactive view of resource use that we have been developing: resources are used within instructional regimes. Conventional resources are not the regime, for they cause nothing. Rather they are used or not

32. The causal effect of treatment A in relation to treatment B is defined as the difference between the potential outcomes of a student under A or B. Causal inferences are thus meaningful only when a student is potentially exposable to alternative treatments (Holland 1986). If a regime were strictly enacted, only one possible "dose" would be conceivable at any moment for a particular student. There is a treatment A but no treatment B! This means that such a student would have only one potential outcome, so that no causal effect can be defined. In practical terms, this means that, within a strictly enforced regime, it is not possible to find or even imagine a student who is similar to the student of interest but who receives a different dose.

33. The renowned "Pygmalion" experiments (Rosenthal and Jacobson 1968) in classrooms can be read as a scheme to change the instruction (read "dose," or "treatment") that teachers offered students by experimentally inflating evidence on students' IQs (for a review, see Raudenbush 1984).

used, in particular regimes. Resource effects depend both on their availability and on their use within regimes. The central focus in research on resources therefore should be the instruction in which resources are used—and how they are used and to what effect—not the resources alone.

Though this line of reasoning has theoretical appeal, it has several vexing aspects. The continuing and nearly always unobserved and unmeasured adjustment of resources within instruction calls into question a vast body of correlational research on relations between discrete instructional behavior and student outcomes, including most of the studies that we discussed earlier. And while research on dynamic treatment regimes may not require randomized experimentation, randomization to regimes would be optimal for causal inference. That suggests a more restricted role for survey research than has recently been the case in education and a larger role for experimental and quasi-experimental research. But if such studies offer a better grip on causality, they are more difficult to design, instrument, and carry out, and more costly.

New Designs for Research

We have discussed two significantly different perspectives on resources that hold different implications for research and policy. From the inherited, dominant perspective, conventional resources are treated as if they were active agents of instruction, and the key problem is to identify and then deploy the resource mix most likely to improve learning. From a more recent, emergent perspective, teachers, and features of their environments, are treated as the active agents of instruction, and the key problem is to identify and mobilize the knowledge, practices, and incentives that will enable them to best use resources. One perspective is grounded in established habits of thought and the durable realities of life in schools and politics, while the other is grounded in studies that probe those realities.

There has been movement between these views. In the last decade or two, some policymakers began to adopt new conceptions of resources, partly in response to research on instruction. For instance, state standards-based reform is premised on the view that schools and policymakers should clarify schools' learning goals and use resources to achieve those goals. Some researchers, and officials in some districts and states, have encouraged schools to focus on the improved use of resources rather than on standard resource inputs.[34] There also has been growing interest in finding more direct measures of teacher quality, to improve teachers' knowledge and skills directly through professional development rather than relying on course titles and degrees. Each of these changes implies that resource use and the conditions that influence it are considered critical factors in education.

Conventional resources nonetheless remain in the foreground of research and policy. Much action and debate focus on class size, teachers' formal qualifications, facilities and equipment, and education budgets. These have long been the established means to weigh quality in schooling. Buildings, books, and teachers—not knowledge, skill, and will—are plainly visible to administrators, policymakers, and parents. It is easier to observe and quantify dollars and class size than teachers' knowledge of mathematics or their skill in using students' work, and it is much easier to associate these conventional resources with the taxes citizens pay.

Policymakers and school managers can much more easily manipulate dollars and class size than teachers' knowledge and skill. Their actions are scrutinized and contested in elections and require justifications that taxpayers and voters can embrace. These things generate demands for evidence, and, as the dominion of research has grown, politicians have turned to it for help. Specialists in education, economics, politics, and sociology have increasingly occupied themselves with the effects of schooling, and they attend chiefly to the visible resources that play a key role in policy, practice, and argument. Data are relatively easy to come by, have face validity, and are of interest to policymakers.

As a result, policymakers and researchers can most easily deal with the resources that are least directly related to students' learning. And the resources that are most likely to be directly related to learning are those with which policymakers and managers can least easily deal. Research could help to bring the two closer together.

The Frame

Given our theoretical position, the overarching research question cannot be "Do resources matter"? No deliberate attempt to learn or teach is conceivable in the absence of conventional resources, and there is

34. See Odden and Busch (1998).

ample evidence that teaching is causally related to learning. The overarching question must be: "What resources matter, how, and under what circumstances?"

The required resources are significantly a function of the desired result. This question can only be answered once an educational goal, and a strategy to achieve it, have been adopted. Thus a better question is: "What do educators need to do the job?" Putting it that way helps to make clear that the answer would depend strongly on what "the job" was, that is, what needs to be taught and how best to teach it. The requisite conventional resources are not prescribed simply by defining an instructional goal, for there is considerable scope for debate: could the instructional tasks required to achieve any given goal be accomplished with somewhat less skilled teachers, somewhat larger classes, or a somewhat smaller budget for materials and equipment, or by investing somewhat less instructional time than might seem ideal?

This line of reasoning implies that the question for research should not be the one that most researchers concerned with school effects or the economics of education have asked, namely, "How do the available resources affect learning?" Rather, the first question should be: "What instructional approach, aimed at what instructional goals, is sufficient to ensure that students achieve those goals?" A second question follows: "What resources are required to implement this instructional approach?" It may be necessary to modify desired instructional goals if the available resources turn out to be insufficient to achieve the goals; educational policy and practice inevitably involve negotiation among goals, instructional means, and resources. But if resource levels constrain instructional aims and methods, it is logically incoherent to conceive of resources as the "cause" and learning as the outcome. Instructional regimes are the direct cause, and resources are facilitators or inhibitors of instruction.

These ideas entail a sort of Copernican revolution, elements of which have been developing for several decades. Rather than placing conventionally defined resources at the center of inquiry, and trying to identify how each affects performance, or what the best mix is, we would place teaching and learning at the center of inquiry and try to devise ways to identify the resources that best support particular instructional goals. Resources are means, and they can only work in relation to instructional ends. It could not be otherwise unless we envisioned One Embracing Outcome, which all resources would produce, and we cannot imagine either such an outcome or the resources.

This frame brings a kind of theory of relativity to analysis and discussion of resources. For if we are roughly correct, one can only conceive the effect of resources in relation to a specified instructional aim, and a strategy to achieve it. Building a new lab may be essential to one approach to science instruction but irrelevant to another. Class size probably is salient to literacy instruction if it entails frequent, high-quality feedback on student writing and serious class discussion of the writing, but that approach also requires literate, motivated teachers. Class size probably would be less important for other educational aims and means. Research on resources would be more fruitful if it was grounded in conjectures about such relationships and evidence on them.

Active and Passive Research Programs

It follows that in conceiving programs of research on instructional resources, one should place well-defined instructional regimes in the foreground. One example of such a regime might be a program carefully designed to improve reading in the primary grades, which links curriculum and teaching of phonemic awareness, text recognition, and comprehension to specific assessments in those areas. Dynamic treatment regimes in instruction would have several critical features, in this case and others. One is outcome measures that would require students to present the academic performances that the regime is designed to help them learn. Another is the required optimal features of the treatment that is intended to produce those outcomes. That would include more or less elaborated versions of the academic tasks that were central to the regime, and optimal versions of whatever instructional media—books, computer software, and so forth—would be needed to enact those tasks. A third feature would be optimal descriptions, more or less elaborated, of the teaching that is intended to help students use the tasks and materials to produce the desired performances, including descriptions, more or less elaborated, of how teachers would be expected to deal with students' responses to the tasks.

Dynamic treatment regimes require much more consistency in instruction than has been common in the United States. For without such consistency it would be impossible, within regimes, either to validly estimate their effects or to systematically vary some resource constraints while holding other elements of the regime constant. There are very different ways to achieve such consistency. Instruction could be relatively tightly scripted at one extreme, while at another communities of practice could be built around agreed-upon elements of instruction, using intensive communication among teachers about examples of students' and teachers' work, developing or learning criteria of quality, and the like. In the former case, consistency would be created by teachers closely following detailed directions, while in the latter it would be created by developing rich professional knowledge and norms around a skeleton of objectives and tasks. Instruction within regimes could be consistent in either case, but the means to achieve consistency, and quite likely the content of instruction itself, would vary between the two. Combinations of the two methods, and others, also could achieve the consistency that these regimes would require.

It is important to notice that, though any such regime would contain articulate rules that regulated or characterized instruction, there could be enormous variability among regimes in the range of instructional behavior that are governed by such rules. Teaching and learning school subjects are ill-structured domains, and even in the most constrained regimes, rules could not be made to cover anything approaching the entire range of instructional interactions. A great deal must be left to teachers and students to deal with on the spot, and, in devising regimes, those who would change instruction would have to carefully decide on the features of instruction to which they would attend, and what they would ignore. Some regimes might focus on a very constrained region, like word recognition or multiplication, while others might focus on broader regions, like reading comprehension or place value.

Research on these regimes would address two rather different sorts of questions. A first line of research for any such regime might probe what effects it has for students, with respect to its central outcomes, when resources are plentiful. A second line of inquiry could test the effects of such regimes under various resource constraints, which would allow various modifications of the regime that enable its enactment under different conditions.

Pursuing the two lines of work for any given regime would ultimately yield evidence about its effects under a variety of resource conditions, including those that might be optimal. Pursuing both lines of research for regimes that share outcomes, wholly or in part, would yield evidence about their robustness, generalizability, and ultimately, their cost-effectiveness. As each was tested and modified, the research program would reveal the kinds and amounts of resources needed, as well as the ways in which resources must be coordinated to produce effects, given the regime. Our principle of relativity means that there could be neither "regime-free" answers to questions about levels, combinations, and coordination of resources nor "regime-free" studies of their effects.

This active research agenda does more than passively discern the effects of extant resource configurations; it seeks valid causal inferences about designed instructional regimes. Once the efficacy of a regime is established, resources should be varied to discern the effects under alternative constraints.[35] Such an agenda would have profound substantive and methodological implications. It would give priority to research on designed instructional regimes and thus would depend on excellent programs of regime development, field testing, and revision. A focus on regimes also would imply a high priority on experimental and quasi-experimental tests under varied resources constraints.

Given our analysis of mutual adjustment within instruction, a focus on coherent regimes seems the most reasonable way to probe causal relationships between resources and learning. Our account implies that it would not be useful for researchers to attempt to disassemble regimes into their components and do conventional research on the effects of each component. Our frame improves understanding of the complex relationships within teaching and learning and opens opportunities for more coherent research on instruction and its effects. But it also implies certain limits on some sorts of research that have become conventional.

Our frame also implies both crucial opportunities for, and limits on, passive research. Such inquiry cannot offer strong evidence on the effects of regimes in best-case situations or under resource constraints. If instruction is a system of interaction in which students and teachers continually mutually adjust, it would be extraordinarily difficult either to uncover and delineate how a given resource is actually used, or to empirically distinguish well-defined regimes. Existing instructional arrangements and resources have emerged through historical processes of negotiation and accommodation. It is essential to measure student background and school context and statistically adjust for them in models that relate instruction

35. Medical researchers make a clear distinction between efficacy trials and effectiveness trials. Efficacy trials establish that a new treatment can have significant positive effects in carefully controlled settings with plentiful resources. Effectiveness trials take efficacious treatments to the field where implementation is more challenging and resources are more constrained. Our recommended approach to studies of educational improvement is similar. We recommend, however, that effectiveness trials deliberately vary key resources so that their effects can be rigorously evaluated.

to outcomes, if only survey data are available. But that will probably tell us little about what would happen if instruction were modified in deliberate ways. To the extent that regimes do occur naturally, they have developed in part to cope with the resource constraints of given settings. It would be difficult or impossible to answer the question "What resources are essential, given the regime" because of mutual adjustments around existing resources. Instructional practice within a given setting tends to involve a mix of individualized adaptations, and in natural conditions there would be little possibility of holding the regime constant while varying resources. Ethnographies and surveys can reveal how teachers and students think and act within a setting, but they cannot reveal how things would change if new regimes and resources became available. The deliberate development of regimes, and interventions based on them, would be much more efficient and powerful.

Another limit on passive observational research is that it rarely provides student outcome measures that express the aims of a well-conceived regime. That is hardly surprising, given the difficulty of identifying well-conceived regimes in such studies. A well-conceived and deliberately designed regime will set clear instructional goals, and research on it would require outcome measures that specifically assess achievement of these goals. Broad-purpose achievement tests would be used within the agenda we propose, since it would be important to know both that new regimes help students achieve specifically defined skills and knowledge and their effects on more traditional measures of success. But conventional assessments are unlikely to capture the proximal outcomes of a well-defined instructional regime.

Passive inquiry would play several significant roles in relation to active research agendas. Large-scale surveys could provide estimates of the current range of instructional approaches and related resource availability and use within regimes. They might enable researchers to discern the extent to which anything resembling coherent instructional regimes occurs "naturally" in U.S. schools, and, if they do, to distinguish their configurations and roughly estimate their effects. Survey and ethnographic research could illuminate what students know and can do over a range of naturally occurring instruction and settings, and thereby focus attention on where educational effort might be directed. Microethnographies could suggest specific ways in which instruction could be conceived and enacted for specific subgroups and could yield important knowledge about the configuration and operational features of existing instructional regimes.

When we argue that instruction is so interactive as to preclude treating resources as individual variables, we are not arguing that instructional regimes must remain black boxes. Though complex, there is much to be learned about what makes them tick from careful passive research. Survey and ethnographic research could help to clarify the internal dynamics of instructional regimes. That would be especially useful in comparing instructional dynamics across resource variations within regimes. Our agenda contains important roles for both active and passive research.

An active research agenda of this kind can be justified on several grounds: it would give an explicit definition to regimes and resources, thereby creating a basis for valid causal inference; and it would create a useful context for survey and ethnographic research, which currently float largely free of knowledge-building frameworks. Extant instruction reflects accommodations to currently available resource levels, to views of student background, and to prior achievement. Valid causal inferences regarding instruction and resources are extremely elusive in such webs of mutual accommodation. Economists would describe this as a situation in which the causal variable of interest is "endogenous"; that is, it is determined in part by current levels of outcomes and other unobservable factors that lead educators to make choices and compromises. Such endogeneity makes it extraordinarily difficult to separate effects of the key causal variables from the effects of a host of other observed and unobserved factors. Naturalistic survey and ethnographic research can help to advance understanding in several important areas, but such efforts are not well suited to producing defensible conclusions about causal relationships. Sound causal inference requires that the causal variables be made "exogenous"; that is, they must be varied independently of confounding factors.

The best way to do that is through deliberate and well-defined intervention. Exogeneity can be made complete in the case of randomized experiments. Though the random assignment of students to regimes may be feasible in some instances, we anticipate that schools or classrooms, more often than individual students, would be assigned at random.[36] In

36. For example, in evaluating whole-school reform efforts, one might envision assigning schools rather than students randomly to treatments. This could be done ethically if many schools expressed interest in adopting a reform but resources allowed implementation in only a restricted number of sites at any given time. In this setting, intervenors could

other cases when the regimes are self-selected, a strong effort to explicate the regime and associated resources would be in order, as would more tentative causal inference. In either case, research on the dynamics of instruction within regimes could illuminate the role, and perhaps even the importance of, various influences on instruction.

Resources—teacher skill, instructional time, materials, equipment, and facilities—are essential for the enactment of any instructional regime. A well-articulated regime ought to be clear about the required resources and be able to justify that claim by explaining how resources are used to achieve specific aims. It is possible to rigorously evaluate alternative regimes relative to common goals and to evaluate claims about the necessity of levels or combinations of resources within a regime. It is also possible to evaluate alternative versions of a regime for which resource requirements vary. Not only is such research possible, but we think it is essential to learning how to improve schooling in general, and more specifically to understanding the consequences of investing in resources and making them usable for instruction. The program of research that we draw from this view would use the results of passive research programs to generate plausible regimes and resource allocation within them, and to help explicate their dynamics. At its heart, however, it would be an active program of research, in which deliberate interventions vary resources in relation to well-articulated regimes.

Conclusion

We propose a dramatic shift in educational research, from a frame that gives priority to conventional resources and asks how they affect learning, to one that gives priority to designing coherent instructional regimes and asks how resources are used within them. One premise of this approach is that because resources become active when used in mutual instructional adjustment, they are unlikely to have a fixed value in instruction. Their value is likely to depend on the uses to which they are put, which in turn depends on the ends and means of instructional regimes. In order to understand the nature and effects of resources, research must focus on how instructional ends and means are defined,

---

promise all schools that they would have the opportunity to participate, but the timing of participation would be decided via lottery. A randomized "wait-list" control group of schools would then be available.

and on what resources are crucial to those ends and means. The research program that we have sketched is not a design for all educational research, but for inquiries that focus on resource and instructional effects.

Our proposals have complementary benefits and costs. On the one hand, our picture of instruction as a system of interactive mutual adjustment complicates understanding of the dynamics of teaching and learning and of the ways in which resources influence them. In such a system, the value of resources is likely to depend on the ways they are used. That raises fundamental questions about the value of using conventional research to tease out the causal influence of particular resources, across a great variety of schools and classrooms. Though that may unsettle many researchers, it seems inescapable if our account of instruction is roughly right. On the other hand, our account offers a theoretical frame for research on instructional and resource effects that builds on several decades of research, that opens up promising research agendas, and that creates opportunities to lodge active and passive research within mutually reinforcing knowledge-building structures.

Some might argue that these agendas would be insufficient to illuminate policymakers' decisions. To know what resources are needed to teach a given approach in mathematics does not prescribe what resources are needed in general. Small classes might be needed to enact a given approach in literacy, but teachers' subject matter preparation, rather than small classes, might be the crucial ingredient in teaching an effective math curriculum to the same grade. Small classes taught by highly knowledgeable teachers may not be a fiscally feasible objective either. Hence various studies would tend to send mixed signals about how many teachers to hire and what qualifications to require. But in fact, that is exactly what nonexperimental research on class size has done. Our argument is that one of the chief tasks of a coherent educational research agenda is to make just such trade-offs visible as the result of sound empirical study. If our approach is correct, policymakers would be well advised to adopt more complex approaches to resource allocation that capitalize on the role of resource use.

Others might argue that developing such an agenda is infeasible because well-specified instructional regimes could not be devised or because experiments could or should not be done, or because the entire enterprise would be too complex or costly. We disagree. The last decade's work in reading at the National Institute for Child Health and Development (NICHD) and in some whole-school reforms has produced impressive evidence that carefully designed experimental research programs are possible and that instructional regimes can be designed and developed.[37] There would be many difficulties in doing the sort of work that we propose, but if educators and researchers took the ideas seriously, a great deal that seems difficult today could become feasible. One reason for our confidence is the rising demand for solid evidence on the effects of such interventions; it suggests that there may be a market for just such work. Another is the recent experience with reading research and some whole-school reform models. Still another is the success of several seemingly impossible experiments in health care, housing, and welfare. And another is the enormous progress in evidence-based medicine, which faced similar problems.

The sorts of research and instructional design that we have sketched would take careful planning because such work must be strategic. Researchers cannot investigate everything; the goal of our proposal is to investigate a few key issues well. It also would require a broad and energetic constituency that included public and nonpublic supporters and more capable management than educational research has yet had. All of this could be done if researchers and others concerned with education turned their attention to the work. The resulting research would not prescribe decisions about resources, for those require interactions among a range of persons and groups whose qualifications to decide are civic rather than scientific, and whose values often differ. Research on instructional resources could provide a stream of credible evidence regarding the resources required to attain a variety of educational aims and, thus, informing thought and debate about the aims of schooling and levels of investment in education. Over time, it might tend to close out unfruitful arguments as well as highlight new problems. Research could inform but never replace a broad discourse about schooling and school improvement.

References

Brophy, J., and T. Good. 1986. "Teacher Behavior and Student Achievement." In *Handbook of Research on Teaching*, 3d ed., edited by M. C. Wittrock, 328–75. Macmillian.

Bryk, A., V. Lee, and P. Holland. 1993. *Catholic Schools and the Common Good.* Harvard University Press.

37. Cook and others (1999).

Coleman, J. 1966. *Equality of Educational Opportunity Survey.* Washington: Government Printing Office.
Cook, T. D., and D. Campbell. 1979. *Quasi-Experimentation.* Rand McNally.
Cook, T. D., H. D. Hunt, and R. F. Murphy. 1999. "Comer's School Development Program in Chicago: A Theory-Based Evaluation." Unpublished paper, Northwestern University.
Cooley, W., and G. Leinhardt. 1978. *Instructional Dimensions Study.* University of Pittsburgh, Learning Research and Development Center.
Dewey, J. 1905. *The Child and the Curriculum, and School and Society.* University of Chicago Press.
Dweck, C. S. 1986. "Motivational Processes Affecting Learning." *American Psychologist* 5: 1179–87.
———. 1988. "Children's Thinking about Traits: Implications for Judgments of the Self and Others." *Child Development* 69 (2): 391–403.
Edmonds, R. 1979. "Effective Schools for the Urban Poor." *Educational Leadership* 37: 15–27.
———. 1984. "School Effects and Teacher Effects." *Social Policy* 15: 37–39.
Englert, C. S., T. E. Raphael, L. M. Anderson, H. M. Anthony, and D. D. Stevens. 1991. "Making Strategies and Self-Talk Visible: Writing Instruction in Regular and Special Education Classrooms." *American Educational Research Journal* 28 (2): 337–72.
Ferguson, R. F. 1991. "Paying for Public Education: New Evidence on How and Why Money Matters." *Harvard Journal on Legislation* 28: 465–98.
Finn, J., and C. Achilles. 1990. "Answers and Questions about Class Size: A Statewide Experiment." *American Educational Research Journal* 27: 557–77.
Hanushek, E. A. 1981. "Throwing Money at Schools." *Journal of Policy Analysis and Management* 1: 19–41.
———. 1989. "The Impact of Differential Expenditures on School Performance." *Educational Researcher* 18 (4): 45–65.
Hedges, L. V., R. D. Laine, and R. Greenwald, R. 1994. "Does Money Matter? A Meta-Analysis of Studies of the Effects of Differential School Inputs on Student Outcomes (An Exchange: Part I)." *Educational Researcher* 23 (3): 5–14.
Holland, P. 1986. "Statistics and Causal Inference." *Journal of the American Statistical Association* 81 (396): 945–60.
Jencks, C., and others. 1972. *Inequality.* Basic Books.
Lampert, M. M. 2001. *Teaching Problems and the Problems of Teaching.* Yale University Press.
Leinhardt, G., N. Zigmond, and W. Cooley. "Reading Instruction and Its Effects." *American Educational Research Journal* 18 (3): 343–61.
McLaughlin, M., and J. Talbert. Forthcoming. *Professional Community and the Work of High School Teaching.* University of Chicago Press.
Mosteller, Frederick. 1995. "The Tennessee Study of Class Size in the Early School Grades." *Future of Children* 5 (2): 113–27.
Newmann, F. M., and G. G. Wehlage. 1995. *Successful School Restructuring: A Report to the Public and Educators.* OERI. R117Q00005-95. Washington: U.S. Department of Education.

Odden, A., and C. Busch. 1998. *Financing Schools for High Performance: Strategies for Improving the Use of Educational Resources.* San Francisco: Jossey-Bass.

Palinscar, A. M. 1986. "The Role of Dialogue in Providing Scaffolded Instruction." *Educational Psychologist* 21: 73–98.

Palinscar, A. M., and A. Brown. 1984. "Reciprocal Teaching of Comprehension-Fostering and Comprehension-Monitoring Activities." *Cognition and Instruction* 1: 117–75.

Raudenbush, S. W. 1984. "Magnitude of Teacher Expectancy Effects on Pupil IQ as a Function of the Credibility of Expectancy Induction: A Synthesis of Findings from 18 Experiments." *Journal of Educational Psychology* 76 (1): 85–97.

Robins, J. M., S. Greenland, and F. Hu. 1999. "Estimation of the Causal Effect of a Time-Varying Exposure on the Marginal Mean of a Repeated Binary Outcome." *Journal of the American Statistical Association* 94 (447): 687–701.

Rosenholz, S. J. 1985. "Effective Schools: Interpreting the Evidence." *American Journal of Education* 93: 352–88.

Rosenthal, R., and L. Jacobson. 1968. *Pygmalion in the Classroom.* Holt, Rinehart and Winston.

Rubin, D. B. 1974. "Estimating Causal Effects of Treatments in Randomized and Nonrandomized Studies." *Journal of Educational Psychology* 66: 688–701.

Rutter, M., B. Maughan, P. Mortimore, M. Ousten, and A. Smith. 1979. *Fifteen Thousand Hours: Secondary Schools and Their Effects on Children.* Harvard University Press.

CHAPTER FIVE

Missing in Practice? Development and Evaluation at the U.S. Department of Education

MARIS A. VINOVSKIS

PEOPLE HAVE COMPLAINED periodically about the lack of systematic development and rigorous educational program evaluations. Sometimes these protests have led to major efforts to restructure how the federal government organizes and operates its applied research and development efforts; but usually such reform initiatives have not had much lasting effect on the nature and quality of federal development and program evaluations. Rather than just examining the absence or presence of more scientifically sound development and program evaluations today, I will also analyze those practices in the past in order to see what factors have assisted or hindered improving educational research and development. The aim in what follows is to understand how to improve the quality of research and to suggest better approaches to its organization.

Early Federal Research, Evaluation, and Development

Nineteenth-century state and local educators frequently used educational statistics both to help formulate educational policies and to prod reluctant taxpayers to greater exertions on behalf of public schooling.[1] While the federal government provided some incentives for state and local

1. For a discussion of how Horace Mann used statistical information to further his educational efforts, see Glenn (1988); and Vinovskis (1995). For a very useful introduction to nineteenth-century education in general, see Kaestle (1983).

schooling, it did not become very involved in the various antebellum common school reform movements.[2] But just after the Civil War a bill to create a Department of Education was passed that called for a federal role in collecting and disseminating educational data and information.[3] Unfortunately, Henry Barnard, one of the most distinguished nineteenth-century educators and the first commissioner of education, was a poor administrator and an ineffective politician.[4] The Department of Education barely survived and was almost immediately demoted to a Bureau of Education in the Department of Interior.[5] By the end of World War I, the Bureau of Education was a small, but expanding federal agency that performed a variety of administrative and nonadministrative functions.[6]

Federal involvement in educational research and development continued during World War II at the U.S. Office of Education (USOE), but it was not seen as particularly vital to the war effort.[7] While research in other fields, such as science and medicine, increased dramatically during World War II, education research at USOE actually decreased and was relegated to playing a secondary role. But faced with the Soviet threat after World War II, the Congress and the military boosted funding for scientific and medical research.[8] Public and legislative enthusiasm for scientific and medical research in the immediate postwar years did not extend to the social sciences.[9] And research and statistics in USOE fared even worse in the decade after World War II.[10]

The U.S. Office of Education continued to collect state educational statistics and to investigate some problems in education. Most of the

2. On the role of the federal government in education in the late eighteenth and nineteenth centuries, see Zook (1945); Lee (1949); Tyack, James, and Benavor (1987); and Berube (1991).

3. Cohen (1974, vol. 3, p. 1406). The best book on the origins of the U.S. Bureau of Education is Warren (1974).

4. MacMullen (1991).

5. Warren (1974).

6. For a very helpful, but mainly descriptive account of the agency in the early twentieth century, see Smith (1923). During the first half of the twentieth century, private organizations such as the Russell Sage Foundation and the Laura Spelman Rockefeller Memorial Foundation made important contributions to education research. For very useful overviews of some of the strengths and weaknesses of education research during these years, see Lagemann (2000); and Ravitch (2000). For a more general analysis of social science research before World War II, see Bulmer (2001).

7. USOE (1945).

8. Kleinman (1995).

9. Larsen (1992).

10. Ravitch (1983).

research studies, however, were limited to gathering cross-sectional data and then publishing the results often without much rigorous statistical analysis.[11] A small, but in the long term quite a significant, change occurred when Congress passed the Cooperative Research Act of 1954 (P.L. 83-531) to allow USOE to engage in cooperative research efforts with colleges, universities, and state departments of education.[12] With the successful orbiting of Sputnik in 1957, panic about the possible Soviet superiority in science and technology quickly led to increased federal educational funding.[13]

The social and behavioral sciences prospered during the decade of the 1960s.[14] The federal government greatly expanded its domestic social programs—especially as part of President Lyndon Johnson's Great Society programs. Social and behavioral scientists were often involved in helping to create many of the new federal initiatives such as Project Head Start and the Community Action Program.[15]

The social sciences in the late 1950s and 1960s also developed more sophisticated ways of analyzing quantitative data and doing large-scale evaluations. Drawing on the experiences in the Department of Defense (DOD) in the early 1960s, President Johnson called for the implementation of the same planning-programming-budgeting (PPB) system in all federal domestic agencies. While only a few of the federal agencies actually implemented a fully working PPB system, the directive encouraged all federal departments to develop their own planning and evaluation offices and staff.[16]

Increased federal interest and funding for social and behavioral research in the 1960s helped stimulate comparable support for educational research and development. But such work in education continued to be criticized as being conceptually limited and technically unsophisti-

11. Earl McGrath, the commissioner of education, admitted in 1951 that the U.S. Office of Education was not very successful in carrying out its historic data and research mission. See USOE (1951, p. 13).

12. For example, the U.S. Office of Research in 1950 did not have any funds for supporting contract research. USOE (1951, p. 23).

13. USOE (1958, pp. 183–85; 1960; 1965, p. 235).

14. The discussions of the changes in the social sciences and the federal government draw on the work presented in Featherman and Vinovskis (2001).

15. For an introduction to the Great Society programs of the 1960s, see Levitan and Taggart (1976); Kaplan and Cuciti (1986); and Bernstein (1996).

16. Harper, Kramer, and Rouse (1969). On the evolving role of policy analysts in the federal bureaucracy, see Meltsner (1976).

cated, as well as inaccessible to most educators and policymakers.[17] The U.S. Office of Education responded to these criticisms by funding two research and development (R&D) centers in fiscal 1964 in order "to concentrate resources on a particular problem area in education over an extended period of time."[18]

Following the landslide presidential election of Johnson in 1964, more than a dozen influential task forces were created to examine existing federal practices and to suggest bold new ways to improve those services.[19] John Gardner chaired the task force on education, which called for the establishment of at least a dozen large-scale national educational laboratories.[20] The recommendations of the Gardner Task Force on research and development were enacted as Title IV of the Elementary and Secondary Education Act (ESEA) of 1965.[21] Appropriations for USOE, which was designated to oversee the new legislation, soared; and the size of the research budget mushroomed from $3 million in fiscal 1960 to nearly $100 million in fiscal 1967.[22] Yet expectations for large-scale, systematic development were thwarted as Commissioner of Education Francis Keppel and his colleagues emphasized the regional rather than the national orientation of the laboratories.[23]

Besides the work of the R&D centers and the regional educational laboratories, USOE sponsored some important individual research studies. For example, under the Civil Rights Act of 1964 mandate, James Coleman and several other social scientists conducted a massive study of about half a million students, 60,000 teachers, and some 4,000 schools, which reported that minority schools received relatively equal resources and that there was little direct relationship between per-pupil expenditures and academic achievement.[24] In the late 1950s and early 1960s, the

17. For discussions of the state of educational research in this period, see Good (1956); Coladarci (1960); Carroll (1961); Brim (1965); Bloom (1966); and Cronbach and Suppes (1969).

18. USOE (1965, p. 256). For a useful discussion of the creation of the R&D centers, see Dershimer (1976).

19. Kearney (1967).

20. Garner (1964).

21. For a discussion of the origins and passage of ESEA in 1965, see Meranto (1967); and Bailey and Mosher (1968).

22. U.S. Congress (1967, p. 204).

23. For a discussion of the debates within the U.S. Office of Education on the size and function of the regional educational laboratories and the R&D centers in the second half of the 1960s, see Dershimer (1976); and Vinovskis (1993).

24. Coleman and others (1966).

National Science Foundation (NSF) also became increasingly involved in the large-scale development of classroom curricula.[25]

Finally, several important educational program evaluations were completed in the 1960s. In ESEA, Congress mandated that the implementation and effectiveness of Title I of that program was to be evaluated. Although most of the early state and local Title I evaluations were not rigorous or comparable to one another, they did provide some preliminary indications of the ability of schools to help disadvantaged students. Despite efforts to present the best case on behalf of ESEA, the results from these initial Title I evaluations were not encouraging.[26]

Perhaps one of the most visible and controversial evaluations was the 1969 Westinghouse Learning Corporation and Ohio University's evaluation of Head Start, which found that children's IQ gains were small and faded quickly. The evaluation went on to praise some of the noncognitive and nonaffective benefits of Head Start, but these favorable statements were lost as the mass media emphasized the negative findings.[27] There was widespread scholarly criticism of the report for its conceptual and statistical shortcomings; but some scholars and policymakers later candidly acknowledged that many Head Start projects were not very effective at that time.[28]

Changes in Educational Research, Development, and Evaluation in the 1970s

The second half of the 1960s and the early 1970s are sometimes portrayed as the "golden age" for the social sciences.[29] Yet by the mid-1970s there was also a reaction against these social and behavioral efforts. Many of the Great Society programs came under attack as scholars questioned the ability of many of these initiatives to revive urban areas, reduce economic inequality, or eliminate poverty.[30] As the large-scale evaluations challenged some of the overoptimistic expectations of the Great Society programs, analysts now also realized that "research tends to be a conser-

25. Dow (1991).
26. McLaughlin (1975).
27. Westinghouse Learning Corporation (1969).
28. For example, see Smith and Bissell (1970), and the reply by Cicirelli, Evans, and Schiller (1970).
29. Nathan (1988, p. 3).
30. Moynihan (1969); Banfield (1970); and Jencks and others (1972).

vative force because it fosters skepticism and caution by shifting attention from moral commitment to analytical problems that rarely have clear-cut or simple solutions."[31]

In the 1970s conservatives attacked NSF efforts to develop social studies curricula that they charged were subversive and ideologically biased. The fifth-grade anthropological curriculum, MACOS, funded by NSF, was attacked for "mold[ing] children's social attitudes and beliefs along lines that are almost always at variance with the beliefs and moral values of their parents and local communities."[32] Faced with determined congressional opposition against MACOS, NSF quietly terminated support for that program as well as several other curriculum projects. In addition, other members of Congress, like Senator William Proxmire (D-Wisconsin) used his "golden fleece" awards to attack seemingly ludicrous and wasteful federally funded social and behavioral research.[33]

Initially, educational research and development benefited from the new interest in the role of social sciences in designing and improving service programs. The Nixon administration argued that simply spending more money on schooling was not enough; what was needed was a major overhaul of the research and development activities through the creation of a National Institute of Education (NIE).[34] After considerable delays and only lukewarm support from the major education associations, NIE was created in June 1972.[35] Although many of NIE's proponents had hoped for great increases in funding and more support for rigorous, large-scale investigations, congressional hostility to the new agency led to a one-third reduction in its initial budget. Under severe financial as well as political constraints, NIE barely managed to survive.[36]

There were a few large-scale educational evaluations in the 1970s that assessed the effectiveness of improved schooling interventions. The most detailed and rigorous national analysis of Title I of ESEA in the 1970s was the Sustaining Effects Study. Launor Carter, the project director, found that Title I recipients did better than roughly comparable non-Title I students; but those who were the most disadvantaged (and a particular

31. Aaron (1978, p. i).

32. Quoted in Dow (1991, p. 200).

33. For example, see Fields (1980).

34. Finn (1977).

35. For a detailed analysis of the creation and early development of NIE, see Sproull, Winter, and Wolf (1978).

36. Vinovskis (1996).

target of Title I funds) did not receive much benefit. Carter reported that while some of the more moderately disadvantaged students did benefit from the Title I program, their gains were not sufficient to close the gap with the regular students.[37] There were also state analyses of Title I and other programs designed to help students from low-income families. Stephen Mullin and Anita Summers reviewed forty-seven studies and concluded that, while the federal and state programs had a positive but small impact on the achievement of students, the results of those studies were biased upward owing to the statistical procedures employed.[38]

One of the most ambitious and expensive evaluations of early education in the late 1960s and 1970s was the analysis of Follow Through, a program to help sustain the initial positive effects of Head Start on children when they entered the early elementary grades. The Office of Economic Opportunity (OEO) created a small $2.5 million pilot program for Follow Through and transferred that initiative to the USOE in June 1967. Follow Through was slated to become a large $120 million service program, but funding limitations due in large part to the unbudgeted expenses of the Vietnam War reduced its fiscal 1969 budget to $12 million. The initiative was scaled back to an experimental program and adopted a conceptual strategy of planned variation, which was in vogue at that time. Unfortunately, confusion and tension continued to exist between proponents of an experimental approach and those who favored a more service-oriented approach as funding mushroomed to $69.0 million in fiscal 1971 (78,100 students were served in 178 sites). The findings from these evaluations were disappointing as they suggested that overall Follow Through was not an effective way to help at-risk children improve their school performance.[39]

In the early 1970s, the Brookings Panel on Social Experimentation assembled a group of experts to assess the strengths and weaknesses of the planned variation approach that was used in both Follow Through and Head Start Planned Variation (HSPV). The conference organizers, Alice Rivlin and Michael Timpane, summarized the deliberations and pointed to some of the major deficiencies in the existing evaluations.[40] Most conference participants were willing to continue to employ a planned variation approach. But they also called for a more systematic

37. For a discussion of the early evaluations of Title I, see Vinovskis (1997).
38. Mullin and Summers (1983).
39. For an analysis of Follow Through, see Vinovskis (1999b, pp. 89–114).
40. Rivlin and Timpane (1975).

approach to program development and evaluation that included five different stages and would require five to twelve years to complete.[41]

The broad conceptual approach of planned variation was continued in Follow Through, but the serious problems inherent in the existing individual program evaluation designs were not corrected. Yet the program survived until the early 1990s because of strong support from several members of Congress who had Follow Through projects in their districts—sometimes for almost two decades. Efforts to phase out the program in the mid-1970s had been unsuccessful even though Follow Through had in essence become simply a small service program. From fiscal 1967 to fiscal 1992 the federal government spent $1.54 billion (in constant 1982–84 dollars)—just a little more than had been spent on the R&D centers and regional educational laboratories during that period.[42]

During the 1970s most of the educational program evaluations in the federal government were done by the Office of Evaluation and Dissemination (OED) or its predecessor, the Office of Program Budgeting and Evaluation (OPBE). OED in 1980 had a staff of forty professionals and a budget that averaged $21 million over the previous five years. The major exceptions were evaluations done by the Bureau of Education for the Handicapped, the Bureau of Student Financial Aid, and the Follow Through Program. NIE periodically supported evaluation work through its Testing, Assessment, and Evaluation Division.[43]

Congress in 1978 called for the commissioner of education to conduct a comprehensive analysis of the evaluation practices. This task was contracted to Robert Boruch and David Cordray from Northwestern University. They found that while some of the federally funded education evaluations were competent and useful, many would have benefited from better designs, improved implementation, and more rigorous statistical analysis.[44] Boruch and Cordray also urged the newly created U.S. Department of Education to provide for the critique and re-analysis of evaluation results.[45] They went on to make several additional useful, specific recommendations for planning and executing evaluations, setting evaluation standards and guidelines, improving access to the use of evaluation

41. Rivlin and Timpane (1975, p. 18).

42. Vinovskis (1999b, pp. 89–114).

43. For a discussion of the evaluation activities in education in the 1970s, see Boruch and Cordray (1980).

44. Boruch and Cordray (1980, p. 2).

45. Boruch and Cordray (1980, p. 6).

results, and assessing program implementation.[46] Unfortunately, most of their thoughtful proposals were not adequately implemented in the next two decades, either by the Congress or the Department of Education.

The Reagan Revolution and Educational Research, Development, and Evaluation

As noted in the previous section, by the mid-1970s the public and policymakers were becoming disillusioned with the ability of the social sciences to solve the domestic problems besetting the United States.[47] With the election of Ronald Reagan, concerted efforts were made to dismantle many of the federal educational and social welfare programs. The Reagan administration also questioned the value and objectivity of the social sciences for assisting policymakers; and federal funding for social science research and program evaluations were reduced.[48]

Following the failure of the Reagan administration to abolish the recently created Department of Education, there was intense political infighting between incoming Secretary of Education Terrel Bell and his conservative opponents both within the department and the White House. Edward Curran, the newly appointed NIE director, was especially hostile and tried to persuade the president at least to abolish NIE.[49] Bell managed to survive the immediate political challenges to his authority, but he was unable to stem the particularly drastic cuts in the educational research budget.[50] While the Department of Education lost only 11 percent of its budget between fiscal 1981 and fiscal 1988 (in real dollars), NIE lost 70 percent of its funding.[51]

At the same time, NIE lost much of its flexibility for spending the remaining funds. It had planned to reduce funding of the R&D centers and regional educational laboratories proportionately, but the lobbying organization (CEDaR) for those institutions managed to persuade Congress to mandate that these organizations could not have their fund-

46. Boruch and Cordray (1980).

47. "Social Science: The Public Disenchant," *American Scholar* (Summer 1976): 335–59.

48. Palmer (1982); Nathan (1988); Larsen (1992); and Wood (1993, pp. 139–61).

49. Vinovskis (2001, pp. 101–05).

50. For an excellent discussion of NIE's political struggles during the early 1980s, see Zodhiates (1988).

51. Verstegen and Clark (1988, p. 137).

ing cut by more than 10 percent.[52] As a result, other NIE programs had to be cut even more severely. While approximately 55 percent of NIE's research obligations in fiscal 1980 were mandated, by fiscal 1984 that figure had risen to 79 percent.[53]

NIE, now located as a unit within the Office of Educational Research and Improvement (OERI), managed to establish a competitive funding process for the labs and centers and conducted a successful competition in 1985.[54] OERI directives instructed the new regional and educational laboratories to focus more on short-term applied research projects, technical assistance, and dissemination rather than on systematic, long-term development. Similarly, most of the R&D centers downplayed any development activities.[55] Thus large-scale educational development almost completely disappeared at NIE during the Reagan administration; and the overall amount of research and development funded there may have reached an all-time low.

The Reagan years also saw a significant decrease in support for program evaluation. The General Accounting Office (GAO) documented the decline in staff and funding for evaluations in fifteen federal agencies during the early 1980s.[56] Moreover, the nature of those studies changed—from large-scale, rigorous evaluations of federal programs to smaller, internal studies of federal management practices. The GAO also noted that their more in-depth policy analyses all too often found that there was evidence of the "distortion of findings."[57]

Evaluation activities suffered throughout the federal government—including at the Department of Education. The top leadership at the Office of Management and Budget (OMB) during most of the Reagan years was hostile or indifferent to evaluation.[58] Educational evaluation funding already had been declining since 1978, from $71.6 million in fiscal 1978 to $29.6 million in fiscal 1981. By fiscal 1984 Department of Education evaluation funds had dropped to $19.6 million; and by fiscal 1988 they were only $12.9 million.[59]

52. Vinovskis (1998a, pp. 19–23).
53. GAO (1987, p. 76).
54. For a useful analysis of the lab and center competitions, see Schultz (1988).
55. Vinovskis (1993).
56. Chelimsky (1992, pp. 30–31).
57. Chelimsky (1992, p. 32).
58. Havens (1991).
59. PES (1998).

Theoretically, the Planning and Evaluation Service (PES) in the Department of Education was responsible for overseeing all evaluations. But in practice evaluations were funded and supervised in several different agencies throughout the department with little coordination among them. When Secretary William Bennett reorganized the Department of Education in 1985, he reaffirmed that PES was to have primary responsibility for coordinating all evaluation studies—though there was some initial opposition to this directive.[60]

While the Reagan administration generally was hostile to social science research and program evaluations, it became interested in collecting and disseminating student testing scores to spur educational reforms. Building upon the popularity of the dire but controversial portrayal of American education in *A Nation at Risk,* Secretary Bell released annually a wall chart that provided information on how well each of the states was doing in education. The wall chart was very popular among the public and many policymakers; but critics claimed that the use of ACT or SAT scores from college-bound students as an index of the achievement of all students was inaccurate and misleading. The PES staff who had designed and implemented the wall chart acknowledged these shortcomings, but defended its use.[61] The great success of the wall chart, especially within the Reagan administration itself, enhanced the role of PES to policymakers and perhaps reinforced the practice of paying attention to more descriptive, short-term projects than undertaking more complex, large-scale program evaluations.

The Reagan administration also made major improvements in the collection, analysis, and dissemination of educational data at the National Center for Education Statistics (NCES). Under the leadership of OERI, Assistant Secretary Chester Finn, and acting NCES Commissioner Emerson Elliott in the mid-1980s, the statistical capabilities of the Department of Education were greatly enhanced. Comparable progress, however, was not achieved in improving the quality of research and development in the rest of OERI. As a result, while the statistical information available to the public and policymakers improved during the Reagan administration's second term, large-scale systematic development and evaluation continued to suffer.[62]

60. Ginsburg (1992, pp. 39–40).
61. Ginsburg, Noell, and Plisko (1988, p. 1).
62. Vinovskis (1998, pp. 22–23).

Changes in the Bush and Clinton Administrations

The late 1980s and 1990s saw a partial recovery in federal support of the social and behavioral sciences. Overall federal support for academic research in real dollars had declined slightly in the 1970s but rose by almost 20 percent in the 1980s. There was a shift in the nature of that funding; more of the funds were targeted for basic rather than applied research. And while federal support of psychological research increased substantially in the 1980s, federal money for the social sciences decreased from $742 million in 1980 to $563 million in 1990 (in constant 1987 dollars).[63] One of the more encouraging short-term developments, however, was the sizable increase in evaluation funding at the U.S. Department of Education, from $12.9 million in fiscal 1988 to $26.0 million in fiscal 1989 (in constant 1997 dollars)—reaching a high point of $36.8 million in fiscal 1991, before plummeting to $18.3 million in fiscal 1996.[64]

The Planning and Evaluation Service in the late 1980s, under the continued leadership of Alan Ginsburg, tried to repair the earlier erosion of program evaluation work. The agency was assisted by the renewed interest in program evaluation at OMB during the Bush administration.[65] Ginsburg criticized earlier department evaluations for failing to collect information on effective program practices.[66] Ginsburg particularly singled out the need for evaluations based on random assignment of participants and control groups.[67]

Ginsburg's call for the use of random assignments of participants in evaluations did not reflect current practices in the field of education. While randomized controlled experiments were frequently used in public health and medical research, they were rare in education.[68] Interestingly, the few instances in which randomized assignments were used, such as the analysis of class size in Tennessee's Project STAR or the Perry Preschool Project, often had not been developed and supported by federal educational research and evaluation funds.[69]

63. Bureau of the Census (1996, table 968). The cuts in the social sciences were particularly severe during the first term of the Reagan administration and then recovered somewhat afterward. See also Cohen and Noll (1992).

64. PES (1998).

65. Ginsburg (1992, p. 40).

66. Ginsburg, (1992, pp. 38–39).

67. Ginsburg, (1992, p. 41).

68. Boruch (1998).

69. Mosteller (1995); and Schweinhart, Barnes, and Weikart (1993).

Congress also signaled its renewed interest in more rigorous evaluations by mandating a large-scale national longitudinal study of the restructured Chapter 1 program in 1988 (the Title I program had been renamed the Chapter 1 program in 1981). Abt Associates won the contract for the study, which was designated "Prospects: The Congressionally Mandated Study of Educational Growth and Opportunity." The study was a representative longitudinal analysis of three cohorts of public school students in the first, third, and seventh grades who were to be followed over a six-year period (the actual study was terminated after following the students for only three years). The evaluation used a multistage sample stratified by geographic region, degree of urban development, economic disadvantage, and concentration of limited-English-proficiency (LEP) students. Altogether approximately 30,000 students were included in the national sample.[70]

The 1993 interim report of Prospects found that the Chapter 1 program was not sufficient to close the academic achievement gap between at-risk students and their more fortunate counterparts—though the authors speculated that at-risk children might have fared even worse without that program. The disappointing findings were hastily released just as the 103d Congress was debating the reauthorization of the legislation (and months before the actual interim report was completed). The disappointing results played a significant role in the decision to restructure the entire program and rename it once again as Title I of the Improving America's Schools Act (IASA) of 1994.[71]

Congress and PES also indicated interest in ascertaining the relative effectiveness of different model education programs and therefore funded "Special Strategies for Educating Disadvantaged Children." This particular evaluation was modest in scope, however, and methodologically limited. Special Strategies looked at ten strategies in urban and suburban or rural areas. Rather than assembling representative or typical examples of each of these strategies, the evaluators asked the program developers or other knowledgeable persons to nominate well-implemented programs. No special control groups were used to assess the success of these alternative strategies—though the student outcomes were compared with the

70. For some of the details of the statistical design of Prospects, see Puma and others (1993, pp. 1–11, 349–90).

71. Puma and others (1993). Those findings were confirmed in the final report as well. Puma and others (1997). For a useful analysis of congressional politics on education during these years, see Jennings (1998).

results from the Prospects study. Moreover, little effort was made to match the students enrolled or the context in which the programs operated in order to provide more reliable comparative information on the relative effectiveness of the different strategies for helping at-risk children. As a result, while the findings from Special Strategies are interesting, they are not based on a sufficiently rigorous evaluation strategy and design to warrant much confidence in generalizing about the relative ability of these educational interventions to improve the academic achievement of disadvantaged students.[72]

Although most of the program analyses overseen by PES in the late 1980s and early 1990s did not meet the rigorous standards advocated by Ginsburg, the initial evaluation of Even Start by Abt Associates did try to assess the projects using control groups and random assignment of participants. Even Start was intended as a demonstration program to provide simultaneously training in adult literacy and early childhood education. Even Start grew rapidly, from $14 million in fiscal 1989 to $102 million in fiscal 1995 and won widespread, bipartisan support.[73]

The Even Start legislation called for an independent annual evaluation and specified that "when possible, each evaluation shall include comparisons with appropriate control groups."[74] Abt Associates won the five-year evaluation contract, which called for a two-part assessment: (1) the National Evaluation Information System (NEIS) for all Even Start projects and (2) an in-depth study (IDS) of ten projects. In addition, local projects were expected to do their own evaluations as well.[75] The in-depth study of ten purposely selected grantees was an innovative attempt to study the effectiveness of Even Start using randomized control groups.[76]

While the Abt evaluation of Even Start was more rigorous and systematic than most other PES program assessments, it still suffered from some methodological shortcomings. The stringent, but understandable, criteria for selecting the ten sites limited the representativeness of the IDS sites in relation to the other Even Start projects. For example, only thirty-two of the seventy-three first-year grantees expressed interest in participating in the IDS analysis. Moreover, Abt decided that "projects selected for inclusion should be high-quality projects that can reasonably be

72. Stringfield and others (1996).
73. Vinovskis (1999b, pp. 115–42).
74. U.S. Congress (1988, p. 45).
75. St. Pierre and others (1990).
76. Murray and others (1991, p. 4).

expected to be successful at achieving their goals"—thereby potentially biasing the assessment toward a more positive outcome.[77]

One of the best features of the Even Start evaluation was the attempt to implement randomized assignment of the participants and the control group. Initially, the plans called for twenty families to participate at each site with another twenty acting as the control group. Unfortunately, in practice it was difficult to persuade all of the sites to use random assignments. Given an unanticipated high rate of families dropping out of the program, replacements were added to the study who had not been randomly assigned.[78]

Perhaps one of the major reasons for the small number of more rigorous, experimental program evaluations at PES in the 1990s is that the agency frequently was called upon to provide immediate, short-term assistance to policymakers at the Department of Education with only limited staff and funding. William Morrill and Heather Weiss, under contract to the U.S. Department of Education, produced a useful organizational analysis of PES in 1997. They described the large number of PES tasks even though the total number of professional staff had been reduced from forty-five to thirty-eight. Morrill and Weiss praised much of the work of PES—such as its expanded role in strategic planning and the improved dissemination of its products. At the same time, they warned that PES was spending too much time on short-term projects at the expense of its long-term responsibilities.[79]

Morrill and Weiss endorsed the classical evaluation paradigm of rigorous testing and the use of control groups, but they also pointed to the need for more immediate and continuous feedback from programs to improve their performance.[80] Unfortunately, the Morrill and Weiss study did not examine in any detail either the number or the quality of the more classical, rigorous program evaluations at PES. One might argue that the more traditional program evaluations have suffered from relative neglect at PES during the 1980s and 1990s and need much more support and attention today.

The passage of the IASA of 1994 reauthorized existing education programs as well as created new ones; the legislation also mandated evalua-

77. Vinovskis (1999b, pp. 115–42).
78. Vinovskis (1999b, pp. 115–42).
79. Morrill and Weiss (1997, p. iii).
80. Morrill and Weiss (1997, p. iii).

tions of these programs. Many of these evaluation mandates did not have much funding provided so that PES frequently could only commission syntheses of the existing literature or fund small-scale, relatively inexpensive surveys of educators or schools.

The major large-scale evaluation initiative was the five-year Longitudinal Evaluation of School Change and Performance (LESCP) under contract to Westat, Policy Studies Associates, RMC, and the Urban Institute. LESCP is a longitudinal study of third-grade students in seventy-one purposively selected high-level poverty elementary schools in eighteen districts in six states (the states are stratified by their degree of involvement in state-wide standards-based reform). The analysis focused on student achievement in reading and mathematics as well as curriculum and instruction, professional development, and standards-based reform.

The LESCP evaluation could be a valuable and important individual-level cohort analysis of the impact of the Title I program and standards-based reform on third-grade students. Unfortunately, the study does not ascertain which specific educational practices or model programs are particularly effective in helping at-risk children. Nor does it calculate the expenditures on those programs for policy analysts interested in the relative cost-effectiveness of different interventions. Moreover, the lack of funding prevented researchers from following students who moved during the longitudinal study. Therefore, longitudinal information on highly mobile students, who often are the most disadvantaged, is not available.[81]

Unfortunately, PES and the LESCP contractors have delayed analyzing the impact of the Title I program on student achievement and releasing those findings to policymakers. Whereas selected aspects of the first year of results from Prospects, which supported the administration's legislative agenda in 1993, were released even before the interim report had been completed, the comparable LESCP findings have been slow in forthcoming—perhaps because the preliminary data seemed to imply that systemic reform was not as effective as suggested by those who were arguing that Congress should continue to support the current Title I approach.[82] Ostensibly, PES argued that it is improper to release any first-year findings

81. Vinovskis (1999a). See also GAO (2000).

82. The GAO analysis of LESCP pointed out considerable confusion about the purpose of the study among the Department of Education staff, the contractors, and members of the advisory committees. The Department of Education, however, replied "that a study as complex as LESCP had more than one [purpose]. In particular, this study was designed to examine the impacts of standards-driven reforms as well as the impacts of instructional practices

from this longitudinal study (although it had done so with the Prospects data). Yet in its interim report on LESCP based upon just the first-year results, the contractors used and reported those data to study the effects of instructional practices on student achievement.[83]

Yet even when the second-year LESCP data became available, PES and the contractors still failed to provide that analysis on a timely basis. Indeed, Representative Michael Castle (R-Delaware), chair of the House Subcommittee on Early Childhood, Youth and Families, complained to Secretary Richard Riley at a congressional hearing on October 25, 2000, about the long delays in receiving any results about the effectiveness of Title I from the LESCP study and even wondered whether the delay was politically motivated.[84] As a result, unlike Prospects, the $9 million LESCP evaluation did not provide much useful information on the effectiveness of Title I as the 106th Congress completed its deliberations on the ESEA legislation.[85]

PES is looking at specific program operations in several other studies. Work continued on the Even Start programs, but the second phase of the evaluation was marred by a poorly designed questionnaire as well as the lack of an adequate control group. Although the contractors sometimes made statements about the relative effectiveness of different Even Start models or approaches, the findings should be used with caution and considerable skepticism.[86] Fortunately, the third evaluation, now under way, is a much better designed and more rigorous assessment, which includes the use of random assignments for the participants and the control group.

Congressional concern about education also led to the passage of the Obey-Porter legislation, which established a new federal program to provide up to $50,000 annually for three years to help schools adopt com-

---

in high-poverty schools. These two issues are not inconsistent with one another, since a study of the impacts of standards-driven reforms in schools would necessarily take into account, and estimate, differences in impacts due to instructional practices." GAO (2000, p. 25). Given the Department of Education's acknowledgment of the dual purposes of LESCP, it is surprising and disappointing that in the interim report they chose to focus almost entirely on the relative effectiveness of the instructional practices, while ignoring the important issue of the impact of the Title I reforms on student achievement.

83. U.S. Department of Education (1999).

84. U.S. Congress (2001, pp. 39–40).

85. Vinovskis (1999c) See also the reply by PES (1999).

86. I served as a member of the technical advisory panel on the second Even Start evaluation and complained several times in writing about the poorly designed questionnaires as well as the ways in which the contractors were interpreting the flawed data.

prehensive school reforms. In November 1997 Congress provided $150 million for that program and expected approximately 2,500 schools to participate. The legislation specified which comprehensive reform models might be used and stressed the importance of relying on research-based findings.[87] The legislation also called for rigorous evaluations of the programs, and PES is now developing those assessment guidelines. Whether such an ambitious program that tries to combine both service delivery and evaluation at a relatively low cost per project can really succeed in providing rigorous and useful assessments remains to be seen. Previous experiences with mixed service-evaluation programs such as Follow Through demonstrated the inherent tensions and difficulties in carrying out such multiple responsibilities.

PES has the primary responsibility for coordination of all program evaluation activities in the Department of Education. But other units are also expected to promote more in-depth and rigorous program evaluations simultaneously, especially an agency such as the Office of Educational Research and Improvement, which in the past had supported some large-scale demonstration programs. OERI had recovered during the Bush and Clinton administrations from much of its losses in the early 1980s. Its funding rose from $78.2 million in fiscal 1989 to $286.2 million in fiscal 1993, and to $398.1 million in fiscal 1997. Most of the increases in OERI's budget were not in the research account, however, but in the transferred or newly mandated programs designed to improve education more directly. But funding for both the R&D centers and the regional educational laboratories did increase substantially, and one might have expected these institutions to be particularly supportive of long-term program development and evaluation.[88]

While OERI funding increased during these years, the number of staff actually decreased. Following the sizable staff reduction during the Reagan years, there was a small recovery in staff, from 425 full-time equivalents (FTEs) in fiscal 1988 to 448 in fiscal 1992. By fiscal 2000, however, the staff had dropped precipitously to 325 FTEs—a 27.5 percent decline. Moreover, under the department's early retirement buyout program for senior staff, some of the more capable and experienced individuals left. While OERI hired some replacements, the agency continues to have too few distinguished or experienced researchers. For example, in

87. Keltner (1998a).
88. Vinovskis (1998a, pp. 25–31, 34–38).

the closing days of the Clinton administration, Assistant Secretary Kent McGuire decided to appoint permanent directors of the five research institutes—but only one of the five appointees has had extensive research training and personal scholarly experience.[89] As a result, although OERI now has more funds and responsibilities than ever before, its staff is significantly smaller and less research-oriented.[90]

Despite NIE's emphasis on development in the more distant past, the agency has not devoted much attention to program development and evaluation in the late 1980s and early 1990s. A few of the regional educational laboratories did support some program evaluations, but often these efforts were not particularly scientifically rigorous. The innovative "Success for All" program was developed and self-evaluated by one of the R&D centers; but this was unusual as most of the other R&D centers spread their limited resources among many different, small-scale projects rather than concentrating their resources on a few larger, long-term initiatives.[91]

When OERI was reauthorized in 1994, Congress tried to encourage more large-scale, systematic work by defining more precisely what they meant by the concept of development.[92] Although OERI emphasized the need for the systematic development and evaluation of promising educational practices and programs, especially in its request for proposals (RFP) for the regional educational laboratories in 1995, there does not appear to be much work along these lines in the agency as a whole.[93] In 1993 OERI tentatively explored the possibility of undertaking a large-scale program development and evaluation effort to assess the value of systemic reform, but then decided not to pursue that option. One potentially promising area of development and evaluation today is the after-school programs in the 21st Century Schools. In partnership with the Mott Foundation, the Department of Education is developing an evaluation program to assess the work on these entities.

89. Interestingly, while several qualified researchers had applied and were interviewed for some of those positions, OERI decided not to hire them but wanted to appoint some other individuals who did not have the requisite research experience and training. In order to accomplish that task, it was necessary to cancel two of the ongoing searches and redefine the positions to emphasize the need for managerial skills rather than a research and administrative background.

90. Vinovskis (1998a, pp. 34–38).

91. Vinovskis (1993).

92. Public Law 103-227, Title IX, Sec. 912, (1) (4). For a discussion of the meaning and expectations for this directive, see Vinovskis (1998b).

93. Vinovskis (1998a, pp. 44–50).

Rather than focusing on program development and evaluation to reform American education, the Department of Education and Congress have devoted more of their attention and funds to measuring student outcomes and creating expected performance standards through the National Assessment of Educational Progress (NAEP). NAEP was created in 1969 and provided national and regional information about student achievement in several core subject areas. In the late 1980s NAEP was expanded to provide state-level student achievement data, and the National Assessment Governing Board (NAGB) was given the responsibility for overseeing the program, while the National Center for Education Statistics dealt with the more technical and operational issues. Much of the debate over NAEP in the 1990s was over NAGB's work on student performance standards, which involved issues of how to integrate properly the use of particular technical procedures and human judgments in setting those standards.[94]

Many educators and policymakers have viewed NAEP as one of the most effective ways of not only measuring student achievement, but also stimulating educational reforms at the state and national levels. Given the increasingly ambitious agenda expected of NAEP, some argue that the program continues to be seriously underfunded at the $35 million to $40 million it receives annually. Yet over the past three decades, the federal government has invested nearly half a billion dollars (in constant 1996 dollars) in NAEP. Much has been gained from NAEP, and it promises to make even more significant contributions in the future—especially as policymakers pay more attention to improving student achievement at the state level. But NAEP by itself is not a substitute for also developing better ways of teaching at-risk students in classrooms in diverse school settings. Perhaps we need to consider devoting at least as much attention and funds to developing better ways of educating students as to measuring their current knowledge.[95]

Conclusion

Nineteenth- and early twentieth-century policymakers were very interested in collecting and using data on students and schools—both to gauge the extent of educational achievement and to spur additional school

94. Vinovskis (1998c).
95. Vinovskis (1998c).

reforms. They were less convinced of the need for more scientific studies of educational reform. Indeed, while the natural sciences as well as the other social and behavioral sciences expanded rapidly during World War II to help the war effort, educational research was actually reduced at the U.S. Office of Education.

During the 1950s and 1960s the social and behavioral sciences made considerable progress conceptually and methodologically. These advances helped to pave the way for more sophisticated work in program evaluations and encouraged the federal government to try to assess the effectiveness of the Great Society programs.

Educational research and development, however, did not keep pace with the other social and behavioral sciences. A special effort was made in the mid-1960s to set up institutions to foster more rigorous and systemic work. The R&D centers and the regional educational laboratories were created with the expectation that they would avoid the fragmentation and short-term orientation characteristic of most earlier educational research and development. While some progress was made, even these modest gains were lost during the 1970s and 1980s as a result of the cutbacks in educational research funding, the general growing hostility and suspicion of social science research and evaluations, and the political difficulties besetting NIE and OERI. Rather than supporting systematic development and program evaluation, the Reagan administration and Congress focused more on improving testing student achievement and collecting other educational data.

While the overall support for educational research and evaluation has improved considerably at OERI and PES since the early 1980s, the amount and quality of systematic development and rigorous program evaluation remains limited. Although Congress and the Department of Education periodically reaffirm their interest in development and program evaluation, in practice little has been done. The routinely repeated statements advocating better development and program evaluation during recent congressional hearings and the resultant legislation have not led to major improvements yet. Not surprisingly, many analysts are skeptical that the shortcomings in educational development and program evaluation will be successfully addressed in the upcoming reauthorization.

Perhaps it is time to reorganize federal education program evaluations and large-scale development efforts within the Department of Education. Large-scale, systematic development is by and large absent at OERI. Many of the research and development projects at the R&D centers and the regional educational laboratories continue to be too small and uncoordinated; and the scientific quality of much of the existing developmental work leaves considerable room for improvement. At the same time, neither the Planning and Evaluation Service nor OERI is producing a sufficient number of scientifically sound and educationally relevant program evaluations to provide educators and policymakers with the information they need.

Since 1985 PES has had the primary responsibility for conducting program evaluations. But given its limited funding and preoccupation with numerous short-term assignments, PES has not been able to produce many rigorous, in-depth program evaluations in the last fifteen years. For example, PES has had difficulty in conducting an objective and comprehensive third-year assessment of the activities of the regional educational laboratories.[96] And Representative Castle complained: "I am concerned with some of the findings in recent evaluations of the labs and research centers and disappointed that the Department has been less than forthcoming in providing Congress with timely information about the quality of their research and development."[97] Similarly, PES's interim multimillion dollar evaluation of the effectiveness of the current Title I program, the LESCP, has not been done particularly well—indeed, the analysis of the impact of the Title I program on student achievement so far has been less detailed and less statistically sophisticated in some ways than the roughly comparable work for the Prospects evaluation of Chapter 1 almost a decade earlier.[98]

Moreover, the Department of Education has not always delivered timely and objective evaluations of its major programs. When it suits policy purposes, PES sometimes has appeared to publicize selective results from evaluations immediately (such as Prospects)—even before the actual reports have been made available to the public or policymakers. At other times, PES has delayed much too long to release results from evaluations that may challenge current department policies (such as LESCP).[99] Whether intentional or not, PES has sometimes failed to release the results of major evaluations in time for decisionmakers to use their findings fully in their policy deliberations. The third-year evaluation of the labs, for example, was not released until April 2000—well after most of

96. Vinovskis (2001).
97. U.S. Congress (2000, p. 2).
98. Vinovskis (1999c). See also the reply by PES (1999).
99. Vinovskis (1999c).

the hearings on the OERI reauthorization in the 106th Congress had been concluded.[100] And although the Clinton administration decided to eliminate the Comprehensive Regional Assistance Centers, it did not release the evaluation of those entities until early 2001 (and the preliminary indications were that the delayed evaluation of those centers was rather favorable and thereby challenged the department's decision to abolish them).[101]

Occasionally, OERI has also engaged in selectively releasing evaluations to affect policymaking. Some OERI officials in 1993 explored the possibility of trying to suppress my critical assessment of the quality of the work of the labs and centers; and that report was never published by the Department of Education nor shared with legislators during the OERI reauthorization process during 1993 and 1994. More recently, OERI was reluctant to release the third-year evaluations of the R&D centers so that most members of Congress did not have access to them until after the conclusion of the OERI reauthorization hearings.[102]

Given the need for scientifically sound and politically objective program evaluations and large-scale development projects, perhaps an independent federal unit that initiates and oversees a serious evaluation and development program should be created—the National Center for Evaluation and Development (NCED). This agency would handle the major evaluations of education programs—especially those that have important policy implications. Moreover, it would sponsor and oversee large-scale development projects.[103]

A U.S. commissioner of evaluation and development, appointed for a six-year term, would oversee NCED. The professional staff in that unit would be required to be knowledgeable and familiar with the latest work in rigorous program evaluations and large-scale development projects.

100. Vinovskis (2001).

101. As a member of the advisory committee to the Policy Studies Associates' evaluation of the Comprehensive Regional Assistance Centers, I had an opportunity to read and comment on the various drafts of that evaluation. We had reviewed a preliminary draft of the final report in September 1999 and hoped that the evaluation would be released early in 2000. As an advisory committee, we were never asked to review the subsequent drafts of the report for criticisms or suggestions.

102. Vinovskis (2001).

103. This proposal was presented at a recent House hearing on the reauthorization of OERI. See Vinovskis (2000). Parts of this conclusion also are drawn from the concluding chapter of Vinovskis (2001).

The program and development effort would be overseen by an independent, objective group of experts who would not only provide technical assistance but ensure that the design, implementation, and interpretation of the work is scientifically sound as well as useful to educators and policymakers. Moreover, they would help to ensure that the evaluations and development projects done under this unit would be readily and equally available to everyone—and not just to those who control the Department of Education at the time.

Program evaluations should vary according to the types of information needed. For the most rigorous and statistically reliable studies, the use of randomized-assignment control groups should be considered—though the much higher costs of these efforts will limit the number of studies that can be expected to employ this approach. Planned variation projects, building upon the work of the early 1970s in educational evaluation, can be profitably used in many other instances. And more limited and less costly information might be routinely gathered in most other projects to provide guidance and feedback to local areas in order to help them make any necessary improvements.[104]

NCED should set up an initiative for soliciting and implementing large-scale, systematic development. Initially, this program might focus its energies on three to five long-term projects in areas such as developing reading improvement programs or helping at-risk children make a successful transition from early childhood programs into the regular classrooms. Anyone, including the R&D centers or the regional educational laboratories, could compete for these demonstration projects. The open competition would not only spur existing educational research and development providers to produce better proposals, but it might also attract interest from other major social science research organizations such as the Manpower Development Research Corporation (MDRC), Rand Corporation, or the Urban Institute.

While ordinarily Congress should assign the major, large-scale evaluations and development projects to NCED, some smaller and less policy-sensitive programs might be handled by other agencies as well. Smaller and more short-term development projects could be supported elsewhere in the department. And some of the smaller and more applied evaluation studies also could be continued by a restructured PES.

104. For a useful discussion of the value of nonrandomized education evaluations and the need for design competitions, see Slavin (1997).

References

Aaron, Henry J. 1978. *Politics and the Professors: The Great Society in Perspective.* Brookings.

Bailey, Stephen K., and Edith K. Mosher. 1968. *ESEA: The Office of Education Administers a Law.* Syracuse University Press.

Banfield, Edward C. 1970. *The Unheavenly City: The Nature and Future of Our Urban Crisis.* Little, Brown.

Bernstein, Irving. 1996. *Guns or Butter: The Presidency of Lyndon Johnson.* Oxford University Press.

Berube, Maurice R.1991. *American Presidents and Education.* New York: Greenwood Press.

Bloom, Benjamin S. 1966. "Twenty-Five Years of Educational Research." *American Educational Research Journal* 3 (May): 211–21.

Boruch, Robert F. 1998. "Randomized Controlled Experiments for Evaluation and Planning." In *Handbook of Applied Social Research Methods*, edited by L. Bickman and D. J. Rog, 161–91. Thousand Oaks, Calif.: Sage Publications.

Boruch, Robert F., and David S. Cordray. 1980. "An Appraisal of Educational Program Evaluations: Federal, State, and Local Agencies." Final report submitted to the U.S. Department of Education (June 30). Contract 300-79-0467.

Brim, Orville, Jr. 1965. *Sociology and the Field of Education.* New York: Russell Sage Foundation.

Bulmer, Martin. 2001. "Knowledge for the Public Good: The Emergence of Social Sciences and Social Reform in Late-Nineteenth and Early-Twentieth-Century America, 1880–1940." In *Social Science and Policy-Making: A Search for Relevance in the Twentieth Century*, edited by David L. Featherman and Maris A. Vinovskis, 16–39. University of Michigan Press.

Carroll, John B. 1961. "Neglected Areas in Educational Research." *Phi Delta Kappan* 42 (May): 339–46.

Chelimsky, Eleanor. 1992. "Executive Branch Program Evaluation: An Upturn Soon?" In *Evaluation in the Federal Government: Changes, Trends, and Opportunities*, edited by Christopher G. Wye and Richard C. Sonnichsen. San Francisco: Jossey-Bass.

Cicirelli, Victor G., John W. Evans, and Jeffrey S. Schiller. 1970. "The Impact of Head Start: A Reply to the Report Analysis." *Harvard Educational Review* 40: 105–29.

Cohen, Linda R., and Roger G. Noll. 1992. "Research and Development." In *Setting Domestic Priorities: What Can Government Do?* edited by Henry J. Aaron and Charles L. Schultze, 223–65. Brookings.

Cohen, Sol, ed. 1974. *Education in the United States: A Documentary History.* Random House.

Coladarci, Arthur P. "More Rigorous Educational Research." *Harvard Educational Review* 30 (Winter): 3–11.

Coleman, James S., Ernest Q. Campbell, Carol J. Hobson, James McPartland, Alexander M. Mood, Frederic D. Weinfeld, and Robert L. York. 1966. *Equality of Educational Opportunity.* Government Printing Office.

Cronbach, Lee J., and Patrick Suppes, eds. 1969. *Research for Tomorrow's Schools: Disciplinary Inquiry for Education.* Macmillan.

Dershimer, Richard A. 1976. *The Federal Government and Education R&D.* Lexington, Mass.: Lexington Books.

Dow, Peter B. 1991. *Schoolhouse Politics: Lessons form the Sputnik Era.* Harvard University Press.

Featherman, David L., and Maris A. Vinovskis. 2001. "Growth and Use of Social and Behavioral Science in the Federal Government since World War II." In *Social Science and Policy Making: A Search for Relevance in the Twentieth Century*, edited by David L. Featherman and Maris A. Vinovskis, 40–48. University of Michigan Press.

Fields, Cheryl M. 1980. "A Social Scientist Recounts Some Lessons He Learned from Winning Proxmire's 'Golden Fleece.'" *Chronicle of Higher Education* 27 (September 15).

Finn, Chester E., Jr. 1977. *Education and the Presidency.* Lexington, Mass.: Lexington Books.

Garner, John. 1964. "Report of the President's Task Force on Education" (November 14). LBJ Presidential Library, Austin, Tex.

Ginsburg, Alan. "Meeting the Market for Quality Evaluation in Education." In *Evaluation in the Federal Government: Changes, Trends, and Opportunities*, edited by Christopher G. Wye and Richard C. Sonnichsen. San Francisco: Jossey-Bass.

Ginsburg, Alan L., Jay Noell, and Valena White Plisko. 1988. "Lessons from the Wall Chart." *Educational Evaluation and Policy Analysis* 10 (Spring).

Glenn, Charles L. 1988. *The Myth of the Common School.* University of Massachusetts Press.

Good, Carter V. 1956. "Educational Research after Fifty Years." *Phi Delta Kappan* 37 (January): 145–52.

Harper, Edwin L., Fred A. Kramer, and Andrew M. Rouse. 1969. "Implementation and Use of PPB in Sixteen Federal Agencies." *Public Administration Review* 29 (November/December): 623–32.

Havens, Harry S. 1992. "The Erosion of Federal Program Evaluation." In *Evaluation in the Federal Government: Changes, Trends, and Opportunities*, edited by Christopher G. Wye and Richard C. Sonnichsen, 21–27. San Francisco: Jossey-Bass.

Jencks, Christopher, and others. 1972. *Inequality: A Reassessment of the Effect of Family and Schooling in America.* Basic Books.

Jennings, John F. 1998. *Why National Standards and Tests? Politics and the Quest for Better Schools.* Thousand Oaks, Calif.: Sage Publications.

Kaestle, Carl F. 1983. *Pillars of the Republic: Common Schools and American Society.* New York: Hill and Wang.

Kaplan, Marshall, and Peggy Cuciti, eds. 1986. *The Great Society and Its Legacy: Twenty Years of U.S. Social Policy.* Duke University Press.

Kearney, Charles Philip. 1967. "The 1964 Presidential Task Force on Education and the Elementary and Secondary Education Act of 1965." Ph.D. dissertation, University of Chicago.

Keltner, Brent R. 1998. "Funding Comprehensive School Reform." Issue Paper. Santa Monica, Calif.: Rand Education.

Kleinman, Daniel L. 1995. *Politics on the Endless Frontier: Postwar Research Policy in the United States.* Duke University Press.

Lagemann, Ellen Condliffe. 2000. *An Elusive Science: The Troubling History of Education Research.* University of Chicago Press.

Larsen, Otto N. 1992. *Milestones and Millstones: Social Science at the National Science Foundation, 1945–1991.* New Brunswick, N.J.: Transaction.

Lee, Gordon C. 1949. *The Struggle for Federal Aid for the Common Schools, 1870–1890.* New York: Teachers College.

Levitan, Sar A., and Robert Taggart. 1976. *The Promise of Greatness: The Social Programs of the Last Decade and Their Major Achievements.* Harvard University Press.

McLaughlin, Milbrey Wallin. 1975. *Evaluation and Reform: The Elementary and Secondary Education Act of 1965, Title I.* Cambridge, Mass.: Ballinger.

MacMullen, Edith N. 1991. *In the Cause of True Education: Henry Barnard and Nineteenth-Century School Reform.* Yale University Press.

Meltsner, Arnold J. 1976. *Policy Analysts in the Bureaucracy.* University of California Press.

Meranto, Philip. 1967. *The Politics of Federal Aid to Education in 1965: A Study in Political Innovation.* Syracuse University Press.

Morrill, William A., and Heather Weiss. 1997. "Talent, Tensions and Transition: An Organizational Analysis of the Planning and Evaluation Service." Report submitted to the Planning and Evaluation Service, U.S. Department of Education (February).

Mosteller, Frederick. 1995. "The Tennessee Study of Class Size in the Early School Grades." *The Future of Children: Critical Issues for Children and Youths* 5 (Summer/Fall): 113–27.

Moynihan, Daniel Patrick. 1969. *Maximum Feasible Misunderstanding: Community Action in the War on Poverty.* New York: Free Press.

Mullin, Stephen P., and Anita A. Summers. 1983. "Is More Better? The Effectiveness of Spending on Compensatory Education." *Phi Delta Kappan* 64 (January): 339–47.

Murray, Stephen, and others. 1991. "Evaluating Program Effectiveness for the National Even Start Evaluation: Deriving Estimates of Effect from Reference Groups." Cambridge, Mass.: Abt Associates (April 2).

Nathan, Richard P. 1988. *Social Science in Government: Uses and Misuses.* Basic Books.

Palmer, John L., ed. 1982. *Perspectives on the Reagan Years.* Washington: Urban Institute Press.

Planning and Evaluation Services (PES). 1998. "Evaluation Strategy for High Performance: The Education Department's Experience." Paper presented at "Helpful Practices in Program Evaluation" Symposium, National Academy of Public Administration (November 17).

———. (1999). "Response to Maris Vinovskis' Paper Critiquing the Longitudinal Evaluation of School Change and Performance." Unpublished paper (August).

Puma, Michael J., Calvin C. Jones, Donald Rock, and Reberto Fernandez. 1993. *Prospects: The Congressionally Mandated Study of Education Growth and Opportunity, Interim Report.* Bethesda, Md.: Abt Associates.

Puma, Michael J., Nancy Karweit, Cristofer Price, Anne Ricciuti, William Thompson, and Michael Vaden-Kiernan. 1997. *Prospects: Final Report on Student Outcomes.* Cambridge, Mass.: Abt Associates.

Ravitch, Diane.1983. *The Troubled Crusade: American Education, 1945–1980.* Basic Books.

———. 2000. *Left Back: A Century of Failed School Reforms.* Simon and Schuster.

Rivlin, Alice M., and P. Michael Timpane. 1975. "Planned Variation in Education: An Assessment." In *Planned Variation in Education: Should We Give Up or Try Harder?* edited by Alice M. Rivlin and P. Michael Timpane, 1–21. Brookings.

Schultz, Thomas W. 1988. "Behind Closed Doors: Peer Review in the NIE Research Center Competition." Ed.D. dissertation, Harvard University.

Schweinhart, Lawrence J., Helen V. Barnes, and David P. Weikart. 1993. *Significant Benefits: The High/Scope Perry Preschool Study through Age 27.* Ypsilanti, Mich.: High/Scope Press.

Slavin, Robert E. 1997. "Design Competitions: A Proposal for a New Federal Role in Educational Research and Development." *Educational Researcher* 26: 22–28.

———. 2000. Testimony, U.S. Congress, House, Subcommittee on Early Childhood, Youth and Families. *Options for the Future of the Office of Education Research and Improvement.* 106 Cong. 2 sess., pp. 158–63. Government Printing Office.

Smith, Darrell H. 1923. *The Bureau of Education: Its History, Activities, and Organization.* Johns Hopkins University Press.

Smith, Marshall S., and Joan S. Bissell. 1970. "Report Analysis: The Impact of Head Start." *Harvard Educational Review* 40: 51–104.

Sproull, Lee, Stephen Winter, and David Wolf. 1978. *Organizing an Anarchy: Belief, Bureaucracy, and Politics in the National Institute of Education.* University of Chicago Press.

St. Pierre, Robert G., and others. 1990. *National Even Start Evaluation: Overview.* Cambridge, Mass.: Abt Associates.

Stringfield, Sam, and others. 1996. *Special Strategies for Educating Disadvantaged Children, Final Report.* Washington: Office of Policy and Planning.

Tyack, David, Thomas James, and Aaron Benavot. 1987. *Law and the Shaping of Public Education, 1785–1954.* University of Wisconsin Press.

U.S. Bureau of the Census. 1996. *Statistical Abstract of the United States: 1996.* 116th ed. Government Printing Office.

U.S. Congress, House. 1988. *Elementary and Secondary Education: Conference Report to Accompany H.R. 5.* Report 100-567. 100 Cong. 2 sess. Government Printing Office.

U.S. Congress, House, Committee on Education and the Workforce. 2001. *Waste, Fraud, and Program Implementation at the U.S. Department of Education.* 106 Cong. 2 sess. Government Printing Office.

U.S. Congress, House, Special Committee on Education. 1967. *Study of the United States Office of Education.* House Document 193. 90 Cong. 1 sess. Government Printing Office.

U.S. Congress, Subcommittee on Early Childhood, Youth and Families. 2000. *Options for the Future of the Office of Education Research and Improvement.* 106 Cong. 2 sess. Government Printing Office.

U.S. Department of Education, Office of the Under Secretary, Planning and Evaluation Service. 1999. *The Longitudinal Evaluation of School Change and Performance in Title I Schools.* Government Printing Office.

U.S. General Accounting Office (GAO). 1987. *Education Information: Changes in Funds and Priorities Have Affected Production and Quality.* GAO/PEMD-88-4.

———. 2000. *Education for Disadvantaged Children: Research Purpose and Design Features Affect Conclusions Drawn from Key Studies.* GAO/HEHS-00-168.

U.S. Office of Education (USOE). 1945. *Annual Report, 1944.* Government Printing Office.

———. 1951. *Annual Report, 1950.* Government Printing Office.

———. 1952. *Annual Report, 1951.* Government Printing Office.

———. 1958. *Annual Report, 1957.* Government Printing Office.

———. 1960. *Annual Report, 1959.* Government Printing Office.

———. 1965. *Annual Report, 1964.* Government Printing Office.

Verstegen, Deborah A., and David L. Clark. 1988. "The Diminution in Federal Expenditures for Education during the Reagan Administration." *Phi Delta Kappan* 70 (October): 137.

Vinovskis, Maris A. 1993. "Analysis of the Quality of Research and Development at the OERI Research and Development Centers and the OERI Regional Educational Laboratories." Unpub. final OERI report (June).

———. 1995. *Education, Society, and Economic Opportunity: A Historical Perspective on Persistent Issues.* Yale University Press.

———. 1996. "The Changing Role of the Federal Government in Educational Research and Statistics." *History of Education Quarterly* 36 (Summer): 111–28.

———. 1997. "The Development and Effectiveness of Compensatory Education Programs: A Brief Historical Analysis of Title I and Head Start." In *Giving Better, Giving Smarter: Working Papers of the National Commission on Philanthropy and Civic Renewal*, edited by John W. Barry and Bruno V. Manno, 169–92. Washington: National Commission on Philanthropy and Civic Renewal.

———. 1998a. *Changing Federal Strategies for Supporting Educational Research, Development, and Statistics.* Washington: National Educational Research Policy and Priorities Board.

———. 1998b. "Measuring the Interim Performance of the Regional Educational Laboratory's Educational Research and Development Activities." Background paper prepared for the U.S. Department of Education (October 4).

———. 1998c. *Overseeing the Nation's Report Card: The Creation and Evolution of the National Assessment Governing Board (NAGB).* National Assessment Governing Board (November 19).

———. 1999a. "Do Federal Compensatory Education Programs Really Work? A Brief Historical Analysis of Title I and Head Start." *American Journal of Education* 107 (May): 187–209.

———. 1999b. *History and Educational Policymaking.* Yale University Press.

———. 1999c. "Improving the Analysis and Reporting of Policy-Related Evaluations at the U.S. Department of Education: Some Preliminary Observations about the Longitudinal Evaluation of School Change and Performance." Unpublished paper (August).

———. 2000. "Revitalizing Federal Education Research, Development, and Evaluation." Testimony, U.S. Congress, House, Subcommittee on Early Childhood, Youth, and Families. 106 Cong. 2 sess. (May 4). Government Printing Office.

———. 2001. *Revitalizing Federal Education Research and Development: Improving the R&D Centers, Regional Educational Laboratories, and the "New" OERI.* University of Michigan Press.

Warren, Donald R. 1974. *To Enforce Education: A History of the Founding Years of the United States Office of Education.* Wayne State University Press.

Westinghouse Learning Corporation. 1969. "The Impact of Head Start: An Evaluation of the Effects of Head Start on Children's Cognitive and Affective Development." Report presented to the Office of Economic Opportunity. Contract B89-4536.

Wood, Robert C. 1993. *Whatever Possessed the President? Academic Experts and Presidential Policy, 1960–1988.* University of Massachusetts Press.

Zodhiates, Philip. 1988. "Bureaucrats and Politicians: The National Institute of Education and Educational Research under Reagan." Ed.D. dissertation, Harvard University.

Zook, George F. 1945. *The Role of the Federal Government in Education.* Harvard University Press.

CHAPTER SIX

Objecting to the Objections to Using Random Assignment in Educational Research

THOMAS D. COOK
MONIQUE R. PAYNE

MANY FEATURES OF educational research are today healthy, particularly as concerns historical scholarship, the use of surveys to describe districts, schools, classrooms and teachers, the use of individual measures to assess student performance, and the use of longitudinal methods to assess how young people change over time. Educational research has also benefited from the use of qualitative methods to describe and explain dilemmas that arise in relationships among students and staff, and in relationships between students and staff, staff and parents, and districts and unions. In these areas, educational researchers can be proud of their accomplishments. But there is one area where pride is not warranted. It concerns the quality of attempts to evaluate changes or even "reforms" in schools. Discontent with the state of current knowledge of what works in education is widespread, and is evident across all parts of the political spectrum. Much has been spent to evaluate educational innovations, but not much has been learned about what works and can be used to improve schools and student performance.

In statistics and most of the social sciences one particular method stands out for the quality of causal inferences it generates—the experiment. However, theorists of educational evaluation such as Eliot Eisner,

Thomas Cook's contribution was supported by a visiting scholarship at the Max Planck Institute for Human Development, Berlin, Germany, and a grant from the Spencer Foundation.

David Fetterman, Egon Guba, Ernest House, Yvonna Lincoln, Michael Patton, Robert Stake, and David Stufflebeam have explicitly rejected this method. This chapter reviews the major arguments adduced by these theorists for not doing randomized experiments even when the conclusions they want to draw are of the kind random assignment promotes: namely, A causes B.

The objections they raise are many and seem compelling when listed. By now, they have influenced the practice of many generations of young educational evaluators and are probably a major cause of the impoverished current state of knowledge about what reform initiatives in American education have actually achieved. Our hope is that this essay will help put randomized experiments back into the armamentarium of educational evaluation methods, but in a way that complements the methods currently favored without replacing them. We also hope that the essay will dampen the hubris of those overzealous advocates of random assignment who do not acknowledge the full panoply of problems associated with implementing it perfectly in actual research practice. Indeed, analyzing the problems of random assignment through the eyes of its educational critics will later allow us to create a rationale for randomized experiments that is subtly different in important ways from the one most often currently advanced.

Objection 1: Randomized Experiments Suppose an Oversimplified Theory of Causation

Experiments are predicated on a theory of causation that is bivariate and unidirectional. They are usually created so that a no-treatment control group functions as a valid counterfactual against which performance in an experimental or treatment group is contrasted. If random assignment occurs and is implemented correctly, then the two groups are presumed to be equivalent in all ways except for the treatment. All subsequent differences can therefore be attributed to the causal agent under study, A. The purpose of an experiment is to estimate the marginal change in B that can be attributed to A, and the crucial assumption is that the control group represents an unbiased assessment of what the treatment group would have done had there been no treatment.

However, that is not the central assumption that worries critics of the method. Rather, they contend that this notion of causation is oversimplified and incommensurate with how causal forces operate in the real world. They want to understand causation as a multivariate and often reciprocal concept. Their claim is that A often affects B in concert with many other variables, and sometimes in complex nonlinear fashion. With a few exceptions, educational researchers seem willing to postulate that a real world exists, however imperfectly it can be known.[1] They also seem to acknowledge that causal relationships are part of this world, but they believe them to be much more complex than an arrow from A to B.

Critics are correct when they assert that most randomized experiments test the influence of only a small subset of potential causes of an outcome, and often only one. And even at their most comprehensive, experiments can responsibly test only a modest number of the possible interactions between treatments. So, experiments are best when a causal question involves few variables, is sharply focused, and is easily justified. The theory of causation most relevant to this modest task has been variously called the activity, manipulability, or recipe theory.[2] It seeks to describe the consequences of a set of activities whose components can be listed as though they were ingredients in a recipe. These ingredients are then actively manipulated as a package in order to ascertain whether they achieve a given result. This task is fundamentally descriptive, and explanation is only promoted either if the manipulations help discriminate between competing theories or if the experiment collects ancillary measures of those processes that might have mediated between a cause and effect.[3] Otherwise, random assignment is irrelevant to explanation.

Cronbach and his colleagues maintain that multiple causal factors are implicated in all student or teacher change, and often in complex nonlinear ways.[4] Their model of real world causation is systemic in form, more akin to intersecting pretzels than a single causal arrow. No educational intervention fully explains an outcome. At most, it is just one more determinant of the outcome. Nor do interventions have effects that we can assume are constant in size across student and teacher populations, across types of schools and time periods. In this way of thinking, causal contingency is the watchword, and the activity theory of causation seems largely irrelevant because so few causally implicated variables can be simultaneously manipulated.

1. Among the exceptions are Guba and Lincoln (1982).
2. Collingwood (1940); Gasking (1955); Whitbeck (1977).
3. Mackie (1974).
4. Cronbach, and others (1980).

However, experiments were not developed to answer questions about complex causal interdependencies. Their purpose is more narrow and practical—to identify whether one or more possible causal agents actually cause change in a given outcome. Experiments were invented, in Bacon's famous words, to "twist Nature by the tail," to pull apart what is usually confounded.

But this prime purpose does not mean that experimenters are indifferent to the conditions surrounding when a treatment is implemented. After all, it was for this reason that Ronald Fisher took experimental methods outside of the laboratory and into agricultural fields, and he also counseled doing experiments so that they included many diverse sampling particulars.[5] But while the fit between the conditions in which research is done and the realms of desired application is always important in experimentation, it is always invariably secondary. Premier is achieving a clear picture of whether the link between two variables is causal in the activity theory sense. Experiments are ideal for accomplishing this goal, and only this goal.[6]

It is not a trivial goal, as one can see from how educational researchers write about effective educational reform. They postulate some noncontingent causal connections that are true enough, and relevant enough to school life, that they constitute summaries of practical causal knowledge—for example, that small schools are better than large ones; time-on-task raises achievement; summer school raises test scores; school desegregation hardly affects achievement; and assigning and grading homework raises achievement. At an abstract level, critics of the activity theory of causation deny the utility of propositions like these because they are not explanatorily complete. But they seem willing to believe such statements are often true enough to be useful. They also seem willing to accept the validity and relevance of other causal propositions that are bounded by some (but few and manageable) contingencies—for example, that reducing class size increases achievement, provided that the amount of change is "sizable" and to a level under twenty; and Catholic schools are superior to public ones when it comes to graduation rates, but only in the inner city. Commitment to a multivariate, explanatory theory of causation has not stopped school researchers from acting as though educational reform can be usefully characterized in terms of some dependable main effects and

5. Fisher (1926).
6. Campbell (1957).

some dependable and simple interactions. Hence randomized experiments cannot be rejected simply on the grounds that the theory of causation that undergirds them is oversimplified as a means for identifying practical ways to improve school life and student performance.

We have considerable sympathy for those critics of experimentation who believe that biased answers to big explanatory questions are more important than unbiased answers to smaller casual-descriptive questions. However, experiments on educational reform do not necessarily involve small questions, even if they are less general than questions about causal generative mechanisms that might apply to many different applications and settings.[7] Still, proponents of random assignment need to acknowledge that the method they prefer depends on a theory of causation that is less comprehensive than the more multivariate and explanatory theory that most social scientists espouse. Acknowledging this does not undermine the justification for experiments, and it might even encourage experimenters to improve the explanatory yield of their work by adding more measures about possible intervening processes. Black-box experiments are a thing of the past. They were generally not productive yesteryear, and there is no reason to believe that this has changed.

Objection 2: Randomized Experiments Suppose an Oversimplified Epistemology

To philosophers of science, positivism connotes a rejection of realism, the formulation of theories in mathematical form, the primacy of prediction over explanation, and the belief that entities do not exist independently of their measurement. This epistemology has long been discredited. When many educational researchers use the word "positivism," they seem to mean something else: quantification and hypothesis-testing, two essential components of experimentation. Educational evaluators lean heavily on Thomas Kuhn's work for justifying the rejection of a positivist method like experimentation.[8]

Kuhn argued two things of relevance. First is his claim about the "incommensurability of theories"—the notion that theories cannot be formulated so specifically that definitive falsification results. Second is his claim about the "theory-ladenness of observations"—the notion that all

7. Cronbach (1982).
8. Kuhn (1970).

measures are impregnated with researchers' theories, hopes, wishes, and expectations, thus undermining their neutrality for discriminating between truth claims. In refuting the possibility of totally explicit theories and totally neutral observations, Kuhn's work was interpreted as undermining science in general and random assignment in particular. This is why educational evaluators often cite his writings and those of philosophers like Imre Lakatos, Rom Harre, and Paul Feyerabend, whose views on these issues partly overlap with Kuhn's. Also often cited are those sociologists of science whose research reveals laboratory scientists whose on-the-job behavior deviates markedly from scientific norms.[9] All these references are designed to illustrate that meta-science has demystified positivist science, revealing it to be a very naked emperor.

This epistemological critique is overly simplistic. Even if observations are never theory-neutral, this does not deny that many observations have stubbornly reoccurred, whatever the researcher's predilections. As theories replace each other, most fact-like statements from the older theory are incorporated into the newer one, surviving the change in theoretical superstructure. Even if there are no "facts" we can independently know to be certain, there are still many propositions with such a high degree of facticity that they can be confidently treated as though they were true. For practicing experimenters, the trick is to make sure that observations are not impregnated with a single theory. This entails building multiple theories into one's collection of relevant observations, especially the understandings of one's theoretical opponents. It also means valuing independent replications of causal claims, provided the replications do not share the same direction of bias.[10] Kuhn's work complicates what a "fact" means, but it does not deny that some claims to a fact-like status are very strong.

We concede that Kuhn is probably also correct that theoretical statements are never definitively tested, including statements about the effects of an educational program.[11] But this does not mean that individual experiments fail to probe theories and causal hypotheses. When a study produces negative results, for example, the program developers (and other advocates) are likely to present methodological and substantive contingencies that might have changed the experimental result—perhaps

9. See, for example, Latour and Woolgar (1979).
10. Cook (1985).
11. Quine (1951, 1969).

if a different outcome measure had been used or a different population examined. Subsequent studies can probe these contingency formulations and, if they again prove negative, lead to yet another round of probes of whatever more complicated contingency hypotheses have emerged to explain the latest disconfirmation. After a time, this process runs out of steam, so particularistic are the contingencies that remain to be examined. It is as though the following consensus emerges: The program was demonstrably not effective under many conditions, and those that remain to be examined are so circumscribed that the reform will not be worth much even if it does turn out to be effective under these conditions.[12] Kuhn is correct that this process is social and not exclusively logical; and he is correct that it arises because the underlying program theory is not sufficiently explicit that it can be definitively confirmed or rejected. But the reality of elastic theory does not mean that decisions about causal hypotheses are only social and so are devoid of all empirical or logical content.

However, critics of the experiment have not been interested in developing a nonpositivist epistemological justification for experiments. Instead, they have turned their attention to developing alternative methods based on quite different epistemological assumptions. Most of these assumptions have led to stressing qualitative methods over quantitative ones and to hypothesis discovery over hypothesis testing.[13] But others have sought to trace whether the mediating processes specified in the substantive theory of a program actually occur in the time sequence predicted.[14] We analyze these alternatives to random assignment later. But for now, we should acknowledge some of the other theoretical attacks made on random assignment.

Objection 3: Randomized Experiments Are Not Suited to Organizations as Complex as Those in the American Educational System

The American educational system is complex, characterized by an intricate web of politicians, bureaucrats, professional associations, and

12. See Kuhn (1970).

13. See, for example, Guba and Lincoln (1982); Stake (1967); Cronbach (1982); Cronbach and others (1980); House (1993); Fetterman (1984).

14. Connell and others (1995); Chen (1990).

unions, as well as by many school districts, schools, and classrooms, as well as by an array of social relationships within schools and classrooms. The following beliefs seem to be widespread:

—Fundamental change in schooling requires a political consensus that is often elusive, given the countervailing interests of political actors.

—Each unit, be it a district, school, or even classroom, is so complex and established in its structure and functions that it is difficult to implement any changes that will modify its central functions.

—Each organization is so distinctive in its goals and culture that the same change attempt will lead to quite variable responses, depending on a school's history, organization, personnel, and politics.

—Change ideas should come from the creative blending of many different kinds of knowledge—deep historical and ethnographic insight into the district or school under study, craft knowledge about what is likely to improve this particular school or district, and the application of existing general theories of organizational change.[15] Experimental results are rarely part of any story about changing environments as complex as these and are never central to it.

Most educational evaluators see themselves at the forefront of a post-positivist, democratic, and craft-based model of knowledge growth that is superior to the elitist scientific model that they believe fails to create knowledge that school staff can actually use to improve their practice. From this perspective, causal knowledge from experiments will obscure each school's uniqueness, oversimplify the multivariate and nonlinear nature of full explanation, overlook the mostly direct ways in which politics structures educational reform, and be naive about the highly indirect ways in which social science is used for change, if it is used at all.

We are more than willing to admit that each school district, school, and classroom is unique. Nevertheless, many commonalities exist. All schools teach approximately the same material until high school. They all want to socialize young people, and they all involve essentially the same set of actors: administrators, teachers, children, parents, and other local supporters. Finer subdivisions between types of schools enhance the similarity even more, as when poor inner-city schools are compared to each other instead of being lumped in with all the other schools. Randomized experiments can be designed to capitalize on general similarities between

15. Lindblom and Cohen (1980).

schools, often by restricting their implementation to schools of a given type—for example, suburban ones. Or experiments can be arranged to contrast classrooms from within the same school, thus enhancing even more the similarity between units.

However, similarity is not a requirement for experiments. Heterogeneity between units requires only that more attention be paid to ensuring that the sampling design of an experiment allows researchers to determine if a given change attempt is effective across the expected range of variation in units. Statistical power must be sufficient to detect the main effects of treatment, despite all the heterogeneity. And it is even more desirable if the power also allows testing whether treatment effectiveness varies by a particular type of district, school, or classroom. The fact that each unit is undeniably unique does not entail rejecting random assignment. Rather, it calls for careful consideration of the types of units to which generalization is sought and for ensuring that the sample size is large enough for reliable estimation of treatment effects.

Objection 4: Random Assignment Is Premature until a Good Theory of the Program and Its Mediating Processes Has Been Developed

Some scholars maintain that using random assignment often (if not mostly) is premature since it requires: (1) an intervention based on strong substantive theory, (2) well-managed schools, (3) implementation quality that does not vary much between units assigned to the same intervention, and (4) implementation that is faithful to the theory of the program being evaluated. Unfortunately, these conditions are not often met in education. Schools tend to be large, complex social organizations characterized by multiple simultaneously occurring programs, disputatious factions within a school, and conflicting stakeholder goals. Management is all too often weak and removed from classroom practice, and day-to-day politics swamps effective program planning and monitoring. So, many reform initiatives are implemented highly variably across districts, schools, classrooms, and students. Indeed, when several different educational models are contrasted in the same study, the between-model variation is usually small when compared with the variation between schools implementing the same model.[16] It is not possible to assume either standard program

16. Rivlin and Timpane (1975); Stebbins and others (1978).

implementation or total fidelity to program theory.[17] To those whose operating premise is that schools are complex social organizations with severe management and implementation problems, randomized experiments must seem premature.

But random assignment does not require well-specified program theories, or good management, or standard implementation, or treatments that are totally faithful to program theory, even though these features definitely make evaluation much easier. Experiments primarily protect against bias in causal estimates, and only secondarily against the imprecision in these estimates due to extraneous variation. So, the complexity of schools leads to the need for randomized experiments with larger sample sizes. Otherwise, experiments in complex settings tend toward no-difference findings. But researchers rarely let such no-difference findings stand as the sole or major conclusion. Instead, they stratify schools by the quality of program implementation and then relate this variation in implementation to variation in planned outcomes. Internal analyses like these make any resulting causal claim the product of the very nonexperimental analyses whose weaknesses random assignment is designed to overcome. This suggests orienting the research focus so as to (1) avoid the need for such internal analyses by having the initial sample sizes reflect the expected extraneous variation, (2) anticipate specific sources of variation and to reduce their influence via modifications to the sampling design or through measurement and statistical manipulation, and (3) study implementation quality as a dependent variable in order to learn which types of schools and teachers implement the intervention better. Variable implementation has implications for budgets, sample sizes, and the relative utility of research questions. But it does not by itself invalidate randomization.

We must also remember that the aim of experiments is not to explain all sources of variation. It is to probe whether a reform idea makes a marginal improvement in staff or student performance over and above all the other background changes that occur. It is not an argument against random assignment to claim that many reform theories are underspecified, some schools are chaotic, treatment implementation is highly variable, and treatments are not completely theory-faithful. Random assignment does not have to be postponed while we learn more about school management and implementation. However, the more we know about these

17. Berman and McLaughlin (1978).

matters the better we can randomize, the more reliable effects are likely to be, and the more experiments there will be that make management and implementation issues worthy objects of study within the experiments themselves. No advocate of random assignment who assumes treatment homogeneity or setting invariance will be credible in education. School-level variation is large and may be greater than in other fields where experiments are routine. So, it is a reasonable and politic working assumption to assert that the complexity of schools requires large sample experiments and careful measurement of implementation quality and other intervening variables, plus careful documentation of all sources of extraneous variation influencing schools. Also, analyses like those of Joshua Angrist, Guido Imbrens, and Donald Rubin are required that first describe the effects of the treatment respecting the original treatment assignment but then subsequently analyze the effects of the treatment actually received, with the original random assignment being used as an instrumental variable to answer the second kind of question.[18] Black box experiments are out. But eliminating them does not eliminate the need for random assignment per se.

Objection 5: Random Assignment Is Politically Infeasible

Another objection to random assignment in education is that it is politically infeasible. Fearing negative reactions from parents and staff, many school district officials (and union representatives) do not like the focused inequities in treatment that random assignment generates. They prefer it when individual schools choose which changes they will make, or when change is made district-wide and so applies to all schools. Principals and other school staff share these same preferences and have additional administrative concerns, especially about disrupting ongoing routines. And then there are the usual ethical concerns about withholding potentially helpful treatments from those in need. In this climate, random assignment is all the more difficult to mount.[19]

In implementing randomization, political will and disciplinary culture are crucial. Random assignment is common in the health sciences because it is institutionally supported there—by funding agencies, publishing outlets, graduate training programs and the tradition of clinical trials. Con-

18. Angrist, Imbrens, and Rubin (1996).
19. Gueron (1999).

trast this with education. Reports from the Office of Educational Research and Improvement (OERI) are supposed to identify effective practices in primary and secondary schools. But neither the work of Maris Vinovskis nor our own haphazard reading of OERI reports suggests any privilege being accorded to random assignment.[20] Indeed, a recent report on bilingual education repeated old saws about the impossibility of doing experiments and the adequacy of quasi-experimental alternatives. At a recent foundation meeting on teaching and learning, the representative of a reforming state governor spoke about a list of best educational practices his state had developed that was being disseminated to all state schools. He did not care, and he believed no governors care, about the technical quality of the research generating these lists. The main concern was to have a consensus of education researchers endorsing each practice. When asked how many of these best practices depended on results from randomized experiments, he guessed it would be zero. Several nationally known educational researchers were present and agreed with this. No one appeared to be distressed. From experiences like these we surmise that so little will to experiment exists in education because of the belief that opportunities for such studies are rare, and there is little need for them anyway. Less noxious alternatives exist already whose internal validity is adequate for credible (if not valid) conclusions. So long as such beliefs are widespread among the elite of educational research, there can never be the kind of pan-support for experimentation that is currently found in the health sciences.

Yet, there is some hint that things may be changing. Prevention studies tap into the same experimental research culture of the health sciences and are routinely conducted as randomized experiments in school settings. In preschool education there is already a high percentage of experiments that are the product of (1) congressional requirements to assign at random, as with Early Head Start, the Comprehensive Child Care Program and the plan for the new national Head Start study; (2) the high visibility of such experiments as the Perry Preschool Program,[21] the Abecedarian project,[22] and Olds' home visiting nurse program;[23] and (3) the involvement of researchers trained in psychology, human development, medicine, and

20. Vinovskis (1998).
21. Schweinhart, Barnes, and Weikart (1993).
22. See, for example, Campbell and Ramey (1995).
23. Olds and others (1997).

microeconomics, fields where random assignment is highly valued, unlike in education. Finally, the past three decades have seen widespread acceptance of random assignment for testing the effectiveness of social interventions, and the U.S. Congress specifies ever more frequently that such assignment be used in studies of the effectiveness of federally funded programs.[24] All this suggests that randomized experiments may also move toward the center in educational research.

Objection 6: Random Assignment Has Been Tried and Failed

Some detractors argue that randomized experiments have been tried in education and that they have failed there. Educational researchers led the flurry of social experimentation that took place at the end of the 1960s. Evaluations of Head Start,[25] Follow Through,[26] and Title I[27] concluded that there were few, if any, positive effects and there might even be some negative ones. These disappointing results engendered considerable dispute about methods, and many educational evaluators concluded that quantitative evaluation was not useful and so they turned to other methods, such as intensive case studies. Other scholars responded differently, stressing the need to study school management and program implementation in the belief that poor management and implementation had led to the disappointing results.[28]

But none of the most heavily criticized studies involved random assignment. Cronbach and his colleagues re-analyzed some studies from the long lists Riecken and Boruch, and Boruch, had generated in order to demonstrate the feasibility of randomized experiments in complex field settings.[29] In his critique, Cronbach paid particular attention to the Vera Institute's Bail Bond Experiment[30] and to the New Jersey Negative Income Tax Experiment.[31] He was able to show to his own and his followers' satisfaction that each was flawed both in how it was implemented

24. For one overview, see Greenberg and Shroder (1997).
25. Cicirelli and Associates (1969).
26. Stebbins and others (1978).
27. Wargo and others (1972).
28. Berman and McLaughlin (1978); Elmore and McLaughlin (1983); Cohen and Garet (1975).
29. Cronbach and others (1980); Riecken and Boruch (1974); and Boruch (1974).
30. Ares, Rankin, and Sturz (1963).
31. Rossi and Lyall (1976).

as a randomized experiment and in the degree of correspondence achieved between its sampling particulars and the likely conditions of its application as new policy. For these reasons primarily, the case was made that the lists of experiments did not constitute a compelling justification for evaluating educational innovations experimentally.

However, the studies Cronbach analyzed were not from education. Although there were many small experiments on highly specific teaching and learning practices, we know of only three randomized experiments on "large" educational topics available at the time, and only one of these dealt with school-age children. One experiment was on Sesame Street in its second year;[32] another on the Perry Preschool Project,[33] and the third involved twelve youngsters randomly assigned to be in a desegregated school.[34] So, it was not accurate to claim in the 1970s that random assignment had been tried in education and had failed there.

Even so, it may not be any easier to implement randomized experiments in schools than in the areas Cronbach and his colleagues did examine. Implementation shortfalls have arisen in many of the more recent experiments in education. Schools have sometimes dropped out of the different treatment conditions in different proportions, largely because a new principal wants to change what a predecessor recently did.[35] Even in the Tennessee class size study, it is striking that the number of classrooms in the final analysis differs by more than 20 percent across the three treatment conditions, though the original design may have called for more similar percentages.[36] Then, there are inadvertent treatment crossovers. In Cook et al.,[37] one principal in the treatment condition was married to someone teaching in a control school; a control principal really liked the treatment, learned more about it for himself, and tried to implement parts of it in his school; and one control schoolteacher was the daughter of a program official who visited her school several times to address the staff about strategies for improving the building. (Fortunately, these crossovers involved only three of twenty-three schools, and none entailed borrowing the treatment's most distinctive and presumptively powerful components.) In the Tennessee experiment, classrooms of different size were

32. Bogatz and Ball (1971).
33. Schweinhart and others (1993).
34. Zdep (1971).
35. See, for example, Cook, Hunt, and Murphy (1999).
36. Finn and Achilles (1990); Mosteller, Light, and Sachs (1996).
37. Cook and others (1999).

compared, but within the same school rather than between schools. How did teachers assigned to larger classes interpret the fact that some of their colleagues in the same building were teaching smaller classes? Were they dispirited and so tried less? All experiments have to struggle with creating and maintaining random assignment, treatment integrity and treatment independence. These things do not come easily. Yet it is impossible to claim that randomized experiments have been tried in education and have failed there.

Objection 7: Random Assignment Entails Trade-Offs Not Worth Making

Randomized experiments entail trade-offs many educational researchers believe are not worth making. Experiments place priority on unbiased answers to descriptive causal questions—internal validity. To draw such causal conclusions in the conditions of likely application—external validity is given lower priority. Cronbach has strongly argued against the assertion that internal validity is the sine qua non of experimentation.[38] He contends that experiments are often limited in time and space and rely on a biased subset of schools that are willing to surrender choice over which treatment they are to receive and to tolerate whatever operational burdens follow from the need to measure implementation, mediating processes and individual outcomes. What kinds of schools are these volunteer schools? Are they fundamentally different from others? Would it not be preferable, Cronbach asks, to sample from a more representative population of schools even if less certain causal inferences have to result from this? Is internal validity really more important than external validity?

There is no way to solve this age-old dilemma. Random assignment creates a probabilistic equivalence between groups at pretest time, irrespective of how these groups were originally selected. Thus it has no necessary implications for representativeness. Representativeness depends on how units were originally sampled and not on how they got to be in different treatment groups once they were in a study. Of course, it is possible to have experiments with units that are randomly selected prior to being randomly assigned. But these are very rare in any field. And when

38. Cronbach (1982). The assertion is by Campbell and Stanley (1963).

experiments last any time at all, some schools usually drop out and compromise the representativeness originally achieved. But the biggest problem is with how units get to be in the study in the first place. An experimenter can assign schools to whatever conditions she wants, but unless principals and teachers want to cooperate with the experimenter's decision, the experimenter has no way to enforce cooperation. This is why experimenters usually restrict their studies to schools willing to tolerate random assignment and measurement, omitting other schools or using nonexperimental designs in them. However, critics note: Why strive for a gain in internal validity that is likely to be marginal when the loss in external validity is likely to be considerable in relation to nonexperimental alternatives?

The question is a fair one. Advocates of random assignment assert that the alternatives Cronbach prefers produce causal claims that are much worse than those from experiments, thus significantly increasing the chance of ignoring educational reforms that work and of promoting reforms that do not. While the terms of the debate are so imprecise that they preclude a clear answer to Cronbach's question, we should not forget that the external validity being sought concerns the generalization of a causal claim. Critics of random assignment want assurances that a specific causal claim applies broadly within education or that we can clearly delineate its specific realms of application. But does there not have to be a causal claim before it is sensible to raise the issue of its generalization? When the entity to be generalized is a causal claim, is it not best specified through random assignment so that we can be more assured of what we want to generalize?

Of course, steps can and should be taken to minimize the external validity loss. Units that will not agree to random assignment can be studied some other way, with the best available analyses being used to see if the results are generally in the same direction as the experimental findings. Alternatively, past studies with nonvolunteer samples might be carefully scrutinized to see if there are credible correspondences with the experimental results. And if the population is known for which generalization is needed, and if there are some measures of this population shared with the sample, then sample weights can be created that allow extrapolation from the experimental results to the wider population. In all these instances, the extrapolation is more problematic than the experiment itself, making it important to display the experimental results separately—since they depend on fewer untested assumptions.

Objection 8: Random Assignment Is Unethical

Randomized experiments involve withholding possibly beneficial treatments from people who need or deserve them, and this is unpalatable to many. For instance, David Fetterman questioned the ethics of assigning disadvantaged high school dropouts to a no-treatment control when they had expressed interest in a remedial "second-chance" treatment.[39] After all, this second chance might really have been their last chance.

The other side of the argument defends randomization by stressing that researchers frequently do not know which treatment is more effective. Otherwise, they would not do the study. Even when a treatment has a past empirical track record, it is often based on small sample sizes and weaker designs, with only slight effects favoring one treatment. That is why a clinical trial is needed—to get larger samples, better designs, and more trustworthy outcome data. Indeed, a review of randomized trials with medical innovations has shown that the innovation produced better results than the standard treatment only about half the time.[40] Chalmers makes a similar point: "One has only to review the graveyard of discarded therapies to discover how many patients might have benefited from being randomly assigned to a control group."[41] So, presumptions about effectiveness in medicine do not routinely translate into evidence of effectiveness. If it were to be the same in education, there is no guarantee that students will do better from interventions that appear promising than without them.

Even when the chance of a treatment being harmful is slim, ethical arguments for the use of randomized experiments are forceful. This is clearly the case when scarce resources make it impossible to provide treatment to everyone, and also when various alternative treatments are compared to each other and no control group is needed. In the former case, some participants must be deprived of the scarce treatment, and the question is only by what mechanism this should occur. In such situations, it helps if the investigator can offer to provide controls with the treatment, or a refinement of it, at a later date. Done properly, this constitutes a crossover design in which control group participants are given the treatment at the end of the study and the treatment participants become the

39. Fetterman (1982).
40. Gilbert, McPeek, and Mosteller (1977).
41. Chalmers (1968, p. 910).

new post-crossover controls.[42] However, this solution works best when the problem being treated will not do permanent damage because of being in the control group. Thus if a disadvantaged high school dropout with few options is denied entry into a second-chance educational program, this might lead to lifelong damage. However, if there are no indications that the problem will get worse, then delayed access to the treatment by controls ensures that everyone will finally receive the treatment if it is useful.

Another ethical objection notes that, in actual research practice, the choice is usually between assignment by lottery versus assignment by need or merit. The latter mechanisms have much to recommend them. The strongest case for assignment by need is when it is already known that a particular treatment is effective in meeting that need, making it difficult to imagine any circumstances under which it would be ethical to withhold a proven compensatory education program from students attending impoverished inner-city schools. Then, assignment by need seems the only fair alternative. Related examples pertaining to merit are also easy to find, as with National Merit Scholarships being given for high performance on the National Merit Exam. The problem here is with the word "proven," especially in a field like education that relies so heavily on weak quasi-experimental or nonexperimental designs. In practice, professional judgment and political convenience often masquerade behind claims that a proven alternative exists for the most needy or meritorious.

Sometimes, though, there is excessive demand for programs for the needy or meritorious—if not universally, then at least at some sites as with Head Start. Indeed, program operators routinely "deny" services to needy families every year as they decide which families to include. Complicating matters here is that decision about the most needy or meritorious involve subjective decisions. Even if a scale does exist and is used, exceptions often are made since need and merit are also in the eye of the beholder. In actual practice, assignment based on need or merit may be more biased than when randomization occurs. More important, exceptions for some persons can be made even within a randomized experiment. For instance, the random assignment might be restricted to those in the middle part of the need distribution where a small difference in score is as likely to be due to measurement error as a valid difference. Those

42. Fleiss (1986); Pocock (1983).

with greatest need are thus guaranteed a certain number of slots and those with little need would be excluded. Ethical objections must be considered when conducting randomized experiments. Informed consent and other organizational guidelines are a "must." But random assignment may not be any more ethically biased than need or merit assignment is as it is carried out in current educational practice.

Objection 9: Randomized Experiments Are Not Needed Because Alternatives Are Available That Are as Good

It is a truism that no social science method will die, whatever its imperfections, unless a demonstrably better or simpler method is available to replace it. Most researchers who evaluate educational reforms believe that superior alternatives to the experiment already exist, and so they are willing to let it die. These methods are superior, they believe, because they are more acceptable to school personnel, because they reduce enough uncertainty about causation to be useful, and because they are relevant to a broader array of important issues than causation alone. Although no single alternative is universally recommended, intensive case studies, theory-based evaluations, and quasi-experimental designs are among the methods most often preferred.

Intensive Case Studies

A central belief of advocates of qualitative methods is that the techniques they prefer are uniquely suited to providing feedback on the many different kinds of questions and issues relevant to a school reform—questions about the quality of problem formulation, the quality of program theory, the quality of program implementation, the determinants of quality implementation, the proximal and distal effects on students, unanticipated side effects, teacher and student subgroup effects, and ways of assessing the relevance of findings to different stakeholder groups. This flexibility for generating knowledge about so many different topics is something that randomized experiments cannot match. Their function is much more restricted, and the assignment process on which they depend can even impose limits to the generalization of a study's results.

The advantages of case study methods are considerable. However, we value them as adjuncts to experiments rather than as alternatives to them. Case study methods complement experiments when a causal question is clearly central and when it is not clear how successful program implementation will be, why implementation shortfalls may occur, what unexpected effects are likely to emerge, how respondents interpret the questions asked of them, what the casual mediating processes are, and so on. Since it will be rare for any of these issues to be clear, qualitative methods have a central role to play in experimental work on educational interventions. They cannot be afterthoughts.

Advocates for qualitative methods also contend that such methods reduce some uncertainty about causal connections. Cronbach agrees that this might be less than in an experiment, but he contends that journalists, historians, and ethnographers nonetheless regularly learn the truth about what caused what.[43] Needed for a causal diagnosis are only a relevant hypothesis, observations that can be made about the implications of this hypothesis, reflection on these observations, reformations of the original hypotheses, a new round of observations, a new round of reflections on these observations, and so on, until closure is eventually reached. Theorists of ethnography have long advocated such an empirical and ultimately falsificationist procedure, claiming that the results achieved from it will be richer than those from black box experiments because ethnography requires close attention to the unfolding of explanatory processes at different stages in a program's development.[44]

We do not doubt that hard thought and nonexperimental methods can reduce some of the uncertainty about cause. We also believe that they will sometimes reduce all the reasonable uncertainty, though it will be difficult to know when this happens. However, we question whether intensive, qualitative case studies can generally reduce as much uncertainty about cause as a randomized experiment. This is because such methods rarely involve a convincing causal counterfactual. Typically, they do not have comparison groups, which makes it difficult to know how a treatment group would have changed in the absence of the reform under analysis. Adding control groups helps, but unless they are randomly created it will not be clear whether the two groups would have changed at similar rates over time. Whether intensive case methods reduce enough uncertainty about cause to be generally useful is a poorly specified proposition we cannot answer well, though it is central to Cronbach's case. Still, it forces us to note that experiments are only justified when a very high standard of uncertainty reduction is required about a causal claim.

43. Cronbach (1982).
44. See, for example, Becker (1958).

Theory-Based Evaluations

It is fashionable in many foundations and some scholarly circles to espouse a nonexperimental theory of evaluation for use in complex social settings such as communities and schools.[45] The method depends on (1) explicating the substantive theory behind a reform initiative and detailing all the flow-through relationships that should occur if the intended intervention is to impact on some major distal outcome, such as achievement gains; (2) measuring each of the constructs specified in the substantive theory; and (3) analyzing the data as coming from a causal model in order to assess the extent to which the postulated relationships have actually occurred through time. For shorter time periods, the data analysis will involve only the first part of a postulated causal chain; but over longer periods the complete model might be involved. Obviously, this conception of evaluation places a primacy on highly specific substantive theory, high-quality measurement, and the valid analysis of multivariate explanatory processes as they unfold in time.

Several features make it seem as though theory-based evaluation can function as an alternative to random assignment. First, it is not necessary to construct a causal counterfactual through random assignment or creating closely matched comparison groups. A study can involve only the group experiencing a treatment. Second, obtaining data patterns congruent with program theory is assumed to indicate the validity of that theory, an epistemology that does not require explicitly rejecting alternative explanations—merely demonstrating a match between the predicted and obtained data. Finally, the theory approach does not depend for its utility on attaining the end points typically specified in educational research—usually a cause-effect relationship involving student performance. Instead, if any part of the program theory is corroborated or disconfirmed at any point along the causal chain, this knowledge can then be used for interim purposes: to inform program staff, to argue for maintaining the program, to provide a rationale for believing the program could be effective if more distal criteria were to be collected, to defend against premature summative evaluations that declare a program ineffective before sufficient time has elapsed for all the processes to occur that are presumed necessary for ultimate change. So, no requirement

45. Connell and others (1995).

exists to measure the effect end points most often valued in educational studies.

Few advocates of experimentation will argue against the need for the greater use of substantive theory in evaluation; and since most experiments can accommodate more process measurement, it follows they will be improved thereby. Such measurement will make it possible to probe, first, whether the intervention led to changes in the theoretically specified intervening processes and, second, whether these processes could then have plausibly caused changes in distal outcomes. The first of these tests will be unbiased because it relates each step in the causal model to the planned treatment contrast. But the second test will entail selection bias if it depends only on stratifying units according to the extent the postulated theoretical processes have occurred. Still, quasi-experimental analyses of the second stage are worth doing provided that their results are clearly labeled as more tentative than the results of planned experimental contrasts. The utility of measuring and analyzing theoretical intervening processes is beyond dispute; the issue is whether such measurement and analysis can alone provide an alternative to random assignment.

We are skeptical.[46] First, a program theory is not always very explicit. Moreover, it could be made more explicit in several different ways, not just one. Is there a single theory of a program, or several possible versions of it? Second, many of these theories seem to be too linear in their flow of influence, rarely incorporating reciprocal feedback loops or external contingencies that might moderate the entire flow of influence. It is all a little bit too neat for our more chaotic world. Third, few theories are specific about timelines, specifying how long it should take for a given process to affect some proximal indicator. Without such specifications, it is difficult to know whether the next step in the model has not yet occurred or will never occur because the theory is wrong in this particular aspect. Fourth, the method places a great premium on knowing not just when to measure, but how to measure. Failure to corroborate the model could be the result of partially invalid measures as opposed to the invalidity of the theory itself—though researchers can protect against this with more valid measures. Fifth is the epistemological problem that many different models can usually be fitted to any single pattern of data, implying that causal modeling is more valid when multiple competing

46. Cook (2000).

models are tested against each other rather than when a single model is tested.[47]

The biggest problem though, is the absence of a valid counterfactual to inform us about what would have happened to students or teachers had there been no treatment. As a result, it is impossible to decide whether the events observed in a study genuinely result from the intervention or whether they would have occurred anyway. One way to guard against this is with "signed causes," predicting a multivariate pattern among variables that is so special it could not have occurred except for the reform.[48] But signed causes depend on the availability of much well-validated substantive theory and very high quality measurement.[49] So, a better safeguard is to have at least one comparison group, and the best comparison group is a randomly constructed one. That means we are back again with random assignment. Theory-based evaluations are useful as complements to randomized experiments, but not as alternatives to them.

Quasi Experiments

Quasi experiments are identical to experiments in their purpose and in most details of their structure, the defining difference being the absence of random assignment and hence of a demonstrably valid causal counterfactual. Quasi experimentation is nothing more than the search, more through design than statistical adjustment techniques, to create the best possible approximation(s) to the missing counterfactual. To this end, there are invocations to create stably matched comparison groups; to use age or sibling controls; to measure behavior at several time points before a treatment begins, perhaps even creating a time-series of observations; to seek out situations where units are assigned to treatment solely because of their score on some scale; to assign the same treatment to different stably matched groups at different times so that they can alternate in their functions as treatment and control groups; and to build multiple outcome variables into studies, some of which should theoretically be influenced by a treatment and others not.[50] These are the most important elements from which quasi-experimental designs are created through a mixing

47. Glymour, Scheines, Spirtes, and Kelly (1987).
48. Scriven (1976).
49. Cook and Campbell (1979).
50. Corrin and Cook (1998); Shadish and Cook (1999); Shadish, Cook, and Campbell (2002).

process that tailors the design achieved to the nature of the research problem and the resources available.

However good they are, quasi experiments are always second best to randomized experiments. In some quarters, "quasi experiment" has been used promiscuously to connote any study that is not a true experiment, that seeks to test a causal hypothesis, and that has any type of nonequivalent control group or pretreatment observation. Yet some such studies have been labeled as "generally causally uninterpretable."[51] Many of the studies educational researchers call "quasi experiments" are of this last causally uninterpretable kind and lag far behind the state of the art. Reading them indicates that little thought has been given to the quality of the match when creating control groups, to the possibility of multiple hypothesis tests rather than a single one, to the possibility of generating data from several pretreatment time points rather than a single one, or to having several comparison groups per treatment, with some initially outperforming the treatment group and others underperforming it.

Although it is true that the results of a well-designed quasi experiment may not differ substantially from the results of a randomized experiment, the average quasi experiment in education seems to be lamentable in the confidence it inspires in the causal conclusions drawn.[52] Recent advances in the design and analysis of quasi experiments are not getting into educational research, where they are sorely needed. Nonetheless, the best estimate of any quasi experiment's internal validity will always be to compare its results with those from a randomized experiment on the same topic. When this is done systematically, it seems that quasi experiments are less efficient than randomized experiments, providing more variable answers from study to study.[53] So, in areas like education where few studies exist on most of the reform ideas being currently debated, randomized experiments are particularly needed and it will take fewer of them to arrive at what might be the same answer as better quasi experiments might achieve at a later date. But irrespective of such speculation, we can be sure of one thing: that in the eyes of nearly all scholarly observers the answers obtained from experiments will be much more credible than those obtained from quasi experiments.

51. Campbell and Stanley (1963); Cook and Campbell (1979).
52. Boruch (1975).
53. Lipsey and Wilson (1993).

Conclusion

In some quarters, particularly medical ones, the randomized experiment is considered the causal "gold standard." It is clearly not that in educational contexts, given the difficulties with implementing and maintaining randomly created groups, with the sometimes incomplete implementation of treatment particulars, with the borrowing of some treatment particulars by control group units, and with the limitations to external validity that often follow from how random assignment is achieved. A more modest case for random assignment in education is that (1) it provides a logically more valid causal counterfactual than any of its plausible alternatives, (2) it almost certainly provides a more efficient counterfactual in that the few studies conducted to date show that where randomized experiments and their alternatives converge on the same answer, randomized experiments do so more quickly, and (3) it provides a counterfactual that is more credible in nearly all academic circles and increasingly more so in educational policy ones. Taken together, these are compelling rationales for using random assignment even if some external validity losses are incurred thereby.

The objections to random assignment make an impressively long list. It is no surprise, therefore, that most graduates from doctoral programs in educational evaluation are sure of the limits of random assignment and also believe that alternatives to it exist that are much more flexible for answering a wider range of interesting questions—about who is exposed to an educational innovation, how it is implemented, what effects it has, why it is effective, and for whom it is effective. Since experiments prioritize on only one of these questions, it is important to stress the need to extend the measurement, sampling, and analysis frameworks of experiments so as to get at this wider range of interesting questions, but without compromising the random assignment that makes quality answers to effectiveness questions possible. This is a lesson experimenters can learn from their critics.

However, none of the objections that the critics have raised is fundamental in undermining experimentation in education. All the objections have complete or partial refutations. And where an objection cannot be totally refuted, a corrective can usually be built into the experiment. The objections to random assignment, while very credible, are just not valid.

References

Angrist, Joshua D., Guido W. Imbrens, and Donald B. Rubin. 1996. "Identification of Causal Effects Using Instrumental Variables." *Journal of the American Statistical Association* 91: 444–62.

Ares, C. E., A. Rankin, and H. Sturz. 1963. "The Manhattan Bail Project: An Interim Report on the Use of Pre-Trial Parole." *New York University Law Review* 38: 67–95.

Becker, Howard S. 1958. "Problems of Inference and Proof in Participant Observation." *American Sociological Review* 23: 652–60.

Berman, Paul, and Milbrey Wallin McLaughlin. 1978. *Federal Programs Supporting Educational Change.* Vol. 8: *Factors Affecting Implementation and Continuation.* Santa Monica, Calif.: Rand Corporation.

Bogatz, Gerry Ann, and Samuel Ball. 1972. *The Impact of "Sesame Street" on Children's First School Experience.* Princeton, N.J.: Educational Testing Service.

Boruch, Robert F. 1974. "Bibliography: Illustrated Randomized Field Experiments for Program Planning and Evaluation." *Evaluation* 2: 83–87.

———. 1975. "On Common Contentions about Randomized Field Experiments." In *Experimental Testing of Public Policy: The Proceedings of the 1974 Social Science Research Council Conference on Social Experiments,* edited by Robert F. Boruch and Henry W. Riecken, 108–45. Boulder, Colo.: Westview Press.

Campbell, Donald T. 1957. "Factors Relevant to the Validity of Experiments in Social Settings." *Psychological Bulletin* 54: 297–312.

Campbell, Donald T., and Julian C. Stanley. 1963. *Experimental and Quasi-Experimental Designs for Research.* Chicago: Rand-McNally.

Campbell, Frances A., and Craig T. Ramey. 1995. "Cognitive and School Outcomes for High-Risk African American Students at Middle Adolescence: Positive Effects of Early Intervention." *American Educational Research Journal* 32 (4): 743–72.

Chalmers, Thomas C. 1968. "Prophylactic Treatment of Wilson's Disease." *New England Journal of Medicine* 278: 910–11.

Chen, Huey-Tsyh. 1990. "Theory-Driven Evaluations." *Sage* 10: 95–103 (Newbury Park, Calif.).

Cicirelli, Victor G. and Associates 1969. *The Impact of Head Start: An Evaluation of the Effects of Head Start on Children's Cognitive and Affective Development.* Vols. 1 and 2: *A Report to the Office of Economic Opportunity.* Ohio University and Westinghouse Learning Corporation.

Cohen, David K., and Michael S. Garet. 1975. "Reforming Educational Policy with Applied Social Research." *Harvard Educational Review* 45.

Collingwood, Robin George.1940. *An Essay on Metaphysics.* Oxford: Clarendon Press.

Connell, James P., Anne C. Kubisch, Lisbeth B. Schorr, and Carol H. Weiss, eds. 1995. *New Approaches to Evaluating Community Initiatives: Concepts, Methods and Contexts.* Washington: Aspen Institute.

Cook, Thomas D. 1985. "Post-Positivist Critical Multiplism." In *Social Science and Social Policy*, edited by R. L. Shotland and M. M. Mark, 21–62. Beverly Hills, Calif.: Sage Publications.

———. 2000. "The False Choice between Theory-Based Evaluation and Experimentation." *New Directions in Evaluation: Challenges and Opportunities in Program Theory Evaluation* 87: 27–34.

Cook, Thomas D., and Donald T. Campbell. 1979. *Quasi-Experimentation: Design and Analysis Issues for Field Settings*. Houghton Mifflin.

Cook, Thomas D., H. David Hunt, and Robert F. Murphy. 1999. "Comer's School Development Program in Chicago: A Theory-Based Evaluation." Working Paper. Northwestern University, Institute for Policy Research.

Corrin, William J., and Thomas D. Cook. 1998. "Design Elements of Quasi-Experimentation." *Advances in Educational Productivity* 7: 35–57.

Cronbach, Lee Joseph. 1982. *Designing Evaluations of Educational and Social Programs*. San Francisco, Calif.: Jossey-Bass.

Cronbach, Lee Joseph, S. R. Ambron, S. M. Dornbusch, R. D. Hess, R. C. Hornik, D. C. Phillips, D. F. Walker, and S. S. Weiner. 1980. *Toward Reform of Program Evaluation*. San Francisco, Calif.: Jossey-Bass.

Elmore, Richard F., and Milbrey Wallin McLaughlin. 1983. "The Federal Role in Education: Learning from Experience." *Education and Urban Society* 15: 309–33.

Fetterman, David M. 1982. "Ibsen's Baths: Reactivity and Insensitivity." *Educational Evaluation and Policy Analysis* 4: 261–79.

———, ed. 1984. *Ethnography in Educational Evaluation*. Beverly Hills, Calif.: Sage Publications.

Finn, Jeremy D., and Charles M. Achilles. 1990. "Answers and Questions about Class Size: A Statewide Experiment." *American Educational Research Journal* 27 (3): 557–77.

Fisher, Ronald A. 1926. "The Arrangement of Field Experiments." *Journal of the Ministry of Agriculture of Great Britain* 33: 505–13.

Fleiss, Joseph L. 1986. *The Design and Analysis of Clinical Experiments*. Wiley.

Gasking, Douglas. 1955. "Causation and Recipes." *Mind* 64: 479–87.

Gilbert, John P., Bucknam McPeek, and Frederick Mosteller. 1977. "Statistics and Ethics in Surgery and Anesthesia." *Science* 198: 684–89.

Glymour, Clark N., Richard Scheines, Peter Spirtes, and Kevin Kelly. 1987. *Discovering Causal Structure: Artificial Intelligence, Philosophy of Science and Statistical Modeling*. Orlando, Fla.: Academic Press.

Greenberg, David, and Mark Shroder. 1997. *The Digest of Social Experiments*. 2d ed. Washington: Urban Institute Press.

Guba, Egon G., and Yvonna Lincoln. 1982. *Effective Evaluation*. San Francisco, Calif.: Jossey-Bass.

Gueron, Judith M. 1999. "The Politics of Random Assignment: Implementing Studies and Impacting Policy." Paper presented at the American Association of Arts and Sciences, Cambridge, Mass.

House, Ernest R. 1993. *Professional Evaluation: Social Impact and Political Consequences*. Newbury Park, Calif.: Sage Publications.

Kuhn, Thomas S. 1970. *The Structure of Scientific Revolutions.* 2d ed. University of Chicago Press.

Latour, Bruno, and Steve Woolgar. 1979. *Laboratory Life: The Construction of Scientific Facts.* Beverly Hills, Calif.: Sage Publications.

Lindblom, Charles E., and David K. Cohen. 1980. *Usable Knowledge.* Yale University Press.

Lipsey, Mark W., and David B. Wilson. 1993. "The Efficacy of Psychological, Educational, and Behavioral Treatment: Confirmation from Meta-Analysis." *American Psychologist* 1181–1209.

Mackie, John Leslie. 1974. *The Cement of the Universe.* Oxford University Press.

Mosteller, Frederick, Richard J. Light, and Jason A. Sachs. 1996. "Sustained Inquiry in Education: Lessons from Skill Grouping and Class Size." *Harvard Educational Review* 66: 797–842.

Olds, David L., John Eckenrode, Charles R. Henderson Jr., Harriet Kitzman, Jane Powers, Robert Cole, Kimberly Sidora, Pamela Morris, Lisa M. Pettitt, and Dennis Luckey. 1997. "Long-Term Effects of Home Visitation on Maternal Life Course and Child Abuse and Neglect." *Journal of the American Medical Association* 278 (8): 637–43.

Pocock, Stuart J. 1983. *Clinical Trials: A Practical Approach.* Wiley.

Quine, Willard Van Orman. 1951. "Two Dogmas of Empiricism." *Philosophical Review* 60: 20-43.

———. 1969. *Ontological Relativity and Other Essays.* Columbia University Press.

Riecken, Henry W., and Robert F. Boruch. 1974. *Social Experimentation: A Method for Planning and Evaluating Social Intervention.* New York: Academic Press.

Rivlin, Alice M., and P. Michael Timpane, eds. 1975. *Planned Variation in Education: Should We Give Up or Try Harder?* Brookings.

Rossi, Peter H., and Katharine C. Lyall. 1976. *Reforming Public Welfare: A Critique of the Negative Income Tax Experiment.* New York: Russell Sage Foundation.

Schweinhart, Lawrence J., Helen V. Barnes, David P. Weikart, with W. Steven Barnett and Ann S. Epstein. 1993. *Significant Benefits: The High/Scope Perry Preschool Study through Age 27.* Ypsilanti, Mich.: High/Scope Press.

Scriven, Michael. 1976. "Maximizing the Power of Causal Investigation: The Modus Operandi Method." In *Evaluation Studies Review Annual, 1,* edited by G. V. Glass, 101–18. Newbury Park, Calif.: Sage Publications.

Shadish, William R., and Thomas D. Cook. 1999. "Design Rules: More Steps towards a Complete Theory of Quasi-Experimentation." *Statistical Science* 294–300.

Shadish, William R., Thomas D. Cook, and Donald T. Campbell. 2002. *Experimental and Quasi-Experimental Designs for Generalized Causal Inference.* Boston: Houghton Mifflin.

Stake, Robert E. 1967. "The Countenance of Educational Evaluation." *Teachers College Record* 68: 523–40.

Stebbins, Linda B., Robert G. St. Pierre, Elizabeth C. Proper, Richard B. Anderson, and Thomas R. Cerba. 1978. "An Evaluation of Follow Through."

In *Evaluation Studies Review Annual, 3*, edited by Thomas D. Cook, 571–610. Beverly Hills, Calif.: Sage Publications.

Vinovskis, Maris A. 1998. *Changing Federal Strategies for Supporting Educational Research, Development and Statistics.* Washington: National Educational Research Policy and Priorities Board.

Wargo, Michael J., G. K. Tallmadge, D. D. Michaels, D. Lipe, and S. J. Morris. 1972. *ESEA Title I: A Reanalysis and Synthesis of Evaluation Data from Fiscal Year 1965 through 1970.* Final Report, Contract OEC-0-71-4766. Palo Alto, Calif.: American Institutes for Research.

Whitbeck, Christine. 1977. "Causation in Medicine: The Disease Entity Model." *Philosophy of Science* 44: 619–37.

Zdep, Stanley M. 1971. "Educating Disadvantaged Urban Children in Suburban Schools: An Evaluation." *Journal of Applied Social Psychology* 1 (2): 173–86.

CHAPTER SEVEN

Randomized Field Trials for Policy Evaluation: Why Not in Education?

GARY BURTLESS

POLICY EVALUATION USING randomized trials has become commonplace in many areas. It is only rarely used to evaluate educational policy, however. This fact raises interesting questions. Why has randomization been used to evaluate welfare policy, adult training, unemployment insurance, job placement, medical interventions, and a host of other policies? Why is controlled experimentation almost never used to evaluate education policy? Is randomization a feasible evaluation strategy for assessing education reform?

It should be clear that random assignment trials do not represent a practical strategy for evaluating some interesting questions pertinent to educational reform. The same can be said, however, for some interesting questions relevant to welfare policy, adult training, and medical interventions. Nonetheless, random assignment trials are common in these areas. Controlled experiments are not used very often to evaluate education policy. What accounts for the difference?

In the following pages I examine the reasons for the scarcity of educational experiments. Chance, social convention, and politics all play a role. Political considerations are probably the dominant factor, however. The remainder of the chapter is divided into three main sections. The first describes the main advantages and drawbacks of controlled experimentation as a research strategy. The second explains why randomization is frequently used to evaluate welfare reform, adult training and job finding programs, and other policy areas that are broadly comparable to education policy. This discussion sheds light on why controlled experiments are only rarely used to evaluate education reform, which is treated in the last section.

Why Conduct Experiments?

Randomized trials have become a popular method for evaluating policy alternatives in a variety of fields. There is one main reason for their popularity. Use of random assignment increases the likelihood that an evaluation will produce a valid estimate of the impact of a policy intervention. In this section, I define randomized trials and describe their advantages and disadvantages in comparison with other techniques for learning about program effectiveness.

DEFINITIONS. The critical element that distinguishes controlled experiments from all other methods of research is the random assignment of meaningfully different treatments to the observational units of study. A randomized field trial (or social experiment) is simply a controlled experiment that takes place outside a laboratory setting, in the usual environment where social, economic, or educational interactions occur. In the simplest kind of experiment, a single treatment is assigned to a randomly selected group (the treatment group) and withheld from the remainder of the enrolled sample (the control or null-treatment group). Many social experiments have tested a variety of different treatments rather than only one. Some have not enrolled a pure control group at all. Instead, the investigators have attempted to measure the differences in effect of two or more distinctive new treatments. The definition of an experiment can include tests of innovative new policies as well as studies that are intended to measure the impact of a current policy in relation to a null treatment.

In the absence of information from social experiments, analysts rely on four main alternatives to experiments to learn about the effectiveness of particular programs or interventions. First, they examine data on the relationship between nationwide or community-wide aggregates, such as test scores and household income. The effect of treatment differences can be calculated by measuring the outcome differences over time or across communities. However, aggregate statistics are inappropriate for analyzing many kinds of detailed relationships, such as the effectiveness of different instructional methods. Second, analysts look at management data collected in the administration of existing programs. However, this almost never provides clues to what the participants' experiences would have been if they had been enrolled in a different program or in no program at all. Third, they consult new survey data. Such data are more costly to obtain than existing programmatic data, but they provide details about the experiences of nonparticipants as well as participants in a program, and thus offer some evidence about likely behavior or outcomes in the absence of treatment. Fourth, analysts examine data generated by special demonstration programs. Like experiments, demonstrations involve the special provision of a possibly novel treatment, data collection about behavioral outcomes, and analysis of treatment effects. Unlike experiments, demonstrations do *not* involve random assignment. What all experiments have in common is that the tested treatments are randomly assigned to observational units, that is, to individuals, companies, elementary school classrooms, or entire communities.

ADVANTAGES OF RANDOMIZATION. The advantages of controlled experiments over other methods of analysis are easy to describe. Because experimental subjects are randomly assigned to alternative treatments, the effects of the treatments on behavior can be measured with high reliability. The assignment procedure assures us of the direction of causality between treatment and outcome. Differences in average outcomes among the several treatment groups are caused by differences in treatment; differences in average outcome have not caused the observed differences in treatment. Causality is not so easy to establish in nonexperimental data. A simple comparison between participants and nonparticipants in a government training program might reveal, for example, that program participants subsequently earn lower wages than eligible workers who never enrolled in the program. Does this indicate the program was unsuccessful? Or does it show instead that the program was very attractive to people who expect to earn very low wages? The poor earnings prospects of some workers might cause them to enroll. Alternatively, inappropriate or low-quality training might have caused participating workers to earn below-average wages. If eligible workers are assigned at random to the training program, the direction of causality would be known with certainty.

Random assignment also removes any systematic correlation between treatment status, on the one hand, and observed and unobserved participant characteristics, on the other. Estimated treatment effects are therefore free from the selection bias that potentially taints all estimates based on nonexperimental sources of information (see the next section). In a carefully designed and well-administered experiment, there is usually a persuasive case that the experimental data have produced an internally valid estimate of average treatment effect.[1]

Another advantage of experiments is that they permit analysts to measure—and policymakers to observe—the effects of environmental changes and new kinds of treatment that have not previously been observed. In many cases the naturally occurring variation in policies is too small to allow analysts to infer reliably the effects of promising new policies. Some people believe, for example, that classroom teachers would perform more effectively if they received money bonuses linked to the test-score gains achieved by their students. If a bonus system of this kind has never been tried, it is impossible to predict how teachers would respond to a particular bonus scheme. Of course, new policies can be tested in demonstration projects, too. But in comparison with most sources of nonexperimental information, experiments permit analysts to learn about the effects of a much wider range of policies and environmental changes.

The Canadian government recently examined the feasibility of offering public assistance recipients a substantial incentive to take full-time jobs. The program, known as the Self-Sufficiency Project, offered to pay public aid recipients one-half the difference between their actual wages and roughly $34,000 (US$23,000) a year.[2] Canadian aid recipients could only receive the wage supplement if they worked in a full-time job and entered the job within one year of being offered the supplement. Because Canada had never previously offered a work incentive nearly this generous, the government would have found it difficult if not impossible to predict the consequences of the incentive using information available when the Self-Sufficiency Project was launched. Wisely, Canadian officials decided to test the supplement in a small-scale randomized trial.

1. An "internally valid" estimate is an unbiased measure of the treatment effect in the sample actually enrolled in an experiment. An "externally valid" estimate is a treatment-effect estimate that can be validly extrapolated to the entire population represented by the sample enrolled in the experiment. Some experimental estimates may not be internally valid, possibly because treatment has not been assigned randomly or because attrition produces treatment-group and control samples that are not comparable (that is, that are not drawn form an identical population). In addition, some internally valid estimates may lack external validity. One reason is that a treatment offered to a small experimental sample may not correspond to any treatment that could actually be provided to a broad cross section of the population.

2. See Michalapoulos and others (2000).

Finally, the simplicity of experiments offers notable advantages in making results convincing to other analysts and understandable to policymakers. A carefully conducted experiment permits analysts to describe findings in extremely straightforward language: "Relative to teachers in the control group, teachers eligible for test-score-linked bonuses boosted their students' achievement scores by X percent." This kind of simplicity in describing results is seldom possible in nonexperimental studies, where research findings are subject to a bewildering range of qualifications.

In recent years the last advantage of experiments has turned out to be particularly important for experiments that test practical policy alternatives in medical care, adult training, and welfare policy. Because policymakers can easily grasp the findings and significance of a simple experiment, they concentrate on the implications of the results for changing medical practice or public policy. They do not become entangled in a protracted and often inconclusive scientific debate about whether the findings of a particular study are statistically valid. Voters and politicians are more likely to act on results they find convincing.

Two experiments provide vivid illustrations of the persuasive power of randomized trials. In the late 1980s, the U.S. Department of Labor followed the advice of social scientists and conducted an experimental evaluation of the Job Training Partnership Act (or JTPA). The JTPA experiment produced convincing evidence that many training programs financed by the Department of Labor for sixteen- to twenty-two-year-olds were conspicuously ineffective in boosting participants' earnings.[3] This evidence was found so persuasive that the administration drastically scaled back spending on the youthful target population, reallocating the funds to groups where training was shown to be effective. Congress accepted the administration's reallocation without protest, because the experimental findings left little reason to think the programs targeted on young people were achieving the desired effect. Critics of the administration's decision could not point to methodological doubts about the results in arguing for continued funding of youth training.

A more hopeful illustration of the power of randomized trials is the recent experience of Minnesota with its Family Investment Program for public assistance recipients. Like the Canadian Self-Sufficiency Project, the Minnesota program tested the effects of providing more generous

3. See Orr and others (1996).

incentives for aid recipients to move into full-time jobs. Under the previous Minnesota welfare program, parents who went to work typically lost most of their cash assistance benefits because their monthly grants were reduced nearly one dollar for every dollar they earned in a job. The Family Investment Program allowed recipients to keep most of their grants for an extended period, even after they found jobs that paid modestly good wages. When this incentive was combined with required participation in job-search and other employment-related activities, participants' employment rate increased by one-third and their earnings by one-quarter.[4] If these results were observed in a nonexperimental evaluation, they would have elicited little comment and might not even have been believed. Because they were observed in a randomized trial, news reporters and political observers accepted the findings at face value and focused on their implications for welfare policy. The findings were easy to believe and even easier to understand. They did not become the focus of a protracted debate about the believability of the research methodology that produced them. Minnesota has expanded the program tested in the experiment to cover its entire welfare caseload, and other states may be tempted to follow Minnesota's example.

Of course, an experiment does not completely eliminate our uncertainty about the answer to a well-posed question concerning individual behavior or policy effectiveness. But it can dramatically reduce our uncertainty. More important, the small number of qualifications to experimental findings can be explained in language that is accessible to people without formal training in statistics or the social sciences. This is a crucial reason for the broad political acceptance of findings from recent labor market experiments.

SAMPLE SELECTION. Sample selection is a frequent source of bias in statistical studies that focus on individual behavior. Nonexperimental studies of education and training, for example, usually rely on observations of naturally occurring variation in treatment doses to generate estimates of the effects of training. Analysts typically compare measured outcomes in test scores, employment, or earnings for participants in an educational or training program and for a comparison group of similar people who did not benefit from the educational or training intervention. For example, the value of a college degree is often calculated by comparing the earnings of college graduates with the earnings of people born in

4. Knox, Miller, and Gennetian (2000).

the same year who graduated from high school but did not attend college. Even if the analysis adequately controls for the effects of all measurable characteristics of people in the sample, it is still possible that average outcomes are affected by systematic differences in the unmeasured characteristics of people in the treatment and comparison groups. In the simplest kind of adult training program, for example, people in the sample are exposed to just two potential doses of treatment, say, $T = 1$ for people who enroll in the training program, and $T = 0$ for people who do not enroll. Program participation represents the sample member's decision to choose one treatment dose or the other. Obviously, this decision may be affected by the person's unobserved tastes or other characteristics, which in turn may also affect the person's later employment or earnings. Since these factors are unobserved, their effects cannot be determined. The exact amount of bias in the nonexperimental estimate thus remains uncertain.

Selection bias is a practical estimation problem in most nonexperimental policy studies. Naive analysts sometimes ignore the problem, implicitly assuming that unmeasured differences between program participants and nonparticipants do not exist or do not matter. While one or both of these assumptions might be true, the case for believing either of them is usually weak. Critics of early training evaluations sometimes pointed out, for example, that people who voluntarily enroll in employment training for the disadvantaged might be more ambitious than other disadvantaged workers. Unfortunately, ambition is an unmeasured personal trait. If personal ambition is correlated with a person's later labor market success, it is unclear what percentage of the average earnings advantage of trainees is due to extra training and what percentage is due to the greater average ambition of people who apply for and receive training.

Selection bias can go in the opposite direction. Disadvantaged students who are unlikely to obtain good test scores may be disproportionately enrolled in a compensatory education program. If their assignment to the compensatory program is based on a valid, but unobserved, assessment of their learning potential, we would expect that their test scores in the absence of compensatory schooling would be lower than those of students with identical observable characteristics who are not enrolled in the program.

Our uncertainty about the presence, direction, and potential size of selection bias makes it difficult for analysts to agree on the reliability of estimates drawn from nonexperimental studies. The estimates may be suggestive, and they may even be helpful when estimates based on many competing research strategies all point in the same direction. But if statisticians obtain widely differing estimates or if the available estimates are the subject of strong methodological criticism, policymakers will be left uncertain about the genuine effectiveness of the program. In the case of adult training programs, two studies have shown that this kind of uncertainty was not just a theoretical possibility. Both found that the nonexperimental literature contained an unhelpfully wide range of estimated impacts of the Comprehensive Employment and Training Act (CETA) on earnings.[5] The range of estimates reported in the nonexperimental studies was too wide to permit policymakers to decide whether CETA-sponsored training was cost-effective. It was not clear for some groups whether the impact of CETA training was beneficial at all. As just mentioned, the findings from the later study of Job Training Partnership programs were not subject to the same kinds of criticisms. They were produced in a randomized trial rather than with nonexperimental research methods. Economists and other researchers have broadly accepted the findings of the Job Training Partnership experiment, and policymakers have acted upon them.

COST CONSIDERATIONS. Experiments have three kinds of cost that make them more expensive than most nonexperimental research on the same topic. Of course, running a controlled experiment consumes more real resources than a nonexperimental study that uses existing data sources. An experiment is also costly in terms of time. Several years usually elapse between the time an experiment is conceived or designed and the release of its final report. If policy decisions about a particular policy question cannot be deferred, the usefulness of an experiment is questionable.

In addition, experiments often involve significant political costs. It is more difficult to develop, implement, and administer a new treatment than it is simply to analyze information about past behavior or to collect and analyze new information about existing policies. Voters and policymakers are rightly concerned about possible ethical issues raised by experiments. As a result, it is usually easier to persuade officials to appropriate small budgets for pure research or medium-sized budgets for a new survey than it is to convince them that some people should be systematically denied a potentially beneficial intervention in a costly new study.

5. Ashenfelter and Card (1985); and Barnow (1987).

These disadvantages of experiments are real, but they should be placed in perspective. Some forms of nonexperimental research suffer from identical or similar disadvantages. A demonstration study that lacks a randomly selected control group can easily cost as much money as a social experiment that tests the same innovative treatment. A demonstration will almost certainly take as much time to complete as an experiment. If Canada had chosen to study the work incentive in its Self-Sufficiency Project using a demonstration instead of a randomized trial, it would have saved little money and no time. If a new survey must be fielded to obtain the needed information, the extra time and money needed for an experiment may seem relatively modest.

ETHICAL ISSUES CONNECTED WITH HUMAN EXPERIMENTATION. Many observers are troubled by the ethical issues raised by experiments involving human subjects, especially when the experimental treatment (or the denial of treatment) has the capacity to inflict serious harm. If the tested treatment is perceived to be beneficial, program administrators may find it hard to deny the treatment to a randomly selected group of people enrolled in a study. Except among philosophers and research scientists, random assignment is often thought to be an unethical way to ration scarce resources. If the tested treatment is viewed as potentially harmful, it may be difficult to recruit program managers to run the project and impossible to recruit voluntary participants. It may not be ethical to mount such an experiment in any event. Readers should recall, however, that similar ethical issues arise in studies of new medicines and medical procedures, where the stakes for experimental participants are usually much greater than they are in educational or training experiments. Yet randomized field trials have been common in medicine for far longer than has been the case in social policy. In fact, randomized trials are frequently required as a matter of law or regulation in order to demonstrate that a new medical treatment is safe and effective.

Good experimental design can reduce ethical objections to random assignment.[6] At a minimum, participants in experimental studies should be fully informed of the risks of participation. Under some circumstances, people who are offered potentially injurious treatments or denied beneficial services can be compensated for the risks they face. The

6. See Burtless and Orr (1986), esp. pp. 621–24; and the essays in Rivlin and Timpane (1975).

risks of participation are usually unclear, however, because it is uncertain whether the tested treatment will be beneficial or harmful.

Of course, uncertainty about the direction and size of the treatment effect is the main reason that an experiment is worthwhile. A successful experiment substantially reduces our uncertainty about the size and direction of the treatment effect. The ethical argument in favor of experimentation is that it is preferable to inflict possible harm on a small scale in an experimental study rather than unwittingly to inflict harm on a much larger scale as a result of misguided public policy.

Experiments for Labor Market Policy

Random trials have become a popular method for evaluating program effectiveness in a variety of labor market areas, including welfare, unemployment insurance, worker training, and job placement. The popularity of randomized trials in these fields is the result of the inherent advantages of controlled experimentation as well as the peculiarities of these policy areas. Among the reasons for the wide use of randomization in these areas are the following:

—Randomized trials provide a practical way to obtain believable, understandable results.

—Nonexperimental evaluation methods had glaring defects, and they often produced unreliable (and disbelieved) results.

—Economists and other social scientists favoring randomized trials became influential in determining evaluation policy in several cabinet departments, including the U.S. Departments of Labor and of Health and Human Services.

—Policy areas in which random trials have become common are often areas where the Federal government plays the dominant policy or funding role—approval of new medicines, public assistance, unemployment insurance, and training programs for disadvantaged adults.

—Many target populations are politically weak. Even if many people in these populations object to random assignment, they may lack the political power to stop randomized trials.

—Random assignment, though expensive, has been so widely used and successful in certain policy areas that it has become established as the norm for best-practice policy evaluation. Policymakers and analysts who are influential in determining evaluation strategy in these areas will at least consider using a randomized trial when a practical policy question must be answered.

Before discussing randomized trials in education, it is worth considering these points in some detail. In 1968 randomized policy trials were an unknown quantity. No one knew whether experiments could be implemented or whether their results would be useful or informative. For many labor market policies, experimentation has turned out to be practical, and it has often provided timely findings that are helpful in influencing policy.

What aspects of labor policy make it peculiarly well suited to experimentation? Many "treatments" in labor policy can be administered to one person at a time. They do not need to be administered to an entire community. (Community-wide policy trials using random assignment can be extremely expensive.) The treatment can easily be withheld from control-group members. The appropriate treatment dose can be administered in a few months or years. The results of the treatment can be observed soon after the treatment is administered. Even if the full effect of a treatment on a person is not apparent within the observation time frame, the analyst can safely predict whether the full effect of the treatment will be bigger or smaller than the effect that is initially observed.[7]

To be sure, it takes a great deal of effort and time to design and implement an experiment, to enroll an experimental sample, and to measure and analyze the sample response. But the alternatives to experiments, described earlier, are also costly and time-consuming. In some cases, they consume almost as much time and money as a controlled experiment. Even when experiments turn out to be costly and time-consuming, the policy questions they are designed to answer are often relevant for many years after the study has been completed.

FEASIBILITY. The experience of the past quarter century shows it is feasible to attract competent administrators and organizations willing to implement labor market and other policy experiments. In some cases, the

7. One approach, used in the negative income tax (NIT) experiments, was to randomly enroll people into different NIT plans, with some plans lasting just three years, others lasting five years, and others lasting twenty years (see Burtless and Greenberg 1982). By seeing whether the impact of the long-duration plans differed from that of the short-duration plans, the evaluators could predict the likely impact of a plan that would last indefinitely. In the case of training programs, this complication may be unnecessary. What is needed instead is a practical and inexpensive method for collecting information about participants' earnings long after their participation in the training program has ended.

organizers and administrators are drawn from specialized research organizations—examples are Abt Associates, Mathematica Policy Research (MPR), and the Manpower Development Research Corporation (MDRC). More commonly, the experiments are administered by ordinary program managers drawn from existing public agencies. The data from the experiments are then collected and analyzed by economists or other social scientists from the specialized research organizations.

To be sure, even the best experiments fail to answer *all* the questions one might raise regarding program effectiveness. Even if a small-scale experimental study shows that a particular job placement strategy helps job-seekers find employment faster than they otherwise would, can it be inferred that the same result would be observed if placement assistance was offered to *every* disadvantaged worker in a local job market? Or is it possible that the treatment simply moves a handful of lucky job seekers to the front of the queue, giving treatment-group workers an advantage they would not enjoy in a full-scale implementation of the same policy?

That is a critical and challenging question. Fortunately, we do not need to know the answer if it turns out the tested job placement strategy hurts workers in their search for a job. (This outcome has actually been observed in several experiments.) Although the tested treatment in this case proved unsuccessful, the experiment was completely successful in uncovering the futility of the strategy. It is irrelevant for researchers to discover the general-equilibrium consequences of a full-blown implementation of the tested placement strategy. The experiment has answered the only policy question that in this case requires an answer, namely, does the policy increase workers' chances of obtaining a job?

WEAKNESSES OF THE ALTERNATIVE RESEARCH STRATEGIES. A cynic once observed that "it is not enough to succeed. One's friends must also *fail*." Similarly, it is not enough that experimentation has proved useful in practice. Nonexperimental methods also proved conspicuously *un*successful in answering crucial questions about labor market policy.

Sometimes the futility of nonexperimental methods is obvious even before a study is undertaken. Because Canada had never offered work incentives to public assistance recipients as generous as the ones it offered to people enrolled in its Self-Sufficiency Project, Canadian policymakers found it hard to guess how successful the incentives would be if offered to all public aid recipients. Under these circumstances, nonexperimental methods cannot uncover the likely impact of the proposed incentives on recipients' job-finding success.

In some cases, randomized trials produce very unexpected results, even though specialists believe they can guess the likely direction of a program's impact. Almost every U.S. labor economist in 1975 would have predicted that employers would look favorably on the applications of job-seekers who bring wage vouchers that can be redeemed by the employer for cash. One way to provide cash to employers is to promise them that if they hire vouchered job applicants, the government will reimburse the employer for one-half of the worker's first-year wages. It seems plausible to believe employers would hire vouchered job-seekers in preference to similar job-seekers who do not possess vouchers. In 1975 economists were uncertain only about the size of the employment gain that vouchered job-seekers would enjoy. When wage vouchers were actually tested in randomized trials, economists' intuition about the likely impact of vouchers proved incorrect: wage vouchers *reduced* job seekers' chances of obtaining employment.[8] This result highlights the limits of simple economic theory as well as nonexperimental methods. Nonexperimental research on the likely impact of vouchers had not indicated that their effects would be harmful. Simple theory yielded the prediction that vouchers would help disadvantaged workers in their search for a job. In practice, wage vouchers inflicted harm on disadvantaged job-seekers.

Even when a particular policy has been tried in the past, nonexperimental approaches to evaluation can yield unreliable results. In the area of health insurance, for example, do we know whether generous coinsurance subsidy rates encourage sick people to get more costly health care? Or do the sickest people get insurance plans with generous coinsurance rates because they anticipate large medical bills? In this case, it is not clear which way causality runs. Does generous insurance cause people to spend heavily on care? Or does heavy anticipated spending on medical care cause consumers to seek out generous insurance coverage?

Sample selection raises particularly troubling statistical issues for nonexperimental studies of adult training programs. In nonexperimental studies conducted before 1985, analysts did not know whether the groups they compared in order to infer treatment effects were drawn from identical populations. People who enrolled in government-financed training programs might have been drawn from a hard-working and ambitious population, while those who refrained from enrolling might have been

8. Masters and others (1982); and Burtless (1985).

drawn from a lazy population. In the nonexperimental data sets available to researchers, analysts did not know how much of the earnings difference between trainees and nontrainees was due to training and how much was due to differences in the average laziness of the two groups.

This problem was so severe in the work-welfare area that a National Academy of Sciences panel and a high-level commission appointed by the Secretary of Labor urged labor officials to discontinue further nonexperimental studies of training programs and focus instead on designing and implementing randomized trials.[9] The Secretary of Labor followed this advice, primarily because the earlier, nonexperimental studies failed to produce a set of findings on which researchers and policymakers could agree.

One clear finding from the earlier nonexperimental studies of training programs is that it is difficult—and perhaps impossible—for analysts to agree on an appropriate nonexperimental methodology. When researchers do not agree, and when competing nonexperimental methods yield differing results, policymakers are left to choose among competing evaluation findings. Few of them are equipped to do this.

ECONOMISTS' INFLUENCE. Perhaps by chance, economists reached influential positions in the U.S. Departments of Health, Education, and Welfare, Housing and Urban Development, and (especially) Labor in the late 1960s and 1970s. Economists and like-minded policy analysts are usually taught to think hard about the cost-effectiveness of policy. How can the stated goals of a policy be achieved at the least cost? How can the money allocated for a particular function be used in the most effective manner?

Economists and other social scientists inside and outside the government thought carefully about a number of concrete policy questions: Can we reduce poverty in a cost-effective way by changing the way welfare recipients' benefits are scaled back as they earn more wages? Can we improve poor families' shelter more cheaply by subsidizing their rents in existing, private apartments rather than by building new, publicly owned housing?

Only a handful of social scientists hold strong views about the pros and cons of different human-service strategies. If an enthusiast for a particular approach promises us a cheaper or more effective way to train

9. Betsey, Hollister, and. Papageorgiou (1985); and Stromsdorfer and others (1985).

people, many policy analysts are prepared to test the idea. If an advocate of a competing approach assures us that her job placement strategy will work better and faster than any training strategy previously attempted, hard-headed social scientists are equally prepared to test *that* idea. In my experience, this open-mindedness combined with tough-minded experimental evaluation has demonstrated that some innovative ideas can be successful. The demonstration of their success has led in turn to wide adoption of some effective training and job search policies. Hard-headed evaluation has also proved that some bad ideas and policies can have unexpected and undesirable consequences.

THE FEDERAL ROLE. For several reasons, the influence of federal decisionmakers in a policy area seems to be important in the adoption of experimental methods. Because it is much bigger than state and local governments, the federal government has vastly more resources to evaluate current or proposed policies. Experiments are more costly than most nonexperimental research strategies, so perhaps it is natural that randomization is more commonly used in federally funded evaluations than in those that are sponsored by state and local governments. Even adjusting for scale, however, the federal government devotes more effort and ingenuity to evaluation than do state and local governments.

Ambitious researchers, many of whom are also talented social scientists, are frequently attracted to federal service. They may find state and local governments less appealing as a stepping-stone to academic renown or political advancement. Innovative social scientists may be needed in order to push a government department down the road toward a new and possibly risky evaluation strategy. Such people are more likely to seek jobs in Washington rather than in Baton Rouge, Columbus, or Little Rock. This may help account for the greater popularity of randomized trials in federal as opposed to state and local program evaluations.

THE IMPACT OF ETHICAL CONSIDERATIONS. Social experiments raise ethical issues. If we want to test a treatment that is expected to help people, it seems unethical to most Americans (though not to statisticians) to deny helpful services to people in the control group. If we wish to test a treatment that is likely to *hurt* people, it seems unethical to force people to accept such a treatment based on the flip of a coin. That ethical objection is sometimes overcome by offering people the *choice* of participating and then by compensating them with money for the supposed harm inflicted by the treatment.

These ethical issues often present the biggest practical obstacle to performing experimental trials. For this reason, most social experiments have focused on providing innovative services or depriving people of potentially helpful services in populations that are politically weak. Unwed mothers, public assistance recipients, disadvantaged job-seekers, and unemployment insurance claimants do not have much political clout. Perhaps the ethical objections to experimentation do not occur to members of these populations, although that seems doubtful. It is more likely that people in these groups are too inarticulate and weakly organized to resist government and foundation efforts to test a policy through random assignment.

It is worth repeating the simple ethical argument *in favor* of experiments: if the tested policy does real harm, it is far better to find this out in a small-scale trial rather than to inflict harm unwittingly on a large population. If a policy confers tangible benefits, then it is valuable to demonstrate this in a way that persuades policymakers to adopt the tested policy on a wider scale. The ethical case in favor of experiments is rarely persuasive to potential participants in a randomized trial, however. Many would-be participants instinctively recoil from the idea that it is fair to assign people to services on the basis of a coin toss. If opponents to experimentation are politically influential, their influence can doom the effort to use random assignment.

EVALUATION NORMS. Once it was established that random assignment was a feasible and acceptable way to perform policy evaluation, senior researchers and public officials quickly learned that results from random trials could be applied for practical policymaking. Indeed, findings from experimental trials were more likely to affect policy than were results obtained with nonexperimental methods. Randomized trials eventually became the new norm for "best practice" in evaluation studies.

Randomization is now routinely considered a *potential* research strategy whenever evaluation is undertaken in certain policy areas. Because random trials are fairly common, and because the evaluation industry now contains several well-known and reliable firms, randomization is undertaken even by ordinary government functionaries. No daring spirit of reckless abandon is now needed, and no special analytical insight is required. Every federal official connected with evaluating welfare, adult training, and job placement programs is aware that random assignment is a feasible, practical, and often preferable method of learning about program effectiveness. Program evaluation norms have been permanently affected by this realization.

Education Experiments

Why are random trials so rare in the sphere of educational policy? My earlier discussion of random trials in the labor policy field suggests a few possible reasons:

—The federal role in K–12 education is not large. Only 6 percent of funding for K–12 schooling is derived from the federal budget. States and local governments account for the rest of financing, and they jealously guard their authority over schooling decisions. The important role of state and local governments in policymaking means they exercise disproportionate influence over evaluation policy. Evaluation methods that are popular in the federal government do not necessarily find eager users in state and local governments. Most members of Congress are sympathetic with states' views on schooling and educational evaluation policy. Thus even if federal administrators championed the use of randomized trials in education, they could face serious opposition among federal as well as state and local lawmakers.

—Economists and like-minded social scientists have never exercised important influence over education policy evaluation, either in the federal government or at the state and local levels. This may be a historical accident that reflects the unusual influence of education schools on K–12 evaluation methods. As shown in chapter 6, instructors in most of the nation's education schools are deeply skeptical of modern methods of statistical inference.

—Random assignment involves denying potentially beneficial treatments to teachers or students who are almost all regarded as "deserving." Many people will conclude from this that it is ethically unacceptable to deny beneficial services to some of the deserving population on the basis of random assignment.

—Random assignment requires that teachers and administrators become subject to the control of evaluators, who must be given authority over some aspect of curriculum, student enrollment, or pedagogical technique. Most professional people resist surrendering authority to people they do not consider professionally competent to judge their work. Unlike the people who administer public assistance, adult training and job placement programs, or unemployment insurance, American educators are well organized and politically influential.

—The target populations of school policy—teachers, school administrators, and students from all strata of the social and economic spectrum—are far from politically weak. If parents, teachers, and administrators are suspicious of the ethical merits of random assignment or if they are opposed to ceding authority to evaluators, they have many channels through which to register their political opposition.

Educators might be encouraged to cooperate in randomized policy trials if they could be persuaded that tangible benefits will flow from their cooperation. The Tennessee STAR experiment, which tested the effects of smaller class size on student performance in kindergarten through third grade, offers a hopeful sign that educators' cooperation can sometimes be secured. The STAR experiment offered convincing evidence that smaller class size can produce statistically significant and consistent, though modest, gains in student achievement. This result has been widely cited in state and local efforts to shrink class size in the first years of primary school. Even though the trend toward smaller class size was under way for decades before Tennessee experimentally tested the impact of class-size reductions, the STAR experiment results were among the first to be widely cited in the popular press as persuasive evidence that smaller classes could be helpful.

It would be disingenuous to suggest randomized trials will always yield results that are congenial to educators. Controlled experiments often produce unexpected and even unwanted results. Programs that are thought to be beneficial are instead found to have negligible or undesirable effects. It is precisely because experiments can produce unexpected but believable results that they are so valuable. The crucial reason their findings are believable is that policymakers and social scientists find them easier to understand—and ultimately more convincing—than results from other kinds of policy evaluation.

References

Ashenfelter, Orley, and David Card. 1985. "Using the Longitudinal Structure of Earnings to Estimate the Effect of Training Programs." *Review of Economics and Statistics* 67 (November): 648–60.

Barnow, Burt. 1987. "The Impact of CETA Programs on Earnings: A Review of the Literature." *Journal of Human Resources* 22 (Spring): 157–93.

Betsey, Charles L., Robinson G. Hollister Jr., and Mary R. Papageorgiou, eds. 1985. *Youth Employment and Training Programs: The YEDPA Years.* Washington: National Academy Press.

Burtless, Gary. 1985. "Are Targeted Wage Subsidies Harmful? Evidence from a Wage Voucher Experiment." *Industrial and Labor Relations Review* 39 (October): 105–14.

Burtless, Gary, and David H. Greenberg. 1982. "Inferences Concerning Labor Supply Behavior Based on Limited-Duration Experiments." *American Economic Review* 72 (June): 488–97.

Burtless, Gary, and Larry L. Orr. 1986. "Are Classical Experiments Needed for Manpower Policy?" *Journal of Human Resources* 21 (Fall): 606–39.

Knox, Virginia, Cynthia Miller, and Lisa A. Gennetian. 2000. *Reforming Welfare and Rewarding Work: Final Report on the Minnesota Family Investment Program.* New York: Manpower Demonstration Research Corporation.

Masters, Stanley, and others. 1982. *Jobs Tax Credits: The Report of the Wage Bill Subsidy Research Project, Phase II.* University of Wisconsin, Institute for Research on Poverty.

Michalopoulos, Charles, David Card, Lisa A. Gennetian, Kristen Harknett, and Philip K. Robins. 2000. *The Self-Sufficiency Project at 36 Months: Effects of a Financial Work Incentive on Employment and Income.* Ottawa, Canada: Social Research and Demonstration Corporation.

Orr, Larry L., Howard S. Bloom, Stephen H. Bell, Fred Doolittle, Winston Lin, and George Cave. 1996. *Does Training for the Disadvantaged Work? Evidence from the National JTPA Study.* Washington: Urban Institute Press.

Rivlin, Alice M., and T. Michael Timpane, eds. 1975. *Ethical and Legal Issues of Social Experimentation.* Brookings.

Stromsdorfer, Ernst, and others. 1985. *Recommendations of the Job Training Longitudinal Survey Research Advisory Panel.* Washington: U.S. Department of Labor, Employment and Training Administration.

CHAPTER EIGHT

What to Do until the Random Assigner Comes

CAROL H. WEISS

THE CONTRIBUTIONS TO this volume have largely been appreciations of random assignment and its many virtues. I agree that it is ideal for purposes of establishing causality (I'd better, if I don't want to be thrown out of this merry company) because it shows that the intervention was in fact responsible for observed effects. But there are circumstances when random assignment is very difficult, if not impossible, to implement. One of those circumstances arises when the goal of the intervention is to change *not* the individuals in a community but the community itself. Many such programs are currently in existence, programs that aim to "revitalize," "transform," or "develop" the community in the United States, in Europe with the European Community's "social funds," and in developing countries. Ultimately, the purpose of such programs is to improve the well-being of the residents, but the intervention is not directed at individual residents so much as at the conditions and workings of the neighborhood.[1] The obvious solution to the difficulty with randomizing individuals is to randomize communities, that is, to assign communities randomly to program and control conditions. I will

1. I use the word "neighborhood" interchangeably with "community" to vary the language and avoid total boredom. In both cases the term refers to a relatively limited geographical area inhabited by people who may or may not have much in common. Where community programs are being run, the aim is to improve the way the community functions and, by extension, the lot of the residents.

discuss this possibility in a moment. First I want to define the kinds of programs I am talking about.

Community programs have a rich history, from the settlement houses of the early 1900s to the Community Action Program of the War on Poverty to community development corporations of the late 1960s and 1970s. In the late 1980s and early 1990s, national and community foundations began funding a variety of initiatives to promote positive change in family and community circumstances in disadvantaged neighborhoods. Most community initiatives included at least some of the following elements: improvement and expansion of social services such as child care, health and mental health care, economic development, housing rehabilitation and construction, community organizing, adult education, job training, school reform, neighborhood safety, and recreation, and most called for the participation of neighborhood residents in decisionmaking.[2] A number of federal agencies also began funding community programs for such purposes as reducing delinquency and teenage pregnancy and improving training and employment, with emphasis on the involvement of local people. Signature federal programs are Empowerment Zones/Enterprise Communities and Healthy Start.

One reason for the "community turn" in programming is that practitioners and evaluators have found that interventions aimed at changing individual attitudes and behavior are often undermined by community factors hostile to the change. Program effects are swamped by community norms that denigrate school achievement or accept (or even glorify) violence. Furthermore, even when a program succeeds in bringing about change, the changes are not sustained if community factors work in contrary directions. Such factors as rampant criminality or a climate of opinion that views mainstream behavior as "going over to the enemy," can prevent some residents from benefiting from the program at all and induce others to retrogress. As individual-change programs show disheartening inability to make—or sustain—positive change, more program designers are working to change the environments in which people live.[3] Many community initiatives emphasize the participation of neighborhood residents in planning and governing the interventions. The "empowerment" of residents is often viewed as a goal in itself, as well as an instrument for making community services more responsive to local needs.

2. Kubisch and others (1995).
3. Schorr (1997).

The Task for Evaluators

These interventions present problems for evaluation. The evaluator cannot randomly assign individuals or even families or small groups to one condition or another. Agency-level or community-level structures are being changed. Everyone in the neighborhood is expected to be affected. Moreover, a common theme of these initiatives is that people need *comprehensive* services, not single services one at a time. Agencies are expected to coordinate services and collaborate. All residents are eligible for all services and are expected to benefit from all changes. Within a single agency, interventions are meant to affect all clients. Welfare agencies institute staff training programs to change the attitudes of their workers and encourage them to emphasize job placement. All staff are expected to adhere to the new policies. No client can be randomized to a "control" condition.

To conduct a random-assignment evaluation in community-wide programs, the obvious solution is to randomly assign communities. A randomization procedure would determine which communities receive the program and which communities become controls. However, at the community level, randomization faces three almost intractable problems: (1) small numbers, (2) funders' insistence on control of selection, and (3) variability across sites. In terms of numbers, at the current time only a few communities receive grants to conduct each type of program. Numbers are too small for the laws of probability to operate to produce similar sets of communities in treatment and control conditions.

Second, government and foundation funders want to choose the communities that receive the intervention. Foundations often have program expertise that alerts them to the kinds of communities that can benefit from the intervention and those whose history and culture make them unsuitable. Government funders have similar concerns and in addition may have political reasons for favoring some sites over others. The demands of random assignment evaluation do not appear as compelling as the immediate concerns of increasing the likelihood of success for the intervention and gaining and keeping the support of powerful constituencies and leaders.

A third limitation is that treatments are not consistent across sites. In the four sites of the Neighborhood and Family Initiative (NFI) sponsored by the Ford Foundation, for example, Hartford used its funds to add outdoor lighting, run a community garden, and operate a summer program for children. The NFI in Memphis rehabilitated existing housing and constructed new housing. The Milwaukee NFI joined with other organizations to develop an industrial park.[4] Neighborhood initiatives, even when developed and funded by the same sponsor, tend to pursue a dazzling variety of strategies and activities.

Random assignment of communities, where it is possible, is a highly desirable design. But at the community level, it requires a large number of sites. Communities have such unique populations, economic conditions, political arrangements, and histories that small numbers will yield noncomparable groups. Whatever changes occur in outcome are likely to be overwhelmed by differences in communities.

Alternatives to Random Assignment

If evaluators cannot randomly assign communities, what are the alternatives? The strongest tradition is quasi experiments.[5] These designs will guard against some threats to the validity of causal conclusions, although not all. Because there is such a rich literature on quasi-experiments, I will not address this possibility further. But it is a feasible and often sensible choice.

Collateral to quasi experiments are a number of statistical techniques that aim to improve the comparability of nonrandom comparison groups. They include forecasting what the situation would have been in the absence of the program by extrapolating past trends, and then using the forecast as the "comparison group."[6] Other techniques use nonrandom comparison groups and adjust the data to reduce preexisting differences between the groups. Other techniques model the process that selects some units into the program and others into nonrandom comparison groups, and uses the predicted probability that each unit will enter the program rather than the comparison group as a control variable in the analysis.[7] I will not discuss statistical adjustments further here, but they are well worth considering.

Another approach would be to turn to qualitative methods to capture the full richness of changes in community life. Particularly because

4. Aspen Institute (1995).

5. For discussions of the range of comparisons available without random assignment, see Cook and Campbell (1979); and Shadish and others (2002).

6. See Holder and Blose (1988); Garasky (1990).

7. Rosenbaum and Rubin (1983, 1984); Heckman (1989); Heckman and Hotz 1989.

community and organizational change is complex and multidimensional, there is little hope of fully understanding the range of anticipated and unanticipated consequences without richly detailed narratives.

Qualitative evaluators can provide the perspective of local people, preserve the community context, and offer analyses rooted in informants' worldviews.[8] But what should they focus on? What out of all the "bloomin' buzzin' confusion" should the evaluator observe? With small well-defined programs, consensus can be reached about focus, but large, community-wide programs in sprawling communities test the mettle of qualitative evaluation. Some methods are available for bringing comparability to qualitative work, but they seem to depend on central direction of the evaluation, rather than separate evaluators studying their own communities.[9] Collaboration among community evaluators can be useful but it is difficult to manage. Each evaluator is attracted to the events, activities, themes, and patterns that emerge in her own site(s) and is often reluctant to submerge them in a common framework. Thus qualitative evaluation offers the advantage of placing the inquiry in its local context, but it is likely to surrender the chance of comparability across communities. Nor does it generally have comparison (no-program) communities as contrast. Nevertheless, with all its strengths and limits, qualitative evaluation remains an interesting option.

When random assignment is impossible, I would like to suggest two other possibilities. They are much less traditional alternatives to random assignment, but they have appealing potential. They are Theory-Based Evaluation (TBE) and Ruling Out. Neither has the simplicity and elegance of random assignment, but each has feasible properties for evaluation of community programs.

Theory-Based Evaluation

Writing on Theory-Based Evaluation has been flourishing.[10] The main idea is this: evaluators, often in consultation with program stakeholders, lay out the underlying assumptions about how the program is expected to

8. Bogdan and Biklen (1998); Silverman (1993); Maxwell (1996); Strauss and Corbin (1990).

9. Miles and Huberman (1994).

10. Weiss (1967, 1972, 1995, 1997, 1998); Chen and Rossi (1980, 1983, 1987); Chen (1990); Bickman (1987, 1990).

Figure 8-1. *Example of a Program Theory*

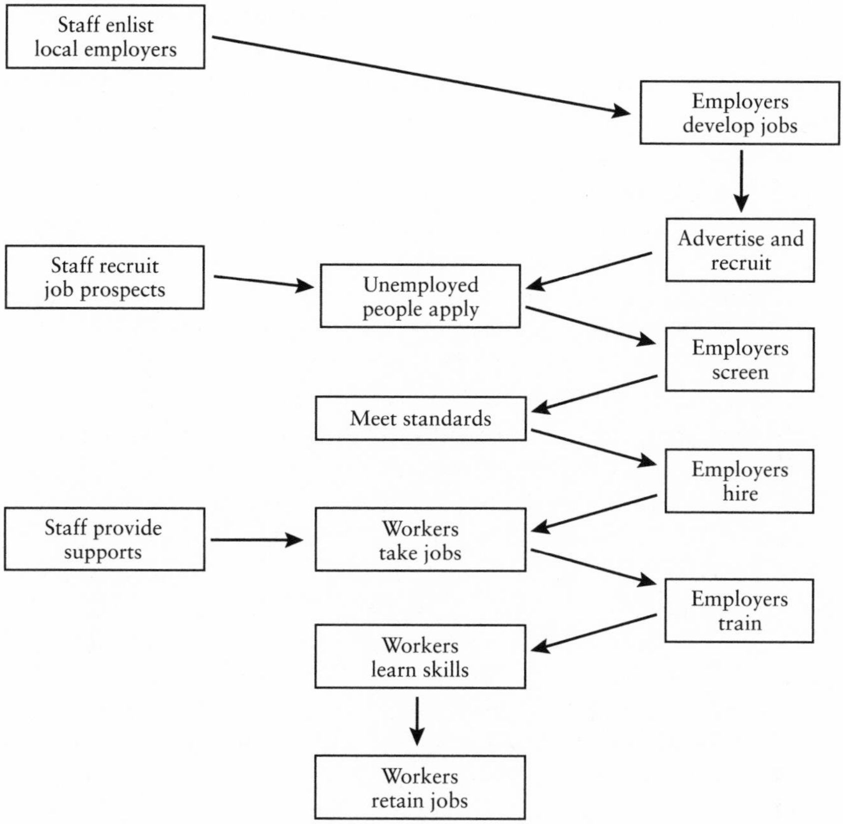

work. This "theory" encompasses not only what the program is expected to do at each stage but also how recipients of service will respond at each stage. Figure 8-1 gives an example of what a program theory might look like. The "theory" comprises a set of linkages that move from original inputs to eventual outcomes. It is a theory of change.[11]

The example is a job creation program in a depressed community. The program is expected to enlist employers in the neighborhood to develop

11. Another term for this procedure is "logic models." It has the advantage of not sounding highbrow, not encompassing expectations for wisdom on the order of Max Weber or Jean Piaget. But in practice logic models are often simplistic and lacking in detail.

jobs suitable for chronically unemployed workers. Employers create such jobs. They advertise them through channels that reach chronically unemployed residents of the neighborhood. Program staff also recruit suitable applicants. The chronically unemployed apply for the jobs. The employer hires those who meet certain standards (for example, employees must be drug-free). Applicants take the jobs. The employer provides training. Workers take the training and learn needed skills. The program provides support. Workers stay on the job and perform adequately.

An evaluator using TBE would follow the trail of these expected linkages and see whether they come to pass. Do staff approach employers? Do they persuade them to cooperate? Do employers create jobs? Does word of the jobs reach the target population? Do chronically unemployed people apply? Do they meet standards? Do employers hire them? And so on.

An advantage of this approach is that without randomly assigned control groups, the evaluator can see the extent to which the assumptions of the program are being borne out—the extent to which the program apparently "causes" the effects it seeks. As Lawrence Mohr has written, "If one billiard ball on the table hits another and sends it scooting away, we feel unequivocally that we have witnessed a causal instance and that we understand the kind of causation involved."[12] Interpreting the effects of social programs is not like watching the carom of a billiard ball, but by tracing events in small steps, the evaluator gets information on whether the assumptions underlying the program are showing up as anticipated. If so, she has a sense that the program is causing subsequent events.

Because the state of social theory is so weak in most of the fields in which evaluators work, program theories often have to be developed, or at least made explicit, at the time of the evaluation. If the world worked more rationally, program *designers* would make their assumptions explicit at the time they crafted the programs. Unfortunately, except in a few areas, planning of social programs proceeds more by the seat of the pants and the example of "what everybody else is doing," than it does by thoughtful and critical review of evidence and experience. Therefore it is usually left to the evaluator to convene and cajole stakeholders to articulate their theories about the way program inputs lead to desired outcomes.

Constructing program theory requires evaluators, usually in conjunction with program designers, managers, practitioners, and perhaps

12. Mohr (1998, p. 4).

clients, to articulate their assumptions about the stages through which the program will work. They have to set out their expectations of what program staff will do and how participants will respond in a sequence of small steps, and why the steps will take place in the order assumed. Most people engaged in programs have never gone through such a mental exercise. The evaluator needs persistence and patience to elicit their tacit theories of the program. They may find it uncongenial and difficult to do. On the other hand, some program people find the experience exhilarating.

Sometimes people engaged in these discussions come to consensus about how, why, and when the program will work to achieve desired effects. When they do, the process is rewarding. If program people can agree on how and why they are conducting the program, they are likely to be concentrating their programmatic efforts on the same set of activities, rather than working at cross-purposes. However, often program people have different assumptions about how and why the program will work. An evaluation can incorporate several theories and see which of them are better supported by the evidence.

Developing program theory for community programs is a more difficult task than developing theory for programs that work with individuals. At the community level the canvas for inquiry is so large and variegated that theory-based evaluation can become a daunting task. But when people are able to define program theory (or theories) at the start, evaluation has strong advantages. For one thing, the evaluation does not have to wait until the end of the program and follow-up to find out how well it is succeeding. Data on the early steps—how well the early stages of the theory are being realized—will give preliminary insights into what is going well and which expectations are not being actuated.

Another advantage shows up in contrast to usual modes of *qualitative* investigation. A TBE qualitative evaluation sets out which events and linkages should be studied. The evaluator does not try to look at everything that goes on but concentrates on the phases of the program that have been defined as critical.[13] In contrast to the usual modes of *quantitative* evaluation, it has the advantage of leading to detailed understanding of what is going on at each phase of the program. If the theory, or one of the posited theories, holds up under examination, it has the advantage

13. Of course, like all evaluators, TBE evaluators have to keep their eyes open to unanticipated consequences. It makes good sense to set out some theories that lead to poor results, not just failures of positive steps but counterproductive processes that the program

of showing not only what happened but how it happened and even why it happened. If none of the theories is borne out by the data, TBE shows where in the sequence the theories broke down.

Of course, there are many problems in making TBE work.[14] One of them is the lack of comparisons. Even if the theory is supported all along the way, something other than the intervention might have caused the sequence of results. In our example, was a favorable economic climate and an accompanying labor shortage responsible for employers' willingness to hire unappealing job prospects? To answer such questions, it would be highly desirable to look at a comparison group of communities. Even when a randomly assigned control group cannot be set up, some comparison with other communities would help to answer the question. If comparison communities show similar rates of hiring chronically unemployed people, we would question the effectiveness of the intervention, even if the assumptions of the theory seemed to be borne out. Comparisons increase the power of TBE.

Examples of Program Theory

Figure 8-2 illustrates a theory of change for a community initiative directed at creating a healthier environment for adolescents. It begins at the point where services of social service agencies have been coordinated and residents have become involved in the activities of the initiative. It follows several assumptions about what is going to happen next to meet program goals. Through a number of different links, the twin emphases of agency coordination and resident participation are expected to lead to more appropriate services for adolescents and a community environment more supportive and nurturing of their development.

---

inadvertently sets in motion. For example, a program that paves roads in a farming community aims to enable farmers to market their produce in the city without having to rely on intermediaries. An unanticipated result may be that richer farmers with efficient vehicles get richer using the paved roads while poorer farmers fail to use the roads and thus make little gain in income; income inequality increases and social divisions rend the community. The more specifically the evaluator can specify counterproductive theories at the start, the better able she will be to follow their development and to pin down unanticipated and undesirable steps and consequences. She can be alert to counterproductive forces early in the program sequence (for example, poor farmers are not marketing their produce in the city), and not have to wait until the end to find out what went wrong.

14. Weiss (1997).

Figure 8-2. *Example of Theory of Change for Comprehensive Community Programs, Positive Consequences*

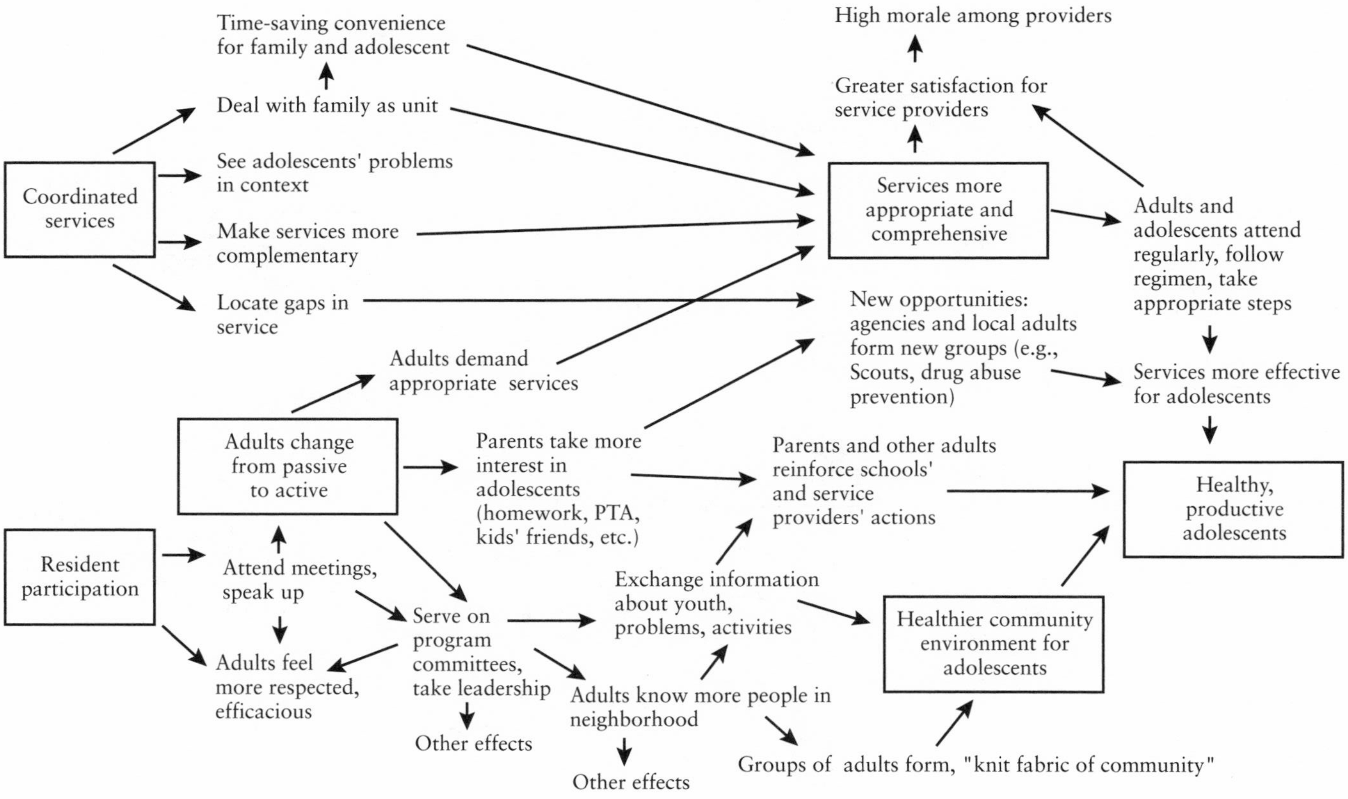

Figure 8-3. *Example of Theory of Change for Comprehensive Community Programs, Negative Consequences*

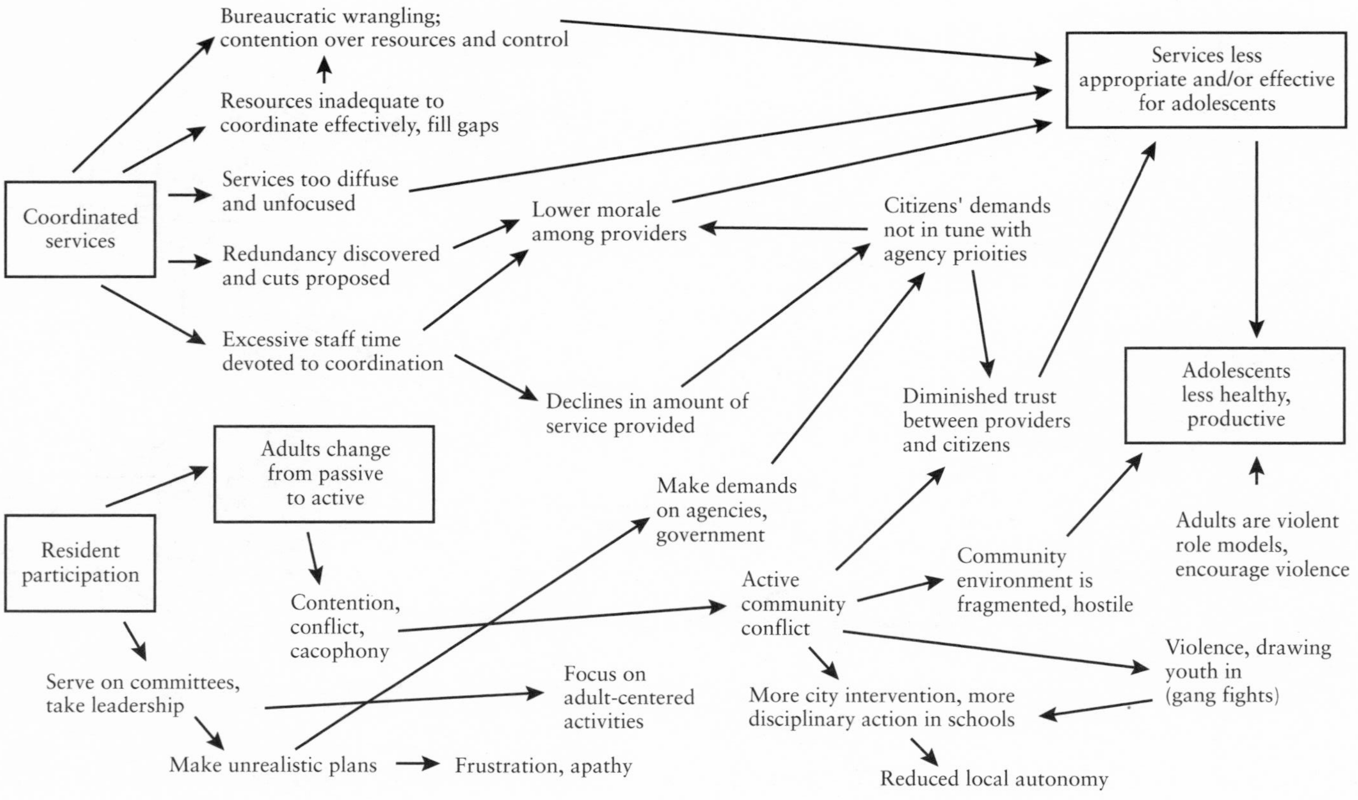

Figure 8-3 is an example of unanticipated consequences of the same initiative. The community intervention may set in motion a variety of unwanted social processes. Attempts to coordinate services may stir up bureaucratic wrangling over resources and control; it may take large amounts of staff time to sit on committees, alter forms and data systems, and stay in contact with other agencies, thus reducing the amount of time available for direct service. Resident participation in the initiative may lead to argument and contention among factions in the community, and their disagreements may spill over into wider community conflict. Through a number of negative links, the result may be a neighborhood less conducive to healthy adolescent development.

Making TBE Practical

TBE can be a large task. If one tried to follow each link of each of several alternative theories, one would be inundated with data and have difficulty analyzing it. To make the task more manageable, the method should be used selectively. First, carefully choose the programs and occasions for which TBE will make the greatest contribution and do not try to use it for every evaluation study. Second, do not always follow every theory from program input to long-range outcomes. Many studies would be valuable if they followed events only to the point of program outputs, that is, to the point at which the program effectively delivers the services it intends to deliver. In the example of the job creation program, this would be the point at which the program places and supports the workers in jobs and provides ongoing support at the job site. Thus it would be mainly a process evaluation.

Third, focus the study on only the most strategic linkages, those that are central to the success of the program and about which the least information is available. Fourth, consider which linkages in the program's theory occur in other program contexts. For example, many kinds of programs tend to assume that conveying knowledge to clients (about the effects of drug abuse, the advantages of college going, and so on) will lead to changes in behavior. The link from knowledge to behavior change is a link that has application in multiple contexts and may well merit study. Let me say a word about each of these conditions.

CHOOSE PROGRAMS CAREFULLY BEFORE UNDERTAKING TBE. Evaluators need to be selective in choosing which studies are candidates for TBE. Much the same criteria can be used for choosing programs for

TBE as should be used for random assignment evaluations. Before undertaking TBE, the evaluator should try to see that the program is adhering to the basic plan that was designed for it (fidelity). It should be carried out with reasonable competence (quality). It should be reasonably stable over time (stability). There should be at least a few clues of positive results (potential success). It is the spendthrift who uses scarce evaluation resources on sophisticated evaluations of programs that do not have at least a modicum of fidelity, quality, stability, and a chance of good outcomes.

DO NOT PURSUE LONG-TERM OUTCOMES IN EVERY STUDY, BUT PURSUE VERY LONG-TERM OUTCOMES FOR WELL-CHOSEN STUDIES. Not every study needs to follow the whole sequence of assumptions to their long-term behavioral conclusion. It may sometimes be enough to find out whether community initiatives did what they intended to do and delivered the outputs that they aimed for. Outputs, as contrasted with outcomes, deal with conditions at the boundaries of the program. For example, did the community development corporation achieve the outputs it sought: build the desired number of units of low-income housing, train numbers of residents in construction skills, set up and maintain resident management of housing units? Not every evaluation needs to pursue program theory to find out whether availability of low-income housing units led to stable families, better health, or improved children's school performance.

Relying on output measures assumes that later links are self-evident, or that somebody else will study these fundamental social processes. Academic researchers, rather than evaluators, can study such questions as whether residents' active engagement in community affairs teaches them skills that upgrade their employment opportunities. Sometimes relevant research is available. The evaluator of a stop-smoking program does not have to study whether stopping smoking leads to good health effects, such as reduction in heart disease. Biomedical research has already established the relationships.

An emphasis on program outputs has parallels with the current emphasis on "performance measurement." Mark Moore contends that organizational managers want to know whether their staffs are performing well and doing the job that they are supposed to do.[15] They are less interested in whether the customers of the organization go on to receive long-term benefits. Business firms measure such things as the length of

15. Moore (1997).

time between customer order and product delivery or the frequency of customer reorders. Nonprofits look at the cultural sensitivity of their services or client satisfaction. Such numbers tell organizational leaders a great deal about how well the organization is performing and help to pinpoint needs for organizational improvement.

However, the social programs that evaluators usually deal with differ in many ways from other organizations. Their aim is not so much to *satisfy* participants' expressed wants as to *change* participants' wants—and their knowledge and behavior. The programs often aim to bring participants' behavior into line with mainstream behavior whether the participants want that outcome or not. Delivering the service is not enough to herald success. Placing workers in jobs does not necessarily lead to stability of employment or family-supporting wages.

Furthermore, evaluators work in terrain where strategies and inputs have not been authoritatively shown to yield desired outcomes. They are not sure that decentralizing neighborhood services will lead to better services or that involvement of residents necessarily leads to services that are more appropriate to the community. Some well-chosen evaluations have to look at the connection between a fully realized decentralization of government services and service quality. Some evaluations will need to go even farther. It is one thing to find a relationship between decentralized services and quality of services and another thing to find a relationship between a *change to decentralization* and *improvement* in quality. Some studies may need to investigate that linkage. In sum, selected evaluations of community programs will have to follow the full sequence of steps of program theory on to long-range consequences.

FOCUS ON ONLY THE MOST STRATEGIC LINKAGES IN THE THEORIES. To make TBE more feasible for day-to-day work, evaluations have to be selective about which linkages to study. I would suggest three criteria for choosing the key element in the theory. First, it should be a link that is central to the success of the program. For example, if a community program expects to reach its results via active engagement of community residents, then that would be a feature to concentrate on. Are residents engaged? Do they develop plans of action to see that needs are met? Do social agencies listen to their demands? If data show that residents have been mobilized and forcefully present demands to social agencies in the community, do the other expected results ensue? Examination of the *crucial* expectation is the most important criterion for deciding where to focus a TBE.

A second criterion for the focus of a TBE is that it should be a link about which little information exists or about which prior information is contradictory. Thus if prior studies have not examined the link between resident mobilization and pressure on agencies to improve the quality of services, this is a point that a theory-based evaluation might take on. Or if earlier studies have yielded discrepant data, again this is a signal that the issue may invite attention. A third possible criterion is that the link(s) should be assumptions that have multiple applications. Thus if many programs assume that involvement of community residents in concerted action will increase government's attention to community needs, that may be a linkage that merits study.

One benefit of examining key linkages is that evaluations of this sort can contribute to changing reigning ideas about program design. If a key assumption is that decentralization leads to improved services, evaluations can seek to confirm or disconfirm that assumption in the fields of health care, education, social services, and transportation. If conclusions converge over time, they can influence policymakers, program designers, administrators, and practitioners. We know from much research on knowledge utilization that the results from evaluations that have the greatest impact are the "ideas." Data are useful and occasionally persuasive (and always useful for advocacy) but what people carry away (if they carry away anything) is the idea. When TBEs can help to confirm or disconfirm an idea in good currency in the world of community programming, they can make an edifying contribution.

Which Kind of Theory?

What should the links in a program theory look like? The studies I am examining illustrate two quite different approaches. One lays out a cascade of program activities and participant responses. Figure 8-1 is an example of this type of theory. The other approach identifies the social and psychological mechanisms that are expected to make program activities work. Figures 8-2 and 8-3 incorporate attention to social and psychological mechanisms alongside theories based on activities and responses.

Consider a theory of change for the same intervention that takes place *prior* to the achievement of coordinated services and resident involvement. An activity-response type of theory would look something like this: the community initiative plans meetings for community residents ➧ many residents attend ➧ initiative staff seek to enroll them in committees that will work on improving welfare, housing, and education services ➧ many residents sign up and meet regularly ➧ they identify a need for greater collaboration across agencies ➧ resident committees and initiative staff contact service agency leaders and arrange conferences ➧ service agency staff meet with resident committees ➧ residents present demands ➧ service staff agree to make changes ➧ they make changes that move toward greater coordination, and so on.

On the other hand, a theory that tries to identify the key psychological and social mechanisms expected to lead to change might focus on one or two particularly problematic elements. In this case, it might well be the agreement of social service agency leaders to *undertake* increased coordination. One mechanism that might lead to such an action is the demonstration of residents' potential political power. Through mobilization, residents show city officials and agency leaders that they have significant potential voting strength, and elected officials might press agencies to satisfy their demands. The key mechanism to be investigated here would be political organization. Figure 8-4 is an attempt to illustrate several mechanisms that might work for and against coordination of services and resident participation.

Whether TBE should take one path or the other is not obvious. The activities-response approach gives a firm backbone to the evaluation. It lays out the points at which information should be collected. It turns up early evidence about expectations that are not being met. It locates the disjunction in the sequence of assumptions, helping to show where the program goes off the expected track.

On the other hand, a problem arises when community initiatives shift their strategies over time. Even when they have gone through an extensive planning process and set out their goals and plans in detail, they may confront new conditions, obstacles, and opportunities. If one line of operation is blocked—say, the local community college fails to follow through on job training opportunities—they may shift their attention to the development of transportation. If the school system is hiring a new school superintendent who appears favorably disposed to strong neighborhood involvement, the initiative may drop something else and become involved with the schools. Search for new funding sources can also lead to a shift in priorities. New funders often have their own agendas that may require the community organization to pursue a somewhat different set of priorities in order to be eligible. Again, the community initiative shifts ground. The ability to shift opportunistically is a strength

Figure 8-4. *Example of Theory of Change That Focuses on Operative Mechanisms*

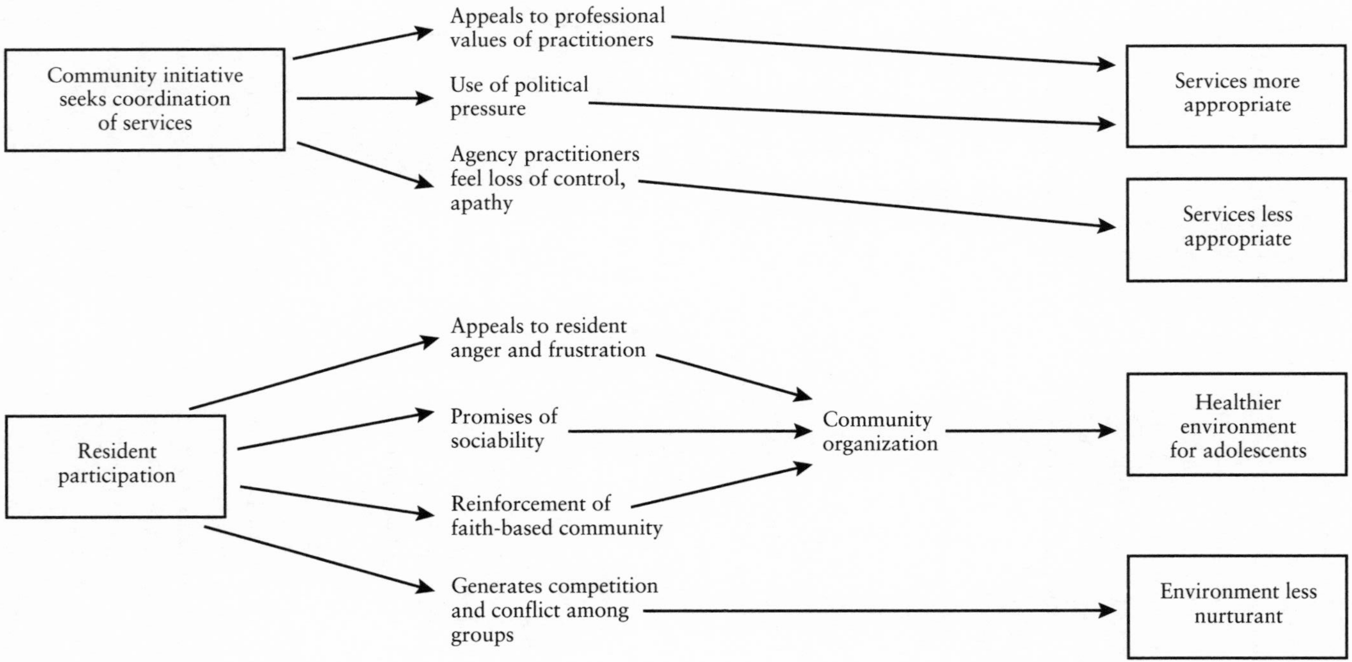

of neighborhood organizations. They need not stay wedded to unproductive activities or dead ends. They can take advantage of sparkling new opportunities. But an evaluator trying to construct and follow a program theory has to keep adapting the theory to changing conditions as windows of opportunity open and shut.

Program theories based on psychosocial or sociopolitical assumptions, on the other hand, try to get to the heart of the matter. Such theories of change are more likely to stay relevant, even under changing programmatic conditions. But they do not give as clear direction for design and conduct of the evaluation. A theory based on social mechanisms does not tell specifically what information should be collected, at which point in program life. Nor is it likely that program people can identify the mechanisms that they implicitly rely on—or would want to divulge them. For example, I recently visited a community initiative where most of the residents on the board, as well as the beneficiaries of the program, were members of local churches. When I interviewed them, neither staff, board members, nor residents spoke about the program being based in communities of faith, and yet I suspected that their common religious affiliation was at least partly responsible for the cohesion of the program and the persistence of program participants in activities directed at changing their behavior. It might take an outsider to get a glimmering of what local people take for granted.

It is important to locate social levers of change. To be more effective in changing community conditions, evaluators need to understand the operative mechanisms. As well as learning from their own studies, they need to keep in touch with research that is investigating the kinds of relationships they are concerned with. They should be learning as much as they can from disciplinary and interdisciplinary research.

At this point, I would recommend that theory-based evaluators develop assessments based on the sequences of expected activities and responses. In time they should supplement this mode of TBE with a conscious search for operative mechanisms. Fortunately, there is some overlap between the two approaches. Community initiatives undertake certain activities precisely because they believe that the activities will activate a lever of change. For example, the mobilization of residents represents latent political power, and even if nobody breathes a word about politics in public, the cognoscenti understand the strength of community organization. A TBE based on an activities-responses theory will follow the steps of resident mobilization. At the same time, the data can help to answer the next question: how effective is community mobilization for securing change in the quality and availability of services?

Ruling Out Alternative Explanations

Another alternative to random assignment is the procedure of systematically ruling out alternative explanations (other than the program) for observed program effects. It can be considered a separate design option or a complement to TBE.

Four conditions appear to be necessary for attributing causality: (1) responsiveness of the outcome (that is, the outcome follows the putative cause), (2) the elimination of plausible alternative explanations, (3) identification of the mechanism that yields the outcome, and (4) replication of the results.[16] Two of these conditions are not of special relevance here. The first condition, that the desired effect comes about following the intervention, is the focus of most evaluation analysis. Evaluators concentrate on seeking change in outcomes. The fourth condition for attribution of causality, replication, requires repeated studies and studies in multiple locations that show the same order of results. If investigators want to be sure that program effects hold over time, place, and population, replication is necessary for *all* evaluations, including those conducted through random assignment.

The third condition, the identification of the mechanism that leads to the outcome, is much more complex. It is a condition that random assignment does not necessarily satisfy. But satisfying it is the exact charge that theory-based evaluation takes on. TBE, particularly in its psychosocial mode, attempts to identify the operative instrumentality that transforms inputs into outcomes. TBE sets forth a candidate theory (or two or three rival theories) at the start of an evaluation, and then collects data to test their efficacy for explaining the evidence. In the current state of knowledge, TBE does not necessarily lead to compelling results, but unlike most other types of evaluation, it takes the task of identifying mechanisms as its central focus.[17]

It is the second condition that concerns us here: ruling out rival explanations. When the evaluator finds it impossible to implement random

16. Hoaglin, Mosteller, and Tukey (1991).
17. Birckmayer and Weiss (2000).

assignment, she can proceed by trying to eliminate plausible interpretations that something other than the program was responsible for observed outcomes. This idea is familiar from the work of Donald Campbell and his colleagues: they assembled an impressive inventory of rival explanations that threaten validity and used the threats to assess the suitability of an array of quasi-experimental designs.[18] They focused mainly on *methodological* problems, misinterpretations caused by such things as unreliability of measures, maturation of subjects, and attrition from treatment groups. The "modus operandi method" is another procedure that essentially seeks the same results.[19]

Robert Yin takes Campbell's ideas about plausible rival hypotheses to the next step. Where Campbell focused primarily on rival explanations stemming from methodological artifacts, Yin proposes to identify *substantive* rival explanations.[20] For example, one possible rival interpretation to the conclusion that the program caused the observed results is that the same results would have appeared in the absence of the program because benefits were received from another policy. In our community example of decentralized services, it may be that agencies produced more effective services not so much because of decentralization as because another policy went into effect at about the same time, and it was the other policy that enhanced agency performance. So alternative policy is a plausible substantive explanation that deserves consideration.

Furthermore, observed results may be due to another practice of the same type as the practice offered by the target program. Similar practices may have been going on simultaneously in other venues, and some recipients took advantage of them. For example, in the evaluation of a community health program, the community intervention may not be the cause of changes in the health status of children. Rather, a similar health intervention conducted in the schools may be responsible. It is incumbent on the evaluator to search for other changes in practice that may be the operative agent.

Another possible substantive rival to the program as causal agent is environmental conditions. It may not have been the program that was

18. Campbell and Stanley (1963); Cook and Campbell (1979); Shadish and others (2002).

19. Michael Scriven (1976).

20. See Yin (2000).

responsible for the employment of former welfare recipients. A booming economy might be the operative agent that was responsible for the observed increase in job-holding.

Yin suggests that a limited number of such rival explanations exist at any one time, and he proposes to identify and codify them.[21] The evaluator can then go down the list, much as she goes down the Cook and Campbell list of threats to validity, and seek to rule them out in each case. The study will collect data to see whether the other substantive explanations are plausible in light of the evidence and accordingly reach a judgment about causal attribution. Knowing whether or not the program was responsible for observed effects will depend on ruling out alternative explanations.

If an evaluation that uses the Ruling Out procedure shows no significant results, no special action is usually required. Generally, it is not interesting to know whether there is a plausible rival interpretation for failure. If no positive effects appear, in all likelihood the program was not effective in its theory or its implementation, or both. In some cases, however, there may be a need to inquire into rival explanations. For example, a nutrition intervention in a developing country may fail not because families did not receive health benefits but because a drought in the area undermined the health benefits that they obtained.

How does an evaluator go about ruling out rival interpretations? The methods of inquiry will be specific to each case. Suppose that one plausible contender for causal agent is political change. And suppose that the intervention is a program to give neighborhood residents greater voice in the direction of government services for their neighborhood (street cleaning, neighborhood policing, trash collection, and so forth). After the so-called empowerment program goes into effect, neighborhood streets and vacant lots are observably cleaner and there are fewer arrests by the police. Was the program responsible for the changes? Fortunately, the evaluator can look at two comparison neighborhoods in the same city that were not exposed to the empowerment intervention. One of them is worse on both dimensions (much as it had been at the start) and the other shows as much decline in law-violating behavior as the target neighborhood, but its streets are not as clean on observational measures. What rival explanation shall the evaluator investigate? And how?

21. Yin (2000).

What would be plausible? That is the key criterion. What other factors could possibly account for the pattern of results observed? The evaluator has to nose around and see what is going on. Perhaps there has been a change in leadership in the police department or the purchase of new sanitation trucks that service particular neighborhoods (and not others) or change in city budget practices or new police policies in some precincts and not others. The evaluator looks around and collects whatever information and qualitative data are relevant to the issue at hand. It is not an elegant design. It is akin to what Campbell called the "patched-up" design, dedicated to the same purpose: to rule out explanations that something other than the program accounted for the changes observed.

Such an investigation would generally take place after the results of the program are known. But the canny evaluator will keep both eyes open to eventualities such as these while the evaluation is in progress. She would ask—and scan local newspapers to find out—about other programs, other policies, environmental conditions (such as changes in unemployment rates, changes in political administration), and social and cultural conditions (for example, increased labor union activity), to see whether any of these factors could have brought about the kinds of outcomes that the target program was trying to effect. If so, she would set up systematic inquiries into the situation.

Like TBE, Ruling Out can be combined with random assignment. Most proponents of random assignment take for granted that a randomly assigned control group represents the counterfactual and all differences between treatment and control groups are due to the program. However, there are times when additional interventions are introduced or changes occur in social and political conditions that affect one group and not the other, particularly when the treatment and control groups are geographically separated. In such cases, a Ruling Out procedure would add important understanding.

Combining Theory-Based Evaluation and Ruling Out

Each of these two alternatives to random assignment can be conducted alone. They can also be combined with random assignment, although the main purpose of random assignment is to obviate the Ruling Out procedure. But what of combining the two of them with each other? Is that redundant or does it buy any further knowledge?

If one refers to Hoaglin, Mosteller, and Tukey's principles for establishing causality, it appears that the combination goes a long way toward satisfying the two key components: identifying a plausible mechanism for change and eliminating alternative explanations.[22] TBE, by tracking the microprocesses by which an intervention leads to success, attempts to demonstrate a causal sequence in fine detail. When TBEs base program theory on psychosocial and sociological *mechanisms* of change, they may be able to make a stronger case. Ruling Out takes as its primary mission the elimination of other explanations for observed effects. It directs all its attention at uncovering other things that might be happening that could have caused the results. The evaluator takes note of political, social, institutional, and cultural changes and analyzes the data with an eye to disconfirming as well as confirming the conclusion that the program was the effective agent.

We come down to standard research advice: look for and take seriously all disconfirming evidence. Do not assume that the program was responsible for observed effects, trumpet the findings, and then write a small disclaimer at the end saying that without random assignment, of course, we cannot be sure about causality. Instead, act as the prosecution, seek out evidence that other causes were at work, wholly or in part, and present all the data about them. Then reach fair judgments about causality.

So far, evaluations based on theories of change have rarely been able to present a convincing case. This situation is due in large part to the weakness of the theories on which programs are designed. Without random assignment, there will always be room for doubt. Evaluators can strengthen their causal case through comparisons with other community interventions, the more similar the better, and through statistical adjustments of the comparative data they collect. They can strengthen the causal attribution even further through Ruling Out.

Conclusion

This chapter has focused on the evaluation of community programs, where random assignment is frequently very difficult and systematic evaluation of all kinds is a problem. The programs aim to change community conditions: upgrade, transform, revitalize, develop the community itself. The long-term goal is to help the people who live in the community, but

22. Hoaglin, Mosteller, and Tukey (1991).

the immediate intervention is designed to change attributes of the community: safety, productivity, norms and beliefs, political mobilization, economic prosperity. In recent instances, efforts to change communities have been sparked by findings that it is difficult to change the attitudes and behavior of individuals when community conditions and beliefs are hostile to the intended result. Therefore program planners direct their attention at changing such things as the availability of alcohol to juveniles, the "acceptability" of teenage drinking to adults, or police patrols around bars patronized by juveniles.[23]

Random assignment is hard to employ in such programs. The numbers of sites are not large enough to satisfy the laws of probability and yield closely similar samples. Furthermore, program funders want to choose the sites that will demonstrate the programs. They seek sites where history, tradition, leadership, organizational auspices, financing, and community support are favorable to the success of the program. Another limitation is the noncomparability of program strategies. Funders usually allow local groups to choose their own strategies. These conditions may render random assignment meaningless. Without random assignment, it is difficult to know whether the program was the cause of whatever results appear.

I propose two alternative means to try to solve the "causality" dilemma. One is theory-based evaluation, which sets out a linked chain of assumptions about what the program does and how it reaches its effects. If there is strong theory and the program does what it plans to do, TBE can give a reasonable approximation of an answer to the causality question. If it were combined with random assignment, it would of course do better on causality, and in addition it would add data (which random assignment does not claim to produce) about how and why the program had the effects that it did. If the program has weak theory, and different people in the program do not agree on what assumptions underlie the program, the evaluation should probably try to pursue several alternative theories. TBE can collect data on each of several theories to see which of them best explains the pattern of results.

If the program does not follow the theoretical assumptions that it originally espoused, TBE has to rush to keep up. In small or contained programs, the evaluator can keep track of the changes, adapt the evaluation design to follow the new assumptions and new activities, and still manage

23. Holder and others (1997).

a reasonable study. In a complex, large, diffuse, and volatile community study, such a course is probably impractical. The evaluator will keep notes on what is going on—a process evaluation will be a good idea—and then collect data down the road on the desired outcomes.

The second method to establish causality I have called Ruling Out. Robert Yin recently began to catalog the rival explanations that a Ruling Out evaluation would have to contend with. The procedure is an eclectic one. It entails figuring out what factors, other than the program, might be causing observed effects, and then collecting systematic data on each of them to see how much they might be affecting the outcomes of concern. It is much like Campbell's "patched-up" design, but it is applied to competing real-world events and conditions and not just to methodological limitations. The conduct of such Ruling Out evaluations at this point is an art. It requires insight into what is really going on, flexibility, and a systematic and open-minded approach to data collection and analysis.

Random assignment has a spare beauty all its own, but the sprawling changeable world of community programs is inhospitable to it. The combination of TBE and Ruling Out may be able to make some inroads on this rocky terrain. None of the nonrandomized designs is very satisfactory in itself, but with a wider array of designs to choose from, evaluators should be able to fashion studies appropriate to the situation. A combination of strategies may be the best way to produce useful results.

References

Aspen Institute, Roundtable on Comprehensive Community Initiatives. 1995. *Voices from the Field: Learning from Comprehensive Community Initiatives.* Appendix D: "Descriptions of Initiatives That Participated in Focus Group Discussions, June–July 1995." New York.

Bickman, Leonard, ed. 1987. *Using Program Theory in Evaluation.* New Directions for Program Evaluation series (no. 33). San Francisco: Jossey-Bass.

———, ed. 1990. *Issues in Constructing Program Theory.* New Directions for Program Evaluation Series (no. 47). San Francisco: Jossey-Bass.

Birckmayer, J. D., and C. H. Weiss. 2000. "Theory-Based Evaluation in Practice: What Do We Learn?" *Evaluation Review*, vol. 24 (4): 407–31.

Bogdan, R. C., and S. K. Biklen. 1998. *Qualitative Research for Education: An Introduction to Theory and Methods.* 4th ed. Boston: Allyn and Bacon.

Campbell, Donald T., and J. C. Stanley. 1966. *Experimental and Quasi-Experimental Designs for Research.* Chicago: Rand McNally.

Chen, Huey-Tsyh. 1990. *Theory-Driven Evaluations.* Newbury Park, Calif.: Sage Publications.

Chen, Huey-Tsyh, and Peter H. Rossi. 1980. "The Multi-Goal, Theory-Driven Approach to Evaluation: A Model Linking Basic and Applied Social Science." *Social Forces* 59: 106–22.

———. 1983. "Evaluating with Sense: The Theory-Driven Approach." *Evaluation Review* 7: 283–302.

———. 1987. "The Theory-Driven Approach to Validity." *Evaluation and Program Planning* 10: 95–103.

Cook, Thomas D., and D. T. Campbell. 1979. *Quasi-Experimentation: Design and Analysis Issues for Field Settings.* Chicago: Rand McNally.

Garasky, Steven. 1990. "Analyzing the Effect of Massachusetts' ET Choices Program of the State's AFDC-Basic Caseload." *Evaluation Review* 14 (6): 701–10.

Heckman, James J. 1989. "Causal Inference and Nonrandom Samples." *Journal of Educational Statistics* 14 (2): 159–68.

Heckman, James J., and J. Hotz. 1989. "Choosing among Alternative Nonexperimental Methods for Estimating the Impact of Social Programs: The Case of Manpower Training." *Journal of the American Statistical Association* 84 (408): 862–80.

Hoaglin, D. C., Frederick Mosteller, and J. W. Tukey. 1991. *Fundamentals of Exploratory Analysis of Variance.* John Wiley.

Holder, H. D., and J. Blose. 1988. "Community Planning and the Prevention of Alcohol-Involved Traffic Problems: An Application of Computer Simulation Technology." *Evaluation and Program Planning* 11: 267–77.

Holder, H. D., R. F. Saltz, A. J. Treno, J. W. Grube, and R. B. Voas. 1997. "Evaluation Design for a Community Prevention Trial." *Evaluation Review* 21 (2): 140–65.

Kubisch, A. C., C. H. Weiss, L. B. Schorr, and J. P. Connell. 1995. "Introduction." In *New Approaches to Evaluating Community Initiatives: Concepts, Methods, and Contexts,* edited by J. P. Connell and others. Washington: Aspen Institute.

Maxwell, J. A. 1996. *Qualitative Research Design: An Interactive Approach.* Thousand Oaks, Calif.: Sage Publications.

Miles, Matthew B., and A. M. Huberman. 1994. *Qualitative Data Analysis: An Expanded Sourcebook.* 2d ed. Thousand Oaks, Calif.: Sage Publications.

Mohr, Lawrence. 1998. "The Case Study as a Design of Abundant Power." University of Michigan. Typescript.

Moore, Mark. 1997. "On Performance Measurement." Talk to the Harvard Evaluation Task Force of the Harvard Children's Initiative (December 3).

Rosenbaum, P., and Donald B. Rubin. 1983. "The Central Role of the Propensity Score in Observational Studies for Causal Effects." *Biometrika* 70: 41–55.

———. 1984. "Reducing Bias in Observational Studies Using Subclassification on the Propensity Score." *Journal of the American Statistical Association* 79: 516–24.

Rubin, Donald B. 1996. "Matching Using Estimated Propensity Scores: Relating Theory to Practice." *Biometrics* 52: 249–64.

Schorr, Lisbeth B. 1997. *Common Purpose: Strengthening Families and Neighborhoods to Rebuild America.* Doubleday Anchor Books.

Scriven, Michael. 1976. “Maximizing the Power of Causal Investigations: The Modus Operandi Method.” In *Evaluation Studies Review Annual*, edited by G. V. Glass, 1: 101–18. Beverly Hills, Calif.: Sage Publications.

Shadish, W. R., T. D. Cook, and D. T. Campbell. 2002. *Experimental and Quasi-Experimental Designs for Generalized Causal Inference*. Houghton Mifflin.

Silverman, David. 1993. *Interpreting Qualitative Data: Methods for Analysing Talk, Text, and Interaction*. London: Sage Publications.

Strauss, A. L., and Juliet Corbin. 1990. *Basics of Qualitative Research: Grounded Theory Procedures and Techniques*. Newbury Park, Calif.: Sage Publications.

Weiss, Carol H. 1967. “Utilization of Evaluation: Toward Comparative Study.” In House of Representatives, *The Use of Social Research in Federal Domestic Programs*, Part III, 426–32. Government Printing Office.

———. 1972. *Evaluation Research: Methods of Assessing Program Effectiveness*. Prentice-Hall.

———. 1995. “Nothing as Practical as Good Theory: Exploring Theory-Based Evaluation for Comprehensive Community Initiatives for Children and Families.” In *New Approaches to Evaluating Community Initiatives*, edited by J. P. Connell, A. C. Kubisch, L. B. Schorr, and C. H. Weiss, 65–92. Washington: Aspen Institute.

———. 1997. “How Can Theory-Based Evaluation Make Greater Headway?” *Evaluation Review* 21 (4): 501–24.

———. 1998. *Evaluation: Methods of Studying Programs and Policies*. Prentice-Hall.

Yin, Robert. 2000. “Rival Explanations as an Alternative to Reforms as ‘Experiments.’” In *Validity and Social Experimentation: Donald Campbell's Legacy*, edited by Leonard Bickman, 239–66. Thousand Oaks, Calif.: Sage Publications.

Conference Participants and Contributors

Deborah Loewenberg Ball, Arthur F. Thurnau Professor, School of Education, University of Michigan

Robert Boruch, University Trustee Chair Professor, Graduate School of Education and Statistics Department, Wharton School, University of Pennsylvania

Gary Burtless, Senior Fellow, Economic Studies Program, Brookings

David K. Cohen, John Dewey Professor, School of Education and School of Public Policy, University of Michigan

Nancy Coles, Former President, Educational Testing Service

Thomas D. Cook, Professor, Department of Sociology, and Fellow, Institute for Public Policy, Northwestern University

Dorothy de Moya, Executive Officer, Campbell Collaboration Secretariat

Judith M. Gueron, President, Manpower Demonstration Research Corporation

Rebecca Herman, Senior Analyst, American Institutes for Research

Howard H. Hiatt, Professor, School of Medicine, Harvard University, and Director, Initiatives for Children, American Academy of Arts and Sciences

Penny Janeway, Administrative Assistant, Initiatives for Children, American Academy of Arts and Sciences

Christopher Jencks, Professor of Public Policy, John F. Kennedy School of Government, Harvard University

Frederick Mosteller, Roger I. Lee Professor in Mathematical Statistics, Emeritus, Harvard University

Monique R. Payne, Graduate Student, Department of Sociology and Graduate Fellow, Institute for Policy Research, Northwestern University

Paul E. Peterson, Henry Lee Shattuck Professor, John F. Kennedy School of Government, Harvard University

Stephen W. Raudenbush, Professor of Education and Statistics, School of Education, University of Michigan

Marshall Smith, Professor, School of Education, Stanford University

Brooke Snyder, Ph.D. Candidate, Center for Research and Evaluation in Social Policy, University of Pennsylvania

Maris A. Vinovskis, Professor, Department of History, Institute for Social Research and the School of Public Policy, University of Michigan

Carol H. Weiss, Professor, Graduate School of Education, Harvard University

Index